D1736073

THE STRUGGLE FOR KIRKUK

THE STRUGGLE FOR KIRKUK

The Rise of Hussein, Oil, and the Death of Tolerance in Iraq

HENRY D. ASTARJIAN

PRAEGER SECURITY INTERNATIONAL
Westport, Connecticut • London

Library of Congress Cataloging-in-Publication Data

Astarjian, Henry D.
The struggle for Kirkuk : the rise of Hussein, oil, and the death of tolerance in Iraq / Henry D. Astarjian.
p. cm.
Includes bibliographical references and index.
ISBN 978–0–275–99589–8 (alk. paper)
1. Karkuk (Iraq)—History. 2. Kurds—Iraq—Karkuk—History. 3. Karkuk (Iraq)—Ethnic relations—History. 4. Astarjian, Henry D. I. Title.
DS79.9.K37A88 2007
956.7′2–dc22 2007014264

British Library Cataloguing in Publication Data is available.

Library of Congress Catalog Card Number: 2007014264
ISBN-13: 978–0–275–99589–8
ISBN-10: 0–275–99589–5

First published in 2007

Praeger Security International, 88 Post Road West, Westport, CT 06881
An imprint of Greenwood Publishing Group, Inc.
www.praeger.com

Printed in the United States of America

The paper used in this book complies with the Permanent Paper Standard issued by the National Information Standards Organization (Z39.48–1984).

10 9 8 7 6 5 4 3 2 1

In the memory of my mentors
Dickran Astarjian (my father)
Levon (Carmen) Stepanian
Haigaz Mouradian
Dr. Papken Papazian
All of whom shaped my political views

"It is that cloud which brought this rain."
(A Bedouin proverb)

Contents

Preface

Battles for this largest and the most ancient oil field in Kirkuk, Baba Gurgur, started around WWI, and continue to date. It is generally accepted that WWI was the progenitor of the one that followed, which, in turn was the progenitor of the cold war, which lasted for a half century.

My father's interest in the news of the WWII, and our exposure to the Allied troops stationed in Kirkuk, evoked my curiosity and captivated my developing mind. The BBC radio channel kept my interest alive.

I was in my early teens when the battle of Stalingrad was waging, and that is my earliest recollection of the war. The Allies, excluding the Soviet Union, had won my heart and mind for their triumphs on the battlefields, as was presented to us by the British propaganda. Winston Churchill became my hero! To have a world leader as a hero may sound strange to an American teenager, whose heroes are Hollywood stars or star athletes, rather than say, Roosevelt; but for Kirkuki, indeed for Iraqi youth, there were no such luminaries to admire, we did not even have national heroes. To us, Churchill and Montgomery were leaders to admire. Ike, Omar Bradley, and General Patten were not; we did not know them, and the United States was not a part of our lives, at that time.

Heroism of the Soviet Union and the sacrifices of its peoples meant little to me! British propaganda had convinced me that Stalin ("Abu-Shwareb" as he was called in Iraq—the "mustachioed man") was Satan, a tyrant who had killed millions of his people (including thousands of Armenians) in Soviet Armenia and had exiled hundreds of thousands to Siberia.

I also hated the Soviets, because they entered Berlin first. I felt that the honor of striking the last blow to Hitler should have been reserved for the British or the American forces; they deserved the sweet taste of victory. Part of that blame went to Ike, because he relinquished the honor of capturing Berlin to the Soviets, thus establishing a Soviet presence in, what later became, East Germany. This is how I reasoned in my teen years, undoubtedly, heavily influenced by British propaganda.

With this mindset, the cold war that followed engaged me in ideological battles with the Leftists, the Communists, and those who opposed the pro-British royal regime within my community.

This book is not a collegiate history book; it is a chronicle of events, which I had witnessed from 1945 until I left Iraq in early 1960s.

To revisit that era is to draw a timeline, which begins with the founding of new Iraq and ends with the demise of the royal regime and the establishment of the Republic of Iraq, the progenitor of Saddam's Iraq.

The ultimate goal of this book is to familiarize Americans with Iraq, where their sons have now gone, risking their lives to establish democracy and engage in nation building.

Americans cannot afford to remain ignorant! They must know Iraq with all its demographic diversity, culture, social graces, and idiosyncrasies. They must arm themselves with knowledge in order to survive the burdens of occupying an alien land thousands of miles away.

Ordinary Americans are not to blame for this ignorance, for Iraq was not on their screen until a group of people, who had their own agenda for the Middle East, put it there, almost instantaneously. Save for a few, Americans did not even know where Iraq was. When I first came to New York, some forty years ago, a sales lady, detecting my accent, asked me where I was from. I said, "Baghdad!" "Oh! India! India!" she exclaimed, "It must be a very beautiful place!" "What ignorance," I thought, "don't these Americans know where Baghdad is? Half their oil comes from there, and they do not know where Baghdad is?"

Some weeks later I learned my lesson; while moonlighting at the Bowery project, in Manhattan, I went to a kosher deli and asked for a ham sandwich and a glass of milk. The man looked at me with disgust! "Is this some kind of a joke?" he asked, "Go somewhere else!" I did not know what kosher was! I left the deli, offended!

When I learned about my faux pas, I remembered the sales lady. I too was ignorant, but my ignorance was not my fault. While she had the means to educate herself, I had no such opportunity; my last exposure to the Jewish culture had been when I was fourteen: we were guests at Gurji's and 'Aabid's house for Sukus. Soon after that holiday, the Jewish community of Kirkuk migrated to Israel, and that was the end of my exposure to the Jewish society. It must have been 1949.

Today, while committing 135,000 of our finest boys to occupy Iraq, and despite our successes and failures, our main problem is unfamiliarity with the country and its people. My book, through a series of real life stories, familiarizes the reader with all that makes Iraq a unique challenge for the United States.

This book however, is not a study of current events: Saddam, Bin Laden, 9/11, Shiites, Sunnis, Kurds, Turkomans, Falluja, or Najaf. Rather, it is the story of the demographic diversity of oil rich Kirkuk, the political currents leading to the demise of the Royal regime of Iraq, and the factors leading to the never-ending battles over the oilfields of Baba Gurgur, Kirkuk. It is the story of colonial Britain, Kurds, Turkomans, Assyrians, preemigration Jews, and postgenocidal Armenians, all of whom called Kirkuk home, and lived together in peace, albeit with deep-seated animosities. Directly or indirectly, they all were involved in surreptitious battles for control over Baba Gurgur. I was both a witness to, and a victim of, some of the battles during this period.

> The book also explores the influences that the British, through the Iraq Petroleum Company (IPC), brought about in shaping Kirkuki society, and my civic and political awareness, but not necessarily direction. Their colonial policies resulted in creating and consolidating an opposition, which hated them, and through them, the ruling royal family. It formed the base for future regime change.

The book goes beyond the obvious in detailing the Soviet attempts to gain access to Baba Gurgur through its surrogates, the Communists, and their efforts to recruit the budding youth, including me, to their cause. It tells the story of my incarceration and torture in a death row cell, at the hands of my childhood friend Adnaan Al-Azzawi, an avowed Communist, whose efforts to indoctrinate me into Communism had failed years before.

The demise of the Hashimite Dynasty in Iraq in 1958, which led to the Communist takeover of the country, touched my life personally. My incarceration with the Ba'th leaders in Al-Rasheed Military Base, gave me a special look at their psyche and a negative sense for the future of Iraq, which influenced my decision to leave the country.

The book pursues the psychological effects of the Iraqi defeat in Palestine (1948) on the Iraqi person and the Armed forces. It details the on-the-spot formation of the Iraqi "Free Officers" movement (whose founders later became my prison mates) and who, a decade later, waged a coup against the Hashimite regime. I witnessed the coup from its first hour.

> I am the only witness to the assassination attempt by Saddam Hussein on Iraq's "sole leader," Abdul-Kareem Qasim, organized by the Ba'th Party.
>
> The book describes the colorful daily life that I witnessed, growing up amongst the Turkomans of Kirkuk and the Kurds of Qalah Dize, where I served as a reserve Army officer. It tells stories of human interest involving the Armenians, Kurds, Turkomans, and the Arabs who formed the demographic mosaic of Kirkuk.

Acknowledgments

On occasion, when in doubt, I have double-checked dates and details with my childhood friend, Mardig Alexandrian of Munich, who, like me, lived under similar circumstances in Iraq. I am grateful for his input.

The late Gregory Avedikian read the early manuscript, made valuable suggestions, and encouraged me, for which I am grateful. Special thanks to William Straub M.D., who read the entire manuscript from the American reader's vantage point, and made valuable suggestions. Thanks also go to Brian O'Sullivan, Ph.D., whose input I value. Lisa Tener, an author in her own right, gave valuable advice and encouragement, for which I am grateful. I thank Tim Defaeo, a freelance writer, for educating me about the intricacies of the publishing world, and who advised me to have patience. Special thanks to Tatul Sonentz Papazian, a man of letters, for his unconditional support and encouragement from the outset.

Cartography by Bookcomp, Inc.

Introduction

It is not an exaggeration to say that after almost a century, the Sykes-Picot Agreement (1916), the Balfour Declaration (November 2, 1917), and the Treaty of Sèvres (1920), continue to be for the Arab nations what 9/11, the London bombings, and 3/11 are for the United States, Britain, and Spain.

These three landmark decisions demolished the twin towers of the Middle East: pan-Arabism and Islam. The area, like America, Britain, and Spain, has never been the same; the impact has been so devastating that its negative effects have lasted for almost a century, and continues to drive the events in the Middle East into the unforeseeable future.

The effects of 9/11 have been of such magnitude that they have mutated the thought processes of the policymakers, indeed that of the man-in-the-street, from logic into negativism and irrationality. In this frame of mind, America belabors to find answers to "Why, America, which was so loved and revered by the world in the past, is now hated?" To get an answer to this question one has to refer to the major political events of the early twentieth century.

In WWI, the colonial powers, and the treaties and agreements that followed, disrupted the established inner milieu of the Middle East, which was at work for centuries. That disruption continues to date with unresolved issues: Syria, Lebanon, and Kurdistan, with its four sectors, Turkey, Kuwait, Iskenderoun, Shatt-El-Arab, and Palestine. Of these treaties, the Sykes-Pico agreement, which shaped the geographic boundaries of the Middle Eastern countries, was instrumental in sowing the seeds of disputes and conflicts. It prepared the ground for additional complications inflicted by the WWII; the disruption continues to date!

Equal in importance was the Balfour Declaration, which paved the way for the creation of Israel. The new geographic arrangements, and the political disorder that resulted, had negative impact on the ordinary people as well as the Arab (Christian and Muslim) intellectuals who felt victimized by the big powers, and deceived by their rulers. They blamed their corrupt regimes for accepting this "cancer" (as the Arabs call Israel) in the body of their nation.

The remedy for this "nakbah" ("tragedy," as it was later labeled), in the minds of Arab intelligentsia and the military, was to resume power and prepare for the war of "Saving Palestine." Within four years of the "nakbah," the Monarchy of Egypt (in 1952), and ten years later, the Monarchy of Iraq (in 1958) were toppled, creating republics. Syria, which was already a republic, had at least six coups in the 1940s and the 1950s, each claiming righteousness and the capability to defeat the Zionists and regain the Holy Land. A new Middle East was born with paramount birth defects!

Despite these "Revolutions," actually coups, which boosted Arab nationalism, the intellectuals, as well as the ordinary people, were angry about their political and socioeconomic structures. There were no Western-style civil rights, human rights, or freedom of the press. The rulers denied their subjects even the rights proscribed by Islam. They blamed the West, especially the United States, for their shortcomings. "It was the West which created Israel in order to control the Middle East, especially Iraq, and its oil," was and still is the dominant, universal thinking of the Arab world. The anger multiplied, and hatred toward America doubled when the Israeli Defense Forces defeated the Arab armies for the third time in 1967.

Arab and Islamic animosity and hatred toward America stems from the notion that she is biased in favor of Israel, not because America is rich and they are poor, as some wanted them to believe. America, they believe, has never been evenhanded, and it is not so now. In order to find satisfactory solutions to complex problems in the region, this basic strategy must change to evenhandedness!

Kirkuk

History knew Kirkuk as "Arapha" (Revue D'Assyrien et d'Archeologie orient, 1926) also as "Karkha d'beth Silokh." Sassanians called this centuries-old city "Garmakan."

Great events have taken place here. Nabuchodonosor, exploiting Jewish captives from Palestine, built the Citadel and a stone bridge leading to it; a great achievement indeed. Alexander the Great, Central Asian tribes of Kara-Qoyunlu, Aq-Qoyunlu, the Seljouks, and numerous other conquering armies have waged wars here to control the trade routes connecting Persia and Istanbul with Baghdad.

In 1732, the Safavid and the Ottoman Empires fought bitter wars over control of Kirkuk; Safavid Nadir Shah won. A year later, the city was in the hands of the Ottoman Empire, to be lost once more in 1743 to the Safavids. Finally, the 1746 peace treaty gave the control to the Turks. Thus, Kirkuk remained under Ottoman domination for a little short of three centuries, until the end of WWI (in 1918), when they lost the war and Iraq.

During these times, and centuries thereafter, lawlessness was the norm in everyday life. With some imagination, one can visualize cavalry waging battle, raising dust and hell, robbing the loaded caravans, or at least collecting taxes in lieu of safe passage. Kirkuk was a dangerous place, a haven for robbers and killers; it also was a mysterious magical city for, a few miles out, in Arafa (new spelling of the ancient name), a patch of land, Baba Gurgur, had eternal flames, which made it a holy place of sorts, a place where miracles could happen. There the land, when scratched, spewed flames, but not always. Pilgrims went to Baba Gurgur, sacrificed lamb for the gods, and begged them to have their wishes come true.

Most pilgrims were infertile women who thought their wombs were possessed. They would spend the night there to dispel the evil and free their wombs of bondage. To find out if their pilgrimage was accepted, they would scratch the ground; if a flame came out, then that meant that the gods had granted their wishes. Lo and behold, they either went home pregnant or became pregnant soon after that. The shepherds nearby made a good business.

The generation before me dispelled that myth when the newly arrived geologists told them that it was the oozing gas, which was burning; the oil wells were only a few miles away! Despite the facts, Baba Gurgur remained a fascinating place to visit, even if it was for the scenery of the surrounding green hills of Arafa. A few miles away were the candelabra of natural gas burning day and night, illuminating the skies of Kirkuk.

Khassa-Su divided the town into two, and the bridge connected them, transgressing centuries of division between the old Citadel and the more recent section of town. The citadel, perched on a hill, had 50-feet high walls, tiny windows, and steps like Jacob's ladder to climb to the top.

God only knows how many attacks had that Citadel fended to protect its inhabitants, the Turkoman bandits, who sought refuge within its walls! How many armies have tried to cross that bridge to gain control over the trade routes! God only knows!

In my time, it was the home of some repentant thieves, ordinary folk, Prophet Daniel Mosque, a Chaldian convent, the Jewish ghetto and synagogue, and Caesar's Bazaar. This covered bazaar had arched gates, passages, entrances, and shops, designed like the signs of the Zodiac, and according to milestones of time: seven gates to signify a week, twelve passages for the months, and 365 shops for the year. This is unique in the world!

The Citadel was rich! The artisans of Kirkuk had their shops there, lining narrow passages and alleys. Dozens of specialized souks crisscrossed the decapitated mountain where businesses and homes lived side by side.

There are the qazanchis, the coppersmiths, who hammered a piece of copper into a pot, providing rhythm to the rising white smoke, sinuously dancing in the air.

Further down the tune changed to another rhythm, this time into the grainy sounds of sand rubbing on metal, whoosh-whoosh, whoosh-whoosh. It was the qalaychi, who, standing in the middle of a huge tray placed on sand, twisted his pelvis like Elvis in concert, or like the wheels of an old-fashioned clock, rotating once to the left, once to the right, to remove rust from an old utensil.

A few shops down, the blacksmiths were busy making the shishes for kebabs and the all-important daggers for men. In that culture, to be a "man" was to wear a dagger (khanjar) in your belt for protection and for wielding power. That, plus the size of one's mustache told the world who one was: sovereign, powerful, and invincible. Christians and Jews would not dare have an oversized mustache or a dagger, lest it be construed as a challenge to the local ethnic dominants. For them survival in that culture necessitated projecting submissive behavior. "There is no need to provoke the rabid dogs," the elders would advise.

As one made a turn around the bend, sights dominated sounds: the sight of beautiful silk and damask, soft and colorful, imported from Damascus and China.

The Citadel. Oil on canvas by the author, 1947.

There were stacks upon stacks of printed cotton for dresses, imported from Egypt. There were bundles of black silk for "aba" (the head-to-toe wrap-around women wear), stacked ceiling high, and dozens of women trying to strike a bargain with the bazergaan (the fabric retailer). They would engage in arguments about the exact yardage of the material, a yard being the length of his arm. Women would whisper, "Don't go to that man, his arm is short and he doesn't use the arsheen" (the yardstick).

A passer-by would slow down, as if looking for something, to admire, the beauty of a kohl-lined single eye exposed through a veil. A woman conveyed a message of seduction—or so it seemed—by sinuous movements of her fingers, while feeling the silk. An occasional giggle added a tune to the mystery of love.

The souk for buttons, threads and needles, dantelles, ribbons, colorful sequins, beads, and the like were the specialty of the next half a dozen or so shops.

The next alley was the exciting world of "spices and herbs." It was truly a festival for one's senses; the cinnamon, the nutmeg, the cloves, the cumin, the cardamom, the chamomile, the mint, the dried jasmine, dried rose petals, and dozens of other exotic medicinal herbs displayed in large and small sacks to be weighed by the "dram" and sold wrapped in folded brown paper. One is good for colds, the other for impotence, guaranteed, and the other for infertility. The same place would display perfumes and essences from India and Egypt, promoted as aphrodisiacs.

But, before that, there were shops selling Aleppo soap made with sage and kaolin to soften hair, and henna to color it, or to color a bride's hands and feet the night before her wedding. The same shop sold an arsenic-based hair remover called Zerneekh, which doubled as an undetectable murder weapon. Many a man has gone to face his creator, compliments of a woman using Zerneekh to remove hair.

Jews monopolized the jewelry market, in its entirety. They were reliable. They handcrafted gold bracelets, rings, necklaces, nose- and earrings, on location. Shops for rice, ghee, dried goods, and many other necessities completed this bazaar.

We went to the Citadel, on occasion, to shop. The place was exotic in its architecture, and intriguing in its ambiance; one could smell antiquity and history, something mysterious, which one could only feel. The narrow alleys barely prevented opposite second-floor windows from kissing each other. Roughhewn wooden doors scattered here and there, some high and narrow, and some wide and low, hiding a whole story of cloistered women and their mustachioed, daggered husbands, who lived behind those doors.

A huge key trying to unlock the door or a man driving a donkey were the only sounds that disturbed the silence. The alley otherwise was quiet, quiet, and quiet—as if echoing the whispers of life frozen in time, waiting to come to life by the charge of attacking horses.

I remember visiting a Muslim family in the Citadel with my father. The head of the family was a very wealthy landlord, Hajji Hassan. In fact, my father was his tenant. Since men did not allow their women to frequent medical or dental offices, my father went to their house to take care of their teeth. I believe Hajji Hassan had three wives, one of them very young and very pretty, or so she seemed to my teenage eyes. The women were not to show their faces to strangers, and not every doctor or dentist had the privilege of seeing or touching them, except when the husband was sure of their professionalism; it was a question of honor,

The Archway in the Citadel. Oil on canvas by the author.

tradition, and religion. Islam forbade a woman from showing her body or a part of it to strangers unless medically necessary, such as in the case of illness. Even then, they would expose the smallest possible area of the body for examination.

Rumor had it that Hajji Hassan was, at one time, a Don of sorts, the head of a robbery gang, which raided caravans transporting valuable merchandise, silk, salt, sugar, coffee, coins, and the like, passing his territory. Or else he taxed them and allowed passage. Now he had repented and gone to Mecca for pilgrimage and returned as a respectable Hajji engaged in legitimate business. He had even rewarded himself with a new young wife to start a clean life, afresh.

I remember the huge doors leading to the huge courtyard of this huge house, where men were tending horses. I can recall that sharp acidic smell emanating from the stables and the sight of rusty swords on the wall alongside a horseshoe, hung there for good luck. I remember the huge well in the center of the courtyard surrounded by a few buckets made out of old Goodyear tires to water the horses. I can still smell the rice being cooked in gigantic cauldrons to feed the horsemen at sundown. I remember the young hand of this woman, tinted with henna and decorated with gold, showing my father, through a partly exposed veil, which tooth hurt.

I met Hajji Hassan once or twice. He had a stern-looking face hiding behind a grayish-white beard and an aggressive mustache. He had wrapped his legs in cloth, even in that heat, to minimize the pain of rheumatism from which he suffered. The gigantic gold-thread-embroidered headdress was perched on his head like a crown, and told of the influence he wielded. Despite his kind words, which he articulated with a raspy voice, and his piercing blue eyes, a kid could not feel at ease in his presence. He did not look kindly! My father said he was. His rental rates were reasonable and he paid his dental bills cash, on the spot.

The Hassan household was at one end of the Citadel, and the Jewish ghetto and Synagogue, at the other. Regardless, Hajji's influence reached those sections and beyond.

Muslims tolerated the other two monotheistic religions, but discriminated against those who practiced them. Moses and Jesus, and especially Virgin Mary, were sacred and holy; that is what the Holy Qur'an has revealed. The belief in Immaculate Conception and the innocence of Virgin Mary (Sourat Meriam-Qur'an) is so deep amongst Muslims that fanatics could kill a doubter, in provinces of Iraq, anyway, and be set free. Additionally, they could kill and be set free if someone argued that Christ is the "Son of God"; Muslims believe that "God was never born and never procreated" (the Holy Qur'an). However, they compromised on the Resurrection issue; "It was the spirit, not the body of Christ which resurrected," they would argue. "That is why we believe that he is alive, and that is why we call him Isa Al-Heiy" (Alive Isa). To them Jesus is a prophet, but not on par with Mohammed who is "The Messenger of God." Muslim folklore has it that Prophet Mohammed too, ascended to heaven from Jerusalem, on a white horse's back.

I never had the chance to visit the convent, or the church, or the synagogue, in the Citadel, but had the opportunity to be in a Jewish home in the ghetto on a happy occasion. My father had a few Jewish friends. He bought gold from them for his work as a dentist. They were a trustworthy bunch and honest traders. They, for instance, would send us, without notice, a 100-kilo sack of rice, or a case of soap, and gallons of ghee, in anticipation of a speculated price hike the following week.

That visit to the Jewish home is very vivid in my memory: The dual horse-drawn carriage picked us up and climbed the hill of the Citadel negotiating open but narrow hairpins and brought us to a point where vehicles could no longer pass.

We had to walk the rest of the way negotiating open sewers, mud, and puddles of discarded laundry water to get to our destination, Gurji's house. He and his brother 'Aabid lived there with their families. It was a solid house built with stone and gypsum, and had high ceilings. There was a courtyard, big and spacious, or so it seemed at the time. In the middle there was a trellis put together with tree limbs tied together with sturdy rope. The ceiling was made out of olive branches and boughs. Bunches of grapes, pomegranates, oranges, and pears hung from it for decoration. The sun filtered through it all, creating a beautiful latticework of shade, shadows, and light, on the compact mud floor.

We sat underneath this cozy structure enjoying the bounty that was presented on trays; a variety of homemade juices, diluted syrups, mint concoctions, walnuts from Howramaan, pistachios from Mosul, fresh dates, figs, and pastry. It was "Chardakh Bayrami," Sukos. The samovar kept the tea brewing just right.

I never paid much attention to the conversation, but I know that Gurji and 'Aabid were talking to my father about not having much future in this country and being tired of living with fear, the fear of a pogrom in revenge for the war in Palestine.

It seemed that they had come to terms with discrimination, and physical assault on their kids just because they were Jews, but they could not tolerate living with fear for their lives. Gurji's son had already gone to Palestine surreptitiously, to serve his people. Gurji, 'Aabid, and the rest of the family wished to join him. All this was secret, and my father asked me to keep my mouth shut.

It all became clear later on, in 1948. Now Israel was a State and Iraq was allowing, some say forcing, the Jews to migrate. Others, believing in conspiratorial theories, thought that the Zionists arranged the forced migration from Iraq through British mediation, in order to populate Israel, and that the Iraqi government had agreed to it a priori. Planeloads of Jews left Baghdad. One day Gurji and 'Aabid sold their house for pennies, said goodbye, and migrated to the newly formed Israel. It was a sad day for us! We never saw them again!

There were no Jews left in Kirkuk, except for two sisters who had set their domicile with the Attorney General of Kirkuk, a Muslim Arab. I knew all three of them, as they were our neighbors.

We missed Gurji and 'Aabid, but I especially missed Saleh, my "savior" as I called him, who also migrated. He had saved my life when I was four or five: I had strayed a block away from home to go to Rasheed's store, where little toy soldiers were on display in the vitrine. As I got there, a man picked me up, put me in a 100-kilo-burlap sack, and carried me on his back, as if he was a porter. Through a hole in the sack, I yelled for help and Saleh, a shoeshine man who was sitting there, heard me. He came, and despite the fact that he was a Jew, had the courage to fight the Muslim kidnapper and rescue me. He took me home, to an anticipated punishment for leaving the house.

When I grew up, he was still around, carrying his box to render services from shop to shop. I used to see him every day and exchange pleasantries. He had become a part of my world. I lost him to Israel!

Iraq was empty of Jews, except for a few hundred who preferred to remain in Baghdad and Basra. The synagogue in Baghdad was operational until Desert Storm. It is my understanding that it is still open to worshippers. Recently I saw a documentary about the Jewish synagogue and community in Baghdad: a handful of old people have remained and they were singing the praises of Saddam Hussein because he had allowed them to worship in the only synagogue left in the country. A few years ago, valuable Hebrew scrolls were smuggled from that synagogue, hidden in truck tires, to Israel.

2

Kurds, Turkomans, Arabs, and the Others

In my time, Kirkuk was a prosperous city of some quarter of a million, though nobody knew for sure. The majority of the inhabitants were Turkomans, or so they claimed. Kurds, who probably were in the majority, had lived there for millennia, but because of centuries of Ottoman occupation, they had pretended to be Turkomans. According to the ancient "Qaamous al-'Ilm" (*Encyclopedia of Science*), written by the famous Ottoman chronologist and lexicographer Shamsaddin Sami, three-fourths of Kirkukis were Kurds, and one quarter Turkoman.

This demographic dominance forms the basis of the present Kurdish claim that Kirkuk is a part of the Federated Iraqi Kurdistan. Arabs and Turkomans disagree. Kirkuk, as in the past, remains a disputed land.

Now, the battle lines are drawn; all parties are struggling to change the demographic make up of this city in order to have control over Baba Gurgur. For the post-Saddam Iraqi government Kirkuk is neither Kurd, nor Turkoman, it is a part of Iraq, not Iraqi Kurdistan, which was the set up when the British founded Iraq, and that is how it should remain.

In the 1940s Arabs were a minor minority in Kirkuk, however one could identify a large group of families who spoke Arabic: These were the Bejaats (Begaat = Plural for Beg, Turkish/Khazar for "Title," e.g., Sir), a tribe from the town of Tikrit where Saddam Hussein was born and raised. Tikrit was also the birthplace of the Kurdish warrior, Salahhadin El Ayoubi (Saladin), who liberated Jerusalem from the Crusaders. Legend has it that at one time the Tikritis were Christians who later converted to Islam. That may or may not be true, but the fact remains that there is not even a trace of Christian culture in their society.

I had a few Tikriti high school classmates; all but one, Mohammed Sabir, were vicious, aggressive, belligerent, and hostile. Yes! It is wrong to generalize but uttering the name Tikriti was enough to run chills down one's spine. They picked up fights for trivial reasons. They beat the schoolteacher, for example, if they did not get good grades. They raised hell in the city: extorting, raping, and destroying property at will. At the time, it was my impression that Tikritis' behavior was cultural and inherent. Saddam's and his Tikriti clan's behavior vindicate my earlier impression.

Turkomans are Turkics who, throughout centuries, had migrated as Ottoman soldiers from Central Asia. In the fifteenth century they had pushed southwest to settle in Kirkuk with their families. History indicates that there have been several waves of such migrations. Some say they are a mixture of Mongols and other Central Asiatic Turkics, yet others exclude the Mongols. It is a fact, then, that Turkomans are ethnically and culturally distinct from the Kurds and the Arabs, although they share the same religion, Islam.

When the new religion was sweeping Mesopotamia in the seventh century, some Turkomans resisted conversion to Islam. They lived in the Citadel (Qal'a) with the Jews, and had their churches; they were Eastern Rights Catholics. Muslims called them "Qal'a Giavouri," Infidels of the Citadel (giavour = infidel), and as such they had no say in the governance of Kirkuk.

Some say there were Turkomans who were Jews, but that remains undocumented.

Unlike the Turkomans and the Kurds, Jews of Kirkuk were Semites. I am not sure whether they spoke Hebrew at home, they most probably did, but in public, they were indistinguishable from the Turkomans in garb and language, and always kept a low profile. In the late 1940s, the Jewish population was 726, all of whom lived in a ghetto in the Citadel and had a synagogue. Most goldsmiths were Jews, so were most of the wholesale merchants. Unlike Baghdad and Basra, there were no Jewish professionals in Kirkuk.

Then there were the Assyrians (Ahthouris). These were small tribes, like the Jeelos and Levis. They claimed to be the descendants of the ancient Assyrian Empire of Nineveh. They were looked upon with disdain because they were fighting on the side of the British army against the Arab nationalist uprisings in the 1920s. Religiously, they were Chaldians.

Other inhabitants of the city were the Armenians who numbered about 3,000; they were the Post-Genocidal Generation, the survivors of 1915–1921 Armenian Genocide. We had a school and a church, which doubled as a cultural center.

My ethnic orientation came from those institutions as well as the conversations, which my father used to have with the parish priest and my godfather. They allowed me to sit in on their after-dinner conversations because it was "good for shaping up one's character as an Armenian." The conversation invariably revolved around the Genocide issue, deportation of the Armenian masses, the Turkish atrocities, and the devastation of the Armenian nation. Telling and retelling depressive horror stories of deaths, death marches, and torture, reflected a collective feeling of self-pity, anger, frustration, and calls for revenge, usually recruiting God to do the job. A curse and casting a bad spell on the Turks were thrown in for good measure near the end. After a while, realizing that they had worked themselves to the ground, they would perk up and pull themselves out of the doldrums. They would talk about the heroism of our defending Fedayees and heroes: Kevork Chavoush, Kerri, Tro, Sepastatsi Mourad, Antranig, and many more. The heroic resistance battles of Zeytoun, Sasoon, Van, and the rest gave all of us a renewed self-respect and confidence. Sitting there and listening, I always felt as if I was a direct extension of that heroism, a victim, as well as a fighter.

God however, was not a part of my Aunt Victoria's repertoire when she read me revolutionary, nationalistic, literature, such as Raffi's *Khente*. She was unforgiving for what God had allowed to happen to a million and a half God-loving, God-fearing Armenians. "There is no God," she would conclude, "if there was one, then why did he allow the Turks to commit this unspeakable Genocide against innocent Christians? Wasn't God supposed to protect the good people? Why didn't he? What was his excuse? Did he want to test our faith and commitment to Christianity? How much more of a believer can one be? There is no God!"

To erase the feelings of self-pity and defeat, she would tell me anecdotes about the valiant resistance fighters who protected the villages, women, and children against the Turks, and how they attacked the army of criminal Turks, and killed them. "One should be brave and work for his nation," she would instruct. At that young age, she implanted in my psyche Armenian revolutionary ideas as well as disdain for the Turks.

Not infrequently, my Godfather Ibrahim Qolchi, would join the secular and the religious duo for dinner and a chat. He was not an Armenian. He was a Chaldian (an ancient, almost extinct race) and his real mother tongue was unknown to me except that his basic language was Arabic. He spoke impeccable Armenian, Turkish, and English. If you lived in the Middle East, you would understand such accommodative complexities of race, religion, and language.

When I was born, Ibrahim Qolchi, following tradition, had reserved the exclusive right of naming me. However, for my liberal-minded Uncle Krikor, tradition meant nothing much, except when it applied to matters Armenian, or when it suited his personal purposes. He lost the battle against my godfather and the church, which, in compliance with Qolchi's wishes, baptized me with an English name.

My Uncle was furious. He was angry with the priest, Qolchi, and especially my father, for their collusion in this terrible conspiracy. "The nation is being destroyed, the Ottomans committed our Genocide, and now we are being subjected to a White Massacre, a massacre of the soul; why would you give him an English name?" he would argue angrily. Now, when I hear Rabbis' complaining about "Good Jewish boys, marrying non-Jews," I remember that story! It seems that nothing much has changed in seventy-five years on the ethnic front.

Godfather's rationale in choosing an English name for me was not without some logic. The British, Dutch, and French oil consortia had started oil production in Kirkuk only a few years before, around 1927. Caloust Gulbenkian, later known as "Mr. Five Percent" had negotiated a deal with Turkey to explore for oil in Kirkuk, on behalf of the British and French companies. He was successful and the Turkish Petroleum Company was acquired and renamed Iraq Petroleum Company (IPC). He was given a 5 percent share in the company, hence the nickname.

My godfather was the agent for the company in charge of land acquisitions, an important position, indeed. He had chosen an English name for me in an effort to, maybe, impress the British that we are Christians, and as such, unlike the "Backward Muslims," we subscribe to the European Christian culture. That seemed to be a good strategy at a time when Britain was at the pinnacle of her imperial power, and when Iraq was a newly formed state. "The future belongs to the British!" he would say, "And we have to take advantage of it."

I don't know whether his strategy helped me or not: Armenians did not like it, the Arabs, the Turkomans, and the Kurds considered it foreign, and therefore questioned my patriotism. So, there existed an ethnic identity problem that continues to date; in Europe I am an American, and here I am European.

Qolchi was right—the future did belong to the British but also to Iraq, although in a different way. Aside from the economic bonanza that befell the Kirkukis, IPC's presence propelled Kirkuk from the medieval ages to the twentieth century.

To complete the picture of an ethnic and religious mosaic, it is interesting to note that the "American brand of Christianity" as the locals called it, had made its way into Kirkuk. There was an elderly couple who, carrying pamphlets and the Bible, walked Shari' al-Awqaaf promoting Jehovah. They invited people to repent and seek salvation. In that Islamic city, absolutely no one obstructed their mission. I don't know how many people listened to them, but they were there every morning around eleven o'clock. They must have been the only Jehovah's Witnesses in town!

Mr. Glassner, who taught Sunday school to Christian children of other denominations in his home, represented another American-style Christianity. He had established the Christian Science Reading Room on the main street of town. It was a shop with a large vitrine where the Bible, some books, and idealized pictures of Jesus and the Holy family, were displayed. Inside was spartan: there was an oblong table surrounded by comfortable chairs. On a desk sat Iliya, a bespectacled, soft-spoken, middle-aged man. Bookcases, filled to capacity, lined the walls. There was no other visible soul in the place, only perhaps invisible ones, or so it felt, floating around in peace and silence, blessing the place with tranquility. He welcomed me with a soft, barely audible voice, so as not to awaken the Satan.

I reciprocated his greeting and sat across his desk respectfully. Though I had no qualms about presenting my case, I was somewhat reserved, making a great effort to present my questions by choosing language that he would not perceive as impolite or vulgar. I had to present to him a paramount teenage problem and hope for vindication: there was no sex education in our curricula at the time.

He listened attentively until I finished then, with great authority, and with the same low tone of voice, conveyed his verdict according to God's Law. "Son," he said, "It is against the will of God; short-term it might give you pleasure, but in the long-term it will give you degeneration of the spine and will liquefy your brain; it is a sin, pray so that you may get out of this dilemma, and have inner peace." I didn't know the term then, but what he did in the name of God was nothing short of a castration, albeit gently.

3

From Tranquility to Conflict

This demographic mosaic of Kirkuk had no political impact on the city when Baghdad was Ottoman. However, upon the creation of modern Iraq in 1921, the newly formed Iraqi Government found the ethnic makeup of this strategically important city unacceptable; there was negligible percentage of Arab presence to call Kirkuk a part of Arab Iraq. Furthermore, they feared that one day, with the majority of non-Arabs, Kurds could claim Kirkuk. They were right! More than three-quarters of a century later, their fears have become a reality; today Kurds are claiming Kirkuk to be a part of the Federated Kurdistan, and the battle over Baba Gurgur is just starting.

These realities called for a long-term remedy; changing the ethnic composition of the city. Successive Iraqi governments have tried different methods, some gentle and some brutal, to do just that! The Royal regime had the gentlest approach of all: the government initiated the "Haweeja Project," an irrigation and land development project in Kirkuk, which served at least three purposes. It would:

(1) Convert land from arid to fertile.
(2) Urbanize the nomadic Arab tribes, Obeyd and Jboor.
(3) Change the ethnic balance of the Kirkuk province in favor of the Arabs.

The plan had limited success. The tribes settled all right, but the ethnic divisions remained. The Kurds and the Turkomans continued their low-intensity covert efforts to dominate and control the region. In appearance, however, the daily life was quite different because of the Iraq Petroleum Company's (IPC) positive socioeconomic effect on society, which kept tensions low; the city was largely prosperous and tranquil.

The July 14, 1958 coup changed all that. The Kurds and the Communists rallied to the side of the "sole leader," General Karim Qasim. The new political climate created an opportunity for the Kurds to assert their authority over Kirkuk. They returned to Kirkuk by the thousands and shifted the ethnic balance in their favor. They openly lay claim to Kirkuk as being a part of Kurdistan. Daily demonstrations, seemingly in support of the "sole leader," gave them the image of a conqueror: powerful, infallible, and in control. Their slogans were antinationalist, anti-Nasser, anti-Arif, and pro-Leftist and Communist.

One year later, in the aftermath of anti-Qasim uprising in Mosul, ethnic tensions in Kirkuk peaked with a pogrom committed by the Kurds, which took the lives of some fifty notable Turkomans. They were buried alive. Three of them were my friends.

Enmity between the two sides was now fully established. It prepared the grounds for further conflict, which continues to date.

Kirkuk remained non-Arab until Saddam took over power in the late 1960s. His Arabization plan was the most ruthless of them all. First, he re-zoned the province to include Arab tribes, changed Kirkuk's name to Ta'meem, and then embarked upon ethnic cleansing by deporting both Kurds and Turkomans from the city and replacing them with Arabs from the south. The newcomers were given subsidized housing and rewarded with cash money.

After Saddam's fall in 2003, the Kurds have returned to Kirkuk en masse, reclaiming their homes and the Kurdish identity of the city. This is, as one can imagine, a major problem indeed for both the new Government of Iraq, and the United States.

This kind of demographic diversity, ethnic loyalties, diverse interests, and divisions, were only a part of young Iraq's internal problems. There were also problems in the structure of the State. Iraq could not rid herself from the tribal system to establish a civil society ruled by law, not men. Even the secular Ba'th regime, which followed the monarchy, transformed into a dynasty: that of Saddam.

Baghdad, itself, was not tribal! The Iraqi ruling class consisted of some 500 or so very wealthy families, including Shi'a, who had inherited affluence and influence from the Ottoman Empire. They ruled every aspect of every individual's life: import-export, finance, personal loans, buildings, construction, rent, imported medicines, cars, furniture, and the rest.

The cabinet members, like that of the Parliament, were selected and recycled from the same old "Qa'ima" (nomenclatura), assembled by the Royal Family and the British Embassy.

Even though the majority of the Muslims were Shiites, the country's de facto rulers were the educated, sophisticated, and secular Sunni Arabs. Despite this arrangement, there was no religious-sectarian dispute between the two factions; it did not matter whether someone was Sunni or Shi'i, they both were Muslims; sect did not matter, ethnicity did. In the eyes of an Arab, a Kurd was a Kurd first, different from him, it did not matter if he was a Sunni or Shi'i, or even a Christian or a Muslim. For a Kurd he was a Kurd first, and a Muslim second. The

Ottoman Turks had a saying "Giavoura baqaraq Kurd Musoulman" (compared to the infidels Kurds are Muslims).

Sunnis belittled the Shi'a because they as a community, compared to the rest of them, were socioeconomically backward, and less secular. Illiteracy, poverty, disease, a primitive way of life, and adherence to unorthodox religious rituals characterized them, and subjected them to ridicule. In the month of Muhharam, for instance, Shi'as observe "ashoura" when they mourn and repent the killings of Hassan and Hussein, the grandchildren of prophet Muhammad, some thirteen centuries ago, by self-flagellation with chains and swords.

With some exceptions, Shi'is retention of the seventh-century reactionary societies, and not changing with the times, was the result of neglect by the ruling Sunnis, the inheritors of the Sunni supremacy of the Ottomans. By imposing their hegemony over Mesopotamia, after defeating Shi'i Persia (Iran) in the centuries past, Ottomans extended their oppression to the Iraqi Shi'as as collaborators of Persia. Today, this centuries-old Iranian-Arab Shi'i kinship is renewed, and it raises big problems for Iraq and the American allied forces. Saddam was aware of this, which was why he butchered the Shi'i community in Najaf and Karbala. It is no wonder then, that Shi'is are so adamant on gaining supremacy in the country where they number 60 percent (or more) of the population.

Arab Shi'is were not the only neglected sect in Mesopotamia; they shared this fate with the Kurds in the North who also were second-class citizens, neglected, and in most cases persecuted. However, in general the quality of their life was much better than that of their Shiite counterpart. The Kurd, though he lived in a feudal system, had better soil to till, better fruit orchards to harvest, cleaner mountain air to breathe, and abundance of waterfalls and springs to quench his thirst. It is fair to say that an average individual Kurd was healthier than an average southern-Arab.

The middle and southern Euphrates and Tigris regions, the malaria infested Al-Ahwaar (swamps) region, which Shi'a inhabited, produced nothing but shannafia rice and palm dates. There was no adequate health care, and infant mortality, tuberculosis, and other parasitic illnesses were rampant, more so than the rest of the nation. There was no economy, in the common sense of the word. Poverty was the norm.

Taking advantage of this situation and the religious affiliation with the Iraqi Shiites, the Iranian Tudeh Party, the most virulent Communist party in the Middle East, was working hard to breed generation after generation of Communists in Iraq. The Holy cities of Iranian Qum and Iraqi Najaf were two ends of a political pipeline utilized to subvert the British-controlled Iraqi entity. Both Communists and the Iranian governments of all regimes, have used this pipeline to exert influence in each other's countries. The current situation in Iraq is no exception.

The same was happening in the North, especially Kirkuk, the plum of the region. The cold war was hot in these regions, destabilizing the British-supported regime.

Under the Ottoman regime, Iraq lived under a corrupt, inept regime, like the rest of the empire. After its fall and establishment of the Hashimite royal regime, the young "Independent" government was struggling to establish itself, and organized opposition to the British mandate was developing. However, right after WWII, the country was in turmoil not only because Israel declared Statehood, but also because of a number of other developments affecting Iraq directly:

In 1948, after losing their crown jewel, India, the British tossed the Portsmouth Treaty into the Anglo-Iraqi political arena. It was nothing short of a political tsunami that hit the country. The treaty was to replace the old neocolonial one, which had been in effect since the British Mandate on Iraq. It was a lopsided treaty, crafted to expand British dominance in the region, at the expense of Iraq. Briefly, the treaty had four major provisions:

(a) To continue use of Habbaniya and Shu'eyba air bases.
(b) To limit Iraq's oil profits to 3 percent.
(c) In time of war, to place the railroads, roads, and all other modes of transportation under British control.
(d) In time of war, to allocate to the British military all livestock and agricultural products.

Roughly, this was the treaty, which was due to be signed by Prime Minister Saleh Jabr (a Shi'a). The political parties, as well as the people were furious at this grand treason and were determined to defeat its ratification.

That year, the Communists, despite the fact that their affiliation was with the Soviet bloc, not China, celebrated Mao's victories. This victory gave them new impetus, and a new prestige, to act more vigorously in collaboration with the other opposition groups (Arab Nationalists, the Kurds, and the disenfranchised). They called for and organized massive demonstrations and strikes in Baghdad and other southern provinces, even safe Kirkuk.

In Baghdad, the police, in an attempt to disperse the crowds, opened fire killing a dozen or so, including Ja'far, the brother of Iraq's famous poet, Mohammad Mehdi Al-Jawahiri, a Shiite.

Now the opposition had martyrs to rally around, and they did! They capitalized on the events and gained further momentum in their push for repeal of the treaty agreement. Not only that: they also demanded the resignation of Prime Minister Saleh Jabr who had succeeded Nouri Sa'id Pasha. In fact, the actual behind-the-scenes architect of the treaty was none other than Nouri Sa'id himself, not Saleh Jabr.

The opposition achieved its dual goals; Salih Jabir's government fell after being in power for only a few days, and that ended talk about the treaty.

Mohammed Sader (the grandfather of the present young cleric, Muqtada), a highly respected long-bearded Shiite cleric formed the new government, but soon his government could not endure either; it was seen as pro-Britain. People were disappointed in him too, and in the street coined the slogan, "We brought you for help/you turned out to be a Pharaoh/Oh nylon-bearded man." Nylon, of course, symbolized the West.

A Communist Offensive

The Communist party leaders, being masters of deception, propaganda, and spin, monopolized the victory of killing the treaty of Portsmouth, as if there were no other political forces, which defeated the project. They let it be known that they did it in the name of all "oppressed proletariat struggling against the imperialists."

This action had geopolitical implications in that it neutralized a potential threat to their employer, the Soviet Union, and defeated a major Western plan of containing the Soviets. An important achievement indeed. The party's reputation soared, earning a huge political capital for them, which they spent a decade later in the 1958 coup d'etat. This was their first victory that boosted their depressed morale, which had paralyzed them after the hanging of their founder, Fahad, a few months earlier.

There was alarm in the British Embassy and IPC circles, and rightly so. The Soviets were using their surrogates to destabilize the region, and were succeeding! They were talking to the Kurds, the Assyrians, some Armenians, and the Arab opposition, and were exploiting their political and national aspirations. Baba Gurgur was once more in danger, and the battle over it had once more entered into an acute phase. It was up to the British to defend it.

In fact, the battle over Baba Gurgur had taken a new form right after WWII. In 1946 under the leadership of Fahad, the Communists had organized different factions to form syndicates and labor unions as a façade, seemingly unrelated to them. They had organized workers, students, teachers, and ordinary folk under the pretence of demanding their labor and political rights. Despite governmental crackdowns, they were successful in playing havoc in the country, especially Kirkuk, where they were organizing the oil industry workers for syndication. That would have been the first step in exerting control over the oil wells of Baba Gurgur, the underbelly of Britain and Iraq.

On July 3, 1946, the oil workers of IPC in Kirkuk began mass gatherings in an olive grove, just outside the town, known as Giavour Baghi (the Grove of the Christians). Normally this was a peaceful grove where families took their kebabs and gigantic Kirkuki watermelons, to picnic. But, on this occasion the oil workers had gathered to listen to their leaders demanding, in their name, their labor rights: work conditions, increases in salary, and benefits. They had gathered there after marching to the Governor's mansion requesting a meeting. Having failed to get a satisfactory answer from him, they had launched a strike, the first ever in Iraq's history, paralyzing oil production and refining. I do not know what impact the shut down had on the world markets, but it is reasonable to assume that Rotterdam was not happy with the shortage of some 2 million barrels a day.

The Communist strategists were successful in dominating the podium, subverting it, and giving it a distinct political face. This turn of events was unacceptable to the authorities, which sought to disperse the gathering that had developed into an antigovernment political demonstration. Police interfered, and the crowd dispersed. The rallies continued the following day, packing in more energy and determination. By the third day, it had taken a purely political character, condemning the government and of course the "Imperialist, colonialist Britain." This first in the history of the Iraqi oil industry shook both Baghdad and London. IPC woke up to the reality that their future was, to a large extent, in the hands of its workers.

The police force, which was there to keep order, tried but could not disperse the crowd peacefully, so they opened fire. Their sergeants, who gave the orders, instructed them to fire at "those who wore white, short-sleeved shirts," the hallmark of the Christian leaders and the strike organizers.

By the time the guns fell silent, six people were dead and fourteen wounded, including an Armenian; "Arab" Ohannes, Mgrdich's brother; a second Armenian, was also shot in the arm.

Kirkuk was a war zone. I could hear the bullets, which sounded like machine gunfire, but it wasn't; it was the sound of many rifles firing single shots in fast succession, and together. A short while later speeding ambulances and horse carriages passed in front of our house, carrying the dead and the wounded to the Majidiyya Hospital. I was both horrified by what I was seeing, and curious to understand what was happening. I saw most of the casualties from our balcony overlooking Shari' Al-Awqaf, the main street of Kirkuk. The date was July 12, 1946.

Instantly, the crackdown began against the subversives, the dissidents, the Communists, their sympathizers, and suspects. The following day IPC fired the "agitators"; it didn't matter if they were Communists or not. This was in violation of their promise to the labor leaders the day before, not to do so. The government arrested many and exiled them to Nugrat Salman, a godforsaken prison in the middle of nowhere in the southern Iraqi desert.

Mr. Chapman, A. J. B. Chapman

Mr. A. J. B. Chapman was the British political officer residing in Kirkuk. His job was to control the area and weed out those who constituted a threat to Baba Gurgur. He was in the trenches waging covert battles for his King and his country. His network of agents was in full swing too, gathering information about the undesirable elements. His immediate team consisted of the Armenian cook and a number of other Armenian and Kurdish "office workers," as they were known, who ran the necessary duties of the office, some in gathering information through a network of agents, and some in shaping the public opinion through misinformation, disinformation, and other methods of psychological warfare. Their ultimate goal was to maintain control over Baba Gurgur, and guarantee the safety of the refinery, which was only a few miles away.

The big job however fell on Mr. Chapman himself. He was a colonialist in the classical sense of the word. As a Political Officer of Great Britain, his ultimate duty was to maintain control over the Kurdish tribes on both sides of the Iraq-Iran border, and control events and preempt unfavorable developments that might endanger the British interests, on both sides of the border.

He spoke Kurdish and other local languages. More importantly, he knew Kurdistan's mountains, valleys, and villages on both sides of Iraq-Turkey-Iran border, and exercised control over them. He was so passionately in love with Kurdistan that he had willed to have his ashes scattered over the mountains of Kurdistan. His team executed his will!

Allan Chapman's control over the Kurds was total. He knew the Aghas individually. He had developed close personal relationships with them, and gained their confidence. He used the information he had obtained to divide and conquer the Aghas through intimidation, bribery, and above all, blackmail. He used to threaten an Agha by spreading rumors about his sexual habits, gender preferences, and scandalous behavior. He was in the habit of divulging the secrets of one Agha to a rival Agha, in order to get concessions. He himself, as the rumor goes, was gay.

Through control of Aghas, he controlled his tribe, and through that, he controlled both sides of the Iran-Iraq border, which gave him a unique opportunity to be in the know about the happenings in Iran.

In Northern and North Eastern Iraq, like many other places in the world, borders are only lines drawn on maps, meaningless. The reality on the ground is different; a tribe may live on both sides of an invisible border, and cross it at will without paying attention to the marker stones separating one country from the other.

Chapman used all the options he had with the Kurds, to keep the Iraqi government in line. He could turn the heat on Baghdad, at will, by having the tribes start trouble, somewhere in the Kurdish areas, like Qalah Dize; a policeman killed here, a soldier there, and a small government checkpoint burnt down somewhere else. Iraq's Second Army Division would then have no choice but to respond and be engaged in unwanted battles. This kind of Chapman instigation would serve a dual purpose: It would engage the army in a diversionary war rendering it incapable of plotting against the British-backed government. Second, it would force Baghdad to adjust its position vis-à-vis a given British policy, out of weakness.

Mr. Chapman lived close to the headquarters of the second army division in Kirkuk. This enabled him to keep a watchful eye on the military's top brass. He, for example, helped cleanse the armed forces in Kirkuk and Mosul from the ultranationalists and the leftists who, given the opportunity, might have plotted to depose the Royal Family, veer Iraq toward an anti-British posture, and work for realization of the Arab dream of unification. Creating such an entity was, and remains, a dream for all Arabs, and a nightmare for the West and Israel.

A United Arab country "From the Ocean to the Gulf," would have created a formidable problem for the West to reckon with. Such a union would have changed borders, the psychodynamics, the geopolitical dynamics, and the political orientation of all the governments in the region; additionally, it would have controlled huge reserves of oil and vast strategic land and waterways, which would have jeopardized the livelihood of the West, its security, and its very survival. Such an entity would have sided, undoubtedly, with the Soviet Union, which in the context of the cold war would have been detrimental to NATO and its allies and friends in the Middle East, such as Turkey, Iran, and Israel.

Under the prevailing circumstances of the 1950s, and in order to preserve her interests, Britain had no choice but to protect the Hashimite Royal regime in Iraq for as long as she could because it was the only asset she had in the region!

For the Iraqi nationalists, however, the prime concern, even superseding the pan-Arab Causes such as Palestine, was the absence of true sovereignty of Iraq. The lopsided Anglo-Iraqi treaty of 1932 favoring Britain, and the "Consultant System" of administration, which they had imposed on Iraq, were the two major telling signs of absence of Iraqi sovereignty. The Consultant System entailed having a British consultant sit in an adjacent room to monitor all the decisions made by a Minister and veto whatever decision he may have made that did not conform to British policies.

To appease the nationalists, Britain modified this system: they removed the consultants but mandated obtaining clearance for major policy decisions, from the Embassy. This, too, was not a satisfactory solution: By the late 1940s the nationalist political parties and nationalist military officers were objecting to this arrangement because, the new system meant proxy-governance by the colonialists, denying the Iraqis their rights to make important policies that dealt with their future. This entire exercise once again affirmed the Iraqi belief that the British did not intend to allow Iraq to pursue a path of her choosing. One way or another British colonialism was there, and Iraq had to remain in its galaxy!

For Iraqis, Britain was the master of deception; "If two fish fight in the sea, be sure it is instigated by the British," was, a common saying in Iraq.

Despite all the opposition, dissent, and noise, Britain continued to succeed in its endeavor: keeping control over Baba Gurgur, and fending it against enemies, such as the Soviet Union and the United States.

Soviet Plans for Baba Gurgur

With Churchill's "Iron Curtain" speech, which marked the inception of the cold war, Soviet propaganda in the world and in the Middle East escalated; they offered Marxism-Leninism as a substitute to corrupt capitalism, a system that exploited the masses for the benefit of a few. They presented themselves as advocates of justice, determined to help the oppressed people bring about radical changes in their lives. This meant overthrowing their regimes, and ridding the region from the colonialist-imperialist domination.

The fact that the Soviets had successfully defended Stalingrad and pushed the German forces all the way to Berlin was a forceful, convincing, propaganda point. So was their entry to Berlin! They stressed this point over and over again, praising the heroism of the Soviet soldier, and the wisdom of their commanders. At the end of the litany, it was all, ultimately, attributed to the superiority of the Communist regime, and the endurance of the Soviet people.

Of all this rhetoric, the one that impressed people most was their capture of Berlin. "If it wasn't for the Soviet Army, the American forces could not have taken Berlin," boasted their local propagandists. I argued against this point of view because it gave my interlocuters, the Communist propagandists in my neighborhood, the upper hand. It mattered to me that the West was not the first to enter Berlin. At the time we did not know that Ike had made a decision to let the Soviet soldier, rather than his, die for Berlin.

Kurds, who were Soviet sympathizers, were very happy and proud with this victory, but the Turkomans of Kirkuk felt sorry for the defeat of the Axis, since most of them were pro-Nazis even after Turkey had shifted alliance from Hitler to the allies.

This kind of Soviet propaganda echoed favorably in the Arab world because it articulated the realities of their daily life, albeit somewhat exaggerated, and because it fortified their belief that British policies had undermined their society in order to rob the riches of Baba Gurgur.

While the Soviet propaganda belabored to convey its message to the Iraqi general population, it did not have to struggle too hard to win the hearts and minds of some diasporan Armenians who were familiar with the Russian rather then the Soviet culture. Russo-Armenian "Friendship" is rooted in history. Armenia was one of the Russian Khanats in the Middle Ages. Their Tzars had given Holy Echmiadzin, the Vatican of the Armenian Apostolic faith in Armenia, their constitution, Bolozhenia. They were Armenia's allies who defended Armenia against the invading Turkish Army in the 1920s.

Armenia was one of the sixteen Soviet Republics, and many an Armenian had served, as top-ranking general or foot soldier, in the Soviet Army and defended the fatherland. Anastas Migoyan, an Armenian, was in the politburo, survived all the politburo purges, later, and became Prime Minister. There was his brother, the creator of the MIG jet. Last, but not least, there was Aram Khachaturian the world famous composer.

The Holy Sea of Echmiadzin was the definition of an individual Armenian's national identity, therefore Soviet or not, Armenia, and by extension the Soviet Union, was their spiritual home.

The Soviets had exploited this relationship to advance their interests, in not only the Armenian community of Kirkuk, but also that of Iraq, Syria, and Lebanon, where hundreds of thousands of post-Genocide Armenians had found a safe haven, and thrived.

In fact, this exploitation was not new; a few years after the Bolshevik Revolution the Soviets recruited some Armenian men of cloth, to implement their great designs for the Middle East. For example, the Armenian Archpishops of Iran and Iraq were agents of OGPU, the predecessor of KGB. The former had authority, which extended to India. In fact, the chief of OGPU in the 1920s was an Armenian who was later liquidated in Paris.

Armenian "Patriots," knowingly or unknowingly, were ready and willing to be a part of this strategy believing that their support would help their motherland to stand in good stead with the Soviets. In fact, in the mid-1940s, a handful of Armenians were in the hierarchy of the Iraqi Communist Party (ICP), and at least one of them was an original founder of the organization.

It was this Communist Armenian network, which smuggled the defecting Kim Philby, the famed Soviet mole in the British Intelligent Service and one of the original CIA advisers, from Beirut to Cyprus and ultimately to the Soviet Union. This defection shook Whitehall and the Western world, handing the Soviets a major victory. Kim Philby was a collaborator of McLean-Burgess et al., the Soviet moles in the British Intelligence Organization.

The Arab world was oblivious to this defection except for Saudi Arabia, which paid a passing attention to the event only because they knew his father, Kim Philby senior, who had converted to Islam and assumed the name "Abdullah." He had been a mole and a top adviser to the Saudi Royal Family. He had been an influential strategist in the battle over Saudi "Baba Gurgur."

In Kirkuk, the Armenian General Benevolent Union (AGBU) Club, for instance, was a theater for Soviet propaganda. This most nationalist, noble, benevolent, conservative, and capitalist Armenian Union, which was established by Boghos Nubar Pasha (the onetime Armenian Prime Minister of Egypt), was hijacked by the Armenian Communists, in the name of love for, and loyalty to, the fatherland.

As a teenager I used to go there. They used to sing and teach the youth songs praising the Soviet way of life. Soviet movies shown to us were about the accomplishments of the Soviet regime: the happy life in the kolkhozes, the giant combines, the rich harvests, the contented farmers, the valiant workers of Soviet Armenia, the gymnasts, the healthy vineyards, the famous Armenian cognac factories, and finally, the brave Soviet soldiers standing on guard to protect the beloved fatherland.

AGBU events started by singing Soviet Armenia's national anthem Sovetagan Azad Ashkhar Hayastan (Free World, Soviet-Armenia). The hammer and sickle studded red flag displayed on stage had substituted the historic red, blue, and peach-colored flag of nationalist Free Armenia.

They told us about how great the Soviet regime has been for Armenia since 1921, when the Bolsheviks toppled the three-year-old free and independent Armenian Republic, and took over the country. They despised the Free Armenian Republic, which in 1918 had risen from the ashes of millennia-old Armenian history and had enjoyed America's patronage; they spat on its tricolor flag. They were proud of the fact that the Reds of Armenia, in collaboration with Lenin's forces, had axed to death thousands of incarcerated nationalists who had waged the failed February Uprising against the regime. They were proud of the Sovietization of Armenia! AGBU was so involved in towing the Soviet line, that the opposition labeled them KGBU. Like Philby's case, Armenian Communists were highly instrumental in the workings of the International Communist movement, and were actively involved in the cold war, which in the Middle East reached its zenith in 1956.

That year, in Beirut, the hub of international espionage and the most important cold war theater, there was a big struggle for control of the Armenian Catholicate, the Great House of Cilicia. They were to elect a new Catholicos. This was of paramount importance to the superpowers because control of the Catholicate meant control of the churches in Syria, Lebanon, Iran, and Cyprus, the all too strategically important countries for the superpowers. Control of the churches, in turn, meant control of its parishioners and supporters, thus denying the Soviets bridgeheads in these countries.

The Soviet and the United States Embassies in Beirut were intimately involved in this duel. The negotiators on both sides, those who preferred the Soviet candidate and those who opposed it, had open lines to their perspective Embassies, receiving minute-to-minute instructions. Finally, after days of haggling, the Soviets lost. Thus, America won another round in the cold war.

Communism and the Youth

In Kirkuk, the AGBU club was not the only arena for Communist propaganda, the battlefield was much bigger than that, and the Communists were on the offensive. Aside from the oil industry workers, they had targeted a select group of dissident high school kids for recruitment and indoctrination, regardless of their socioeconomic status; these were the potential future politicians who could, one day, chart the destiny of Baba Gurgur, and Iraq at large.

There were a handful of such people, in my neighborhood, who were happy to have me as an observer and a potential doctrinaire. In turn, my thirst for general education, and curiosity about the Communist underground made me join them.

We used to gather in the Iraq Pharmacy, owned by my father's friend, Khatchig Terzian. The man himself was old, and absent during lunch hours, but his sons ran the pharmacy and conducted these seemingly innocent meetings. The participants considered themselves intellectuals, and expressed diverse opinions and political hypotheses for discussion. Soon I discovered that the Communists had trapped the group in a pseudointellectual world. However, those who already were converts felt differently; they felt important and proud to be a part of the "Revolutionary Intelligentsia" akin to Lenin. Some were trying to highlight distinctions between Marx-Engel and Lenin philosophies; others discussed Trotsky's deviation, yet all admired Stalin, regardless of his butchery of the Soviet people. Everybody had read Chekhov, Pushkin, and Dostoevsky, or anything Russian for that matter. One of the attendees, Mohammed Abdul-Majeed, a rather reserved man who was a student in Teachers' College of Baghdad, was so absorbed by the doctrine that he used to comb his hair, Anastas Migoyan style, to one side, slightly covering the left forehead, as if to conceal his Leftist ideology from the government agents. The attendees were the very first crop of educated Kirkuki youth who were destined to become the future leaders of Communist Iraq.

Such was the extent of Soviet propaganda's influence on their psyche. For them, being a Communist meant being moral, strong-willed, and dedicated hardened doctrinaires, all characteristics of an honorable man.

I used to go to that pharmacy during siesta time because the owner's second son, Dickran, was my friend. It is there where I met a dissident student, Adnaan Azzawi, an Arab, brother of Kan'aan Azzawi, sons of an army top brass. They both were soccer stars, and both eventually graduated from Military College, the West Point of Iraq. Adnaan appeared to be the leader of the deliberations. Little did I know at the time that in a decade Adnaan was going to play a major role in my life!

Despite their heroic efforts, their propaganda could not penetrate my mind. My political thoughts had already jelled through my family, my father, Uncle Krikor, Aunt Victoria, and Aunt Victoria's brother-in-law, Dickran, who was a true hero. He had dedicated himself to rescuing Armenian girls who were kidnapped by the Kurds during the Armenian Genocide, converted them to Islam, and forced them to marry their boys. This was a common practice. I know at least two dozen Kurds whose grandmothers were Armenians abducted during the Genocide.

Aunt Victoria, my mother's sister, was different from her mother and the rest. Like her sister, Takouhi, she was schooled. Her education was interrupted by fighting waged by the forces of Kemal Ataturk against the Kurds in Anatolia, especially Dikranagerd (Diarbakir), which had dislocated large masses of the population, including hers, from their homeland.

Victoria and her family traveled by raft on the Tigris, and ended up in Mosul, the northern city of Iraq, where she settled. She was a "revolutionary," a fierce Armenian nationalist and a staunch anti-Turk, to the point of being a Chauvinist. She was a disbeliever because she couldn't reconcile God's love and mercy with his "indifference" to the Turkish Genocide of the Armenians. She couldn't understand why God allowed such genocide to befall a deeply Christian, peaceful, God-fearing, God loving, ancient people. She would brush aside arguments that by looking the other way or allowing this to happen "God tested our faith"; "There was no need to test our faith, we had already sacrificed thousands of our boys to defend our faith in Christianity, and we have accepted Jesus as his son. Witness the thousand and one churches we built in Ani in glorification of him, and he allows this to happen?" She would therefore conclude that there was no God!

Advancing this line of argument, she also despised organized church, priests, and all, God's deputies on earth. She used to tell me stories about how some deceptive clergy of the time collaborated with the Ottoman authorities and turned in Armenian Fedayees (freedom fighters) thinking that by doing so they might protect the church from the evil of the Muslim Turk. She used to tell me stories about how the Fedayees, even before ARF (Armenian Revolutionary Federation), had "cleansed" the communities from these "Madnitch Houtahs" (Judases).

I would listen to her with great interest, fear, and anxiety, then feel satisfied and proud that at least our boys "got even" with these "traitors." She would finish her stories with "Makretsin, verchatsav" (they were done with, finished) only to start a new story upon my begging for more. From the beginning there was no doubt in my mind as to who the bad people were!

It was on her knees that I learned about Raffi, Siamanto, Kevork Chavoush, Krikor Zohrab, Vartkes, Nzhdeh, Akhpure Serop, Sossi Mayrig, Antranig, Aram, Vratsian, and the "Fedayees," all Armenian intellectuals and battlefield heroes. Especially Raffi's *Khente*, a solid, colorful novel about Armenian nationalism gave her fire and in turn, she fired my youthful imagination. I couldn't imagine, still can't, how an ancient race like the Armenians could be annihilated by the Turks in this manner, bayoneted, burnt alive by the thousand at a time, and the rest deported to the Syrian desert of Der-El-Zor to die of thirst and hunger. I couldn't imagine how Christian Europe allowed this to happen. Weren't we Christians too?

To me, Aunt Victoria was it, a real Armenian, a real revolutionary, someone who could deliberate logically, albeit laced with anger and emotion. What she did for me was priceless; it set my political orientation for the rest of my life. Her actions could only be matched by Uncle Krikor's efforts in the same arena.

Yes, my ideology had crystallized; nevertheless, I listened to the "intellectuals" of the Iraq Pharmacy to educate myself and satisfy my curiosity. Their attempts to convert me to Left-wing ideology was sure to fail, it was bound to: my hero Winston Churchill, the IPC, my father, Godfather Ibrahim Qolchi, my Aunt Victoria, and the others, had solidly formulated my thoughts a long time earlier, and that clashed with Communism. How can an ignorant criminal Turk be equal to a civilized Armenian? That is what Communism is, isn't it, equality between races? Is an Uzbek equal to a Russian in the Soviet Union? I doubt it! No, this doctrine was not for me! These people couldn't brainwash me! I was a staunch anti-Communist. Adnaan Azzawi knew it and saw his failure in me. That angered him.

Turkoman youth did not belong in this group; they were pro-Turkey, therefore Nazi sympathizers in the beginning, then pro Allies when Turkey got out of the Axis in WWII. Additionally, their belief in Pan-Turanism, which they had inherited from their fathers, directed them away from Communism.

Pan-Turanism is a racist, chauvinist ideological doctrine advocated by the Gray Wolves of Turkey. For them Turks are "Uber allis," the other races are inferior to them. This decades-old Turkish political party calls for unification of Turkey with the Central Asian Turkic countries, which stud the "Silk Trail." In fact, even today, they aspire for geographic and demographic unification of Turkic-speaking peoples, wherever they may be. Turkoman's embrace of such a racist doctrine, in Kirkuk, created a political chasm between them and the Kurds, which remains valid to date. In recent years the United States too has subscribed to such an idea in order to gain access to strategically and economically all-important Central Asia.

Thus, divisions in Kirkuk were along not only ethnic lines, but also ideological: Kurds and Communists of all ethnic groups on one side, and the rest on the other. What specifically distinguished the nonestablishment group from the rest was education and ethnic heritage. For instance, unlike young Arab intellectuals who had very rich history to fall back on, the Turkoman youth had neither history nor a glorious past to call their own. However, they are not to blame for this cultural poverty; their elders themselves had none to pass along to them other than what they had learned, in turn, from their elders in the reactionary Central Asian Yurt tradition: the tradition of Genghiz Khan and Houlako Khan. For instance, when confronted, they could not name a single Kirkuki Turkoman poet, or writer, or an intellectual of consequence, to call their own.

In fact, the most educated, prominent, and benevolent Turkoman families, which formed Kirkuk's aristocracy, were the Naffitchis, the Qirdaars, the Hurmouzis, the Ya'qoubis, and the Awtchis. These families had reached prominence during the Ottoman rule of centuries past. Some of them had distinguished themselves in diplomatic, banking, and scientific arenas. Of these, I should like to remember Dr. Najeeb Ya'qoubi, my professor of neurosurgery; my friend Najdad Safwat Qirdaar, who was an ambassador, a translator to General Qasim, and an established author; Naa'il Ya'qoubi, Ibrahim Nafftchi, and Najeeb Qirdaar, all of whom were dignitaries of Kirkuk, and acquaintances of my father.

The socioeconomic gap between these families and the common folk was immense; despite that, I dare say that there was not a single leftist, let alone a Communist, who was a Turkoman, in Kirkuk.

The majority of the Communists and their sympathizers were Arabs, Kurds, and of course, some small group of Armenians. The Arabs had become Communists to "save" their country from the imperialists: the Kurds, to get a measure of political autonomy, and some Armenians, oddly enough, for nationalistic reasons.

Armenians had no political agenda in Iraq. The four-centuries-old Armenian community in Baghdad enjoyed the same citizenship rights as any Arab in the country. Iraqis loved and respected them, and when in 1915, waves of the Armenian Genocide survivors arrived, the government and the people embraced them and sheltered them. Armenians were grateful to the Arabs for their hospitality. They became loyal citizens and helped build the country technologically. Mechanics, photographers, technicians, doctors, dentists, pharmacists, and other artisans and professionals changed the daily life of Baghdad and the major cities. In turn, Arabs appreciated all that.

It was during this immediate postwar era that a handful of men formed the ICP. Hahpet (his first name) an Armenian, a family friend, whose wedding I had attended as a little kid, was a founding member. We suspected that he was a Communist, but did not know for sure until the government arrested and exiled him to Nugrat Salman, the worst prison there was in the country; it was home for hard core "political criminals," a synonym for Communists, who were held there for years, to be forgotten by society. Many of those never came back! It was only a few years ago that one of Hahpet's cousins confirmed to me the fact that he was indeed one of the five founding members of the Iraqi Communist Party.

While Hahpet's name and identity had remained secret, the illusive, legendary Fahad's (Lion's Cub) name was not. He was the legendary chair of the Central Committee of the ICP and its Spokesman, though no one knew who he really was.

Many years later the authorities identified him as one Salman Yousif Salman, a printer who worked out of the wet dungeons of Baghdad and produced the Al Qa'ida party flyer. This bible of ICP circulated all over the country, including the Iraq Pharmacy, spreading the Communist ideology and inciting people to rise against the colonialist-imperialists, and their puppet, the Royal family.

In mid-February 1949, the government tracked down Fahad, arrested him, and together with three of his comrades swayed him from the gallows; one of them was a Jew named Yehuda Siddiq. The presence of a Jew in the hierarchy of ICP reinforced the common belief that Zionism and Communism are two sides of the same coin.

By his execution, the government disrupted the party's operations, but unintentionally created a legend and a martyr for the ICP. Fahad's execution energized the party, and gave them an additional raison d'etre. They regrouped, reorganized, and chose Adil Salaam as the new leader of the Central Committee.

Fahad's demise did not end the government's fight against the Zionist-Communist historical alliance. The Iraqi establishment, like Hitler, despised both, and struggled against them; Arab intellectuals believed that Hitler's anti-Semitism stemmed from Jewish creation and adoption of Zionism-Communism, whose intent was to subvert Germany. Arab enmity toward the Jews stemmed from the same premise: Rightly or wrongly, they argued that Communists were collaborating with the Zionists to subvert the Arab nation. The proof of their argument was the Communist support in creating Israel, and lack of Arab-Communist opposition to it.

8

1948

Creation of Israel was not the only postwar major international event in 1948. That year was a turbulent year for the Middle East, and also for the world at large: major political and demographic shifts in the region changed the balance of power amongst nations. There was mass deportation of Palestinian Arabs, which created a vacuum, filled by mass immigration of Jews to Israel. There was mass immigration of Armenians from the Levant and Iraq to Soviet Armenia. The rationale of this project was to replenish Armenia's population, which had lost hundreds of thousands in WWII.

In Iraq, the Portsmouth Treaty rocked the country. Globally there was the Chinese Revolution, the disputes over the division of India and Pakistan, the aftereffects of Hiroshima and Nagasaki, the Algerian revolution, the crystallization of the NATO concept, and the cold war in general.

In Syria, the Ba'th Party was born, filling the political vacuum created by serial coups of the Syrian generals. The Middle East, and Iraq, seemed hit by severe atmospheric turbulence; regardless, oil kept on flowing from Baba Gurgur to the Mediterranean to quench Europe's thirst.

In 1948, the Balfour Declaration (some call it promise) of November 2, 1917, which favored "...establishment, in Palestine, a national home for Jews but *without* prejudice to the civil and religious rights of the existing non-Jewish communities" had become a reality, but not along the terms it had specified. The declaration became a reality all right, but *with* prejudice to "the civil and religious rights of the existing non-Jewish communities." Hundreds of thousands of Palestinians lost their "civil and religious rights" and fled or were forced to leave their homes to live in tent-cities created by the United Nations in various parts of the Arab world. Logistically and emotionally, this was a big blow to the Arab Nation. For the

Arab person it was, and still is, a constant source of anger, frustration, and hatred toward America and the West. The general feeling was that America had brought this "al-nakbah" (disaster) upon them. That was not all; they also put the blame on the Arab leaders of the time, specifically the Kings of the Hashimite Dynasty; King Abdullah of Trans Jordan headed that list. King Farouk of Egypt was another culprit who deserved punishment of some sort.

Before all this, Jerusalem had been in hibernation! Since Salahaddin (Saladin, the Kurdish warrior from Tikrit, the birthplace of Saddam Hussein) liberated it from the Crusaders in the thirteenth century, and it had not seen major changes; it had lived under some kind of Islamic-Arab administrations, until the Ottomans incorporated it into their empire.

Jerusalem is the third Holy City in Islam, after Mecca and Medina. That is where Khalif Omar Ibn-Al-Khattaab (Omar Al- 'Aadil = Omar the Just) had prayed, and given permission to build a mosque at the site of his prayer, casting Islamic legitimacy over it. That is where Khalif Al-Waleed Bin Abdul-Malik Bin Marwaan built the Al-Aqasa mosque on the site of Muhammad's alleged landing on a white horse, traveling overnight from Medina.

Regardless of the fact that all three monotheistic religions, including the Armenians, Russians, and Greeks owned a part of the Holy land, for the Muslims "Jerusalem was Muslim!" defending it was not only justified but the duty of all Muslims; Jerusalem was as holy, and as important as Mecca.

On the other hand, some prominent Arabs, like King Abdullah of Trans Jordan, the grandfather of King Hussein of Jordan, were accommodative to the idea of "Jewish immigration to Palestine, to live side-by-side with the Arabs." He, and those who were receptive to the idea were misled by their own ignorance; they did not know the Ashkenazim; they thought they were, like Sephardim, Semites, their cousins. They thought the incoming European Jews, like themselves, were the descendants of Abraham; they were not! They expected the immigrant Jew to be docile, servile, obedient, and loyal to them, like the Semitic Jew; they were not!

It was much later that they studied the letters of the twelfth century Abbasid travelers and "Ambassadors," and realized that the Eastern European Jewish tribes were in fact Khazars, Turkic tribes of Central Asia. In the seventh and eighth centuries, the Chinese had displaced them west toward the river Volga, where they had settled around Kiev, and built a Kingdom.

Originally, Khazars had no religion but in their new location, Byzantines tried to impose Christianity on them through war; so did the Abbasids who fought them in the Caucasus to convert them to Islam; they both failed. Finally, upon the advice of a Spanish-Jewish "Ambassador" they accepted Judaism as a state religion. So says Arthur Koestler in his book, *The Thirteenth Tribe*.

In the tenth century Khazaria was an empire of sorts; they dominated the city of Kiev, the entire Volga river basin, Hungary, the entire Eastern European vicinity, and the south all the way to the Caspian Sea, in fact, the Arabs call the Caspian Sea, "Bahhr al-Khaazaar," the Sea of Khazar.

What follows then, is the argument that Eastern European Jews, who populated Israel, were not Semites, but Turkic Khazars. The dominant opinion in the Arab world, at the time, was that the European Jews were not the children of Abraham; therefore, they are not their cousins. Regardless of what they thought, the argument was just an academic exercise, and had no impact on the realities of the conflict.

Arabs considered establishment of the State of Israel illegitimate, created to keep Western control over, not only Baba Gurgur, but also on all the other Baba Gurgurs of the Arab world. Additionally, in terms of military strategy, Israel was to become a base for the West to contain the Soviet Union from the south. Although the foothold served the West well, it, in and by itself, became a major source of instability, wars, and turbulences in the region and beyond.

Upon creation of the State of Israel, the Arab rulers could not stand by passively doing nothing, which would have been treason. They had to react precipitously and dramatically to satisfy the Arab street, which was demanding removal of this "cancer" from its body. They declared war against Israel, which they knew they could not win. Like Egypt, and the other Arab countries, Syria and Iraq also dispatched their armed forces to liberate Palestine and send the Jews back to where they came from, or better yet, dump them into the sea.

In fact, Jews could not go back to where they came from even if they wanted to, Europe was in disarray, and they had just fled the Holocaust! Even if Europe was stable and prosperous, it did not want them, and that was not new; almost all European countries had expelled Jews from their land in the fourteenth and fifteenth centuries, the last being Spain. They could not go to America either because Congress had adopted the Johnson-Reed law, which forbad Jewish immigration to the United States. America turned away ships carrying Jewish immigrants from the shores of Florida

Arabs, in attacking the newborn Israel, underestimated their enemy. They believed that the Israeli defense forces were composed of Jews like the ones they knew: passive, scared, servile, obedient, and cowards. They were mistaken! They were up against a rude awakening; Israeli defense forces handed them a resounding defeat, which they could not tolerate or forget. It had a sobering effect on the entire Arab world, and the political leaders began to reassess the situation and plan for future actions. Their armed forces were humiliated, and the officers took the shame of defeat personally. The loss tagged their psyche and generated hatred, which became a psychological driving force for every Arab. Seeking revenge was the dominant thinking of the day, which the successive generations inherited and nurtured.

The Nakbah sowed the seeds of the "pan-Arab Revolutionary Movement" in the heart and mind of the Arab person, who demanded action. To begin with there had to be housecleaning of all these "traitors, agents of Britain, who sold their country."

King Abdullah paid with his life while praying in the Al-Aqasa mosque with his grandson, Hussein (later, King Hussein of Jordan).

The Egyptian and the Iraqi military had already formed their own separate Free Officers' Movements. Revenge, which has always been a big Arab tribal custom and an element of the Arab psyche, was a big motivating force in initiating these movements. The Egyptian Armed Forces blamed King Farouk for their defeat, accusing him of treason and corruption and of sending them to war with defective British arms (Al-Aslihhaa al-Faasida), which he had purchased and profited from, a clear proof in their eyes of conspiring with Britain to defeat the Arabs.

On July 25, 1952, just four short years after the Nakbah, the "Free Officers" of Egypt, headed by Mohammed Naguib, deposed King Farouk and exiled him to Italy where he lived in hedonism and died as a drunkard. Egypt was now a republic governed by the Revolutionary Counsel. In a matter of days, however, Mohammed Naguib relinquished the chair, and Nasser became president.

Through his speeches and plots, Nasser succeeded in firing the Arab imagination. In a sense, he was the kindling force, which ignited the long held desires of the ordinary Arab, who was aspiring for union of the Arab countries from the Atlantic to the Arabian (Persian) Gulf. In that, they saw the revival of the old Islamic and Moorish glory. Ironically, what Nasser was demanding then, was not different from what Usama Bin Laden is demanding today: rid the Arab land from foreign influences and control the oil wealth of the Nation. However, Nasser, though a devout Muslim, never called for Shari'a rule of the Arab land, like Usama does.

With his actions, Nasser defied the colonial powers and the United States in particular, and soon became a pan-Arab hero, the torchbearer of the Arab nationalism, which was rapidly developing ideological bastions to achieve that ideal.

The Arab ruling classes and Royalty joined the Western world in vehemently opposing Nasser and his ideology, because in him they saw a great danger threatening their interests and the interests of the establishment in general. The Hashimite Royal family, both in Iraq and Jordan, were parties to this opposition.

In 1948, some four years prior to Nasser's propulsion to prominence, the Arab political world was fermenting yet another political ideology, this time originating in Syria, where two Sorbonists, Akram Horani, a Muslim, and Michele Aflaq, a Christian, pursuing the ideals of the French Revolution, established the Ba'th Party. The party's platform called for rejection of all ethnic, gender, and religious discrimination. They advocated Socialism and the union of all Arab countries.

Nasser's ideology was somewhat similar to that of Ba'th, but not quite. Nasser was an avid Muslim. Ba'th was not. The movement echoed favorably amongst the nationalist minded Arab youth.

In Syria, yet another strong political current, working covertly, was the banned Communist Party. Strongman Khalid Bektash was "Mr. Communist of Syria and the Middle East." He, clearly, was a surrogate of the Soviet Union, whose goals in the region were multiple, not the least of which being control of Baba Gurgur and strategically the all-important Middle East.

So, in the late 1940s and the 1950s there were three strong political currents rocking the Arab ship from side to side: Nasserism, Ba'ithism, and Communism. Additionally there were two reactionary political currents, which had no major programs other than regaining what they had lost throughout the past centuries: Islamic Brotherhood (Ikhwaan el-Muslimeen) and the ruling reactionary forces.

In Iraq, Kurdish nationalism was an additional movement, but it did not concern the rest of the Arab countries for various reasons, not the least of which being the conviction that it pertained only to Iraq and it was not a threat to Arab national interests. How misled were they, today's events are the proof of that. More on this subject later.

After the July 14 revolution in Iraq, when there was talk about Iraq joining Nasser's United Arab Republic, Jalaal Talabani, a major Iraqi Kurdish leader, visited Nasser on two separate occasions to assert his demand for Kurdish rights in Iraq. Nasser had assured Talabani of a satisfactory solution to their national aspirations, within the framework of an Arab entity.

This political diversity of the Arab political structure, though healthy, did not speak of democracy, which was, and is, alien to the Arab world and tradition. Other cultures should understand Islam before trying to change it, as the West is trying to do: The sheikh-serf arrangement inherent in the Arab tribal structure was, with variable degrees, the modus operandi of the entire Arab world. The oppressive reactionary regimes in the Arab land did not allow for an alternative. Besides, the "Shari'a" as outlined by Prophet Muhammad and the Holy Qur'an structures every aspect of a Muslim's life. It defines the social structure of society, delineating each person's rights, responsibilities, and behavior. There are restrictive tenets in that system, which are contrary to Western-style democracy. Islamic society is usually built around a central figure, an elder or a leader, who then has a kind of advisory body of his own choosing, known as "Shoora," which advises the leader. The Holy Qur'an makes a clear distinction between a man and a woman in inheritance and in interpersonal relationships, and gives the man a distinct superiority in decision making; a woman is to obey her husband who has the legitimate right to discipline her, even through capital punishment. A woman is not allowed to file for divorce; only now this is somewhat modified in Egypt.

Implementing this Shari'a are men of cloth, who direct society through "fat-was," the product of their "ijtihaad," research and development of their thoughts. True, Muslim seculars do not adhere to the Shari'a verbatim, true there is flexibility in interpersonal relationships; still, the basic guideline is the Shari'a, and that is not subject to modification.

Although the new diverse political ideologies provided the West with an excellent opportunity to continue its "divide and conquer" policies, it also compounded their worries about growing anti-West sentiments, which if neglected would eventually jeopardize their control over Baba Gurgur.

With this political mess in hand, Nasser joined Yugoslavia's Tito, India's Jawahar Lal Nehru, and Indonesia's Sukarno in creating the "Non Aligned block" advocating "Positive Neutrality," a move that propelled him further into a pan-Arab leadership, which allowed him to galvanize the Arab world. People idolized him; for them he was their undisputed leader, the embodiment of their dreams.

For the Soviets Nasser was it, and for the West, he was it too, though in a different way. The West despised him. His appeal to the Arab masses, his charisma, and his success in awakening, organizing, and galvanizing the Arab street, run the chills down their spine. Rightly or wrongly, they looked at Nasserism as an expansion of Communist ideology, and Egypt as an extension of the Soviet sphere of influence. For the first time in history, the Soviets had a foothold in Egypt, from where they could meddle in the affairs of the Middle East. They were jubilant also because the new regime in Egypt and its dynamic variables helped create a major problem for the West, a distracting battle in the cold war.

In fulfilling a dream, Nasser dared to nationalize the Suez Canal, which led to the 1956 war with Israel, France, and Britain. He lost the war, but won the canal. His stock rose with the Arabs even more, who not only gained control of one of their legitimate possessions but also regained their self-respect; at long last someone had stood up to the "aggressors" and expelled them from their land, similar to Saladin.

Nasser was not fighting only the West; he was constantly after Iraq and other oil producers of the Gulf. He plotted against the Sheikhs and the royal families by agitating the oppositions. Through extortion, he secured a share of the oil revenues for Egypt. He plotted against Saudi Arabia, and even had Prince Talaal Ibn Saud, a senior-ranking Saudi prince, defect to Cairo and work there against his own family, plotting to bring about "change" in the Saudi regime.

Nasser's propaganda machine never ceased functioning: Ahmed Sa'eed from "Sawt Al-Arab min Al-Qaahira" (the Voice of Arabs from Cairo) radio, "Nasser's bugle" had editorials and commentaries to agitate the Iraqi masses against the regime, and against the Imperialists who, by controlling Baba Gurgur, were sucking the Arab nation's blood. Nasser considered Arab oil wealth as the property of the entire Arab nation. To him oil was a weapon to fight the West with; he too was waging battle over Baba Gurgur.

Still in the Middle East, Syria experienced a long period of instability suffering multiple, successive, military coups within a decade: that of Shukri Al-Quwatli, Husni Za'eem, Chichekli, Hannawi, Abdul-Hameed Al-Sarraaj, and others.

Thus, in the decade of the 1950s three countries had changed the political landscape of the Middle East: the Egyptian revolution against the Khidevis (1952), the Iraqi army's revolts against the Hashimites (1958), and the Syrian multiple coup d'etats (1948–1958). These revolutions in three major Arab countries had two main common threads, which were:

a) Humiliating defeat of their armies against the Israeli armed forces in 1948, for which they blamed the ruling monarchies and factions.
b) The negative influences of the colonial powers, which supported the corrupt regimes.

One could say that the famed macho Iraqi army felt the bitterness of failure and the shame of defeat the most. The officers were furious. They were bitter, they were restless, and they felt betrayed to say the least.

In war, they had to their credit the "Battle of Jeneen," where they had mercilessly slaughtered a lot of civilian Jews, but that was hardly enough to claim victory. They had lost, period!

Despite their resounding defeat, upon their return to the country, they held a victory parade in Kirkuk, the home of the second Army division. It passed by our house on Shari' Al-Awqaf. I was fourteen at the time, had a Kodak box camera in my hand, and shot pictures of the parade, pretending to be a journalist.

Despite the commotion, the marchers, and the bands, the returning men did not look like heroes, nor did they behave like heroes. From the looks in their eyes and their demeanor, one could tell that they were not parading with heads high; they had the looks of a defeated, rather than a victorious army.

In the parade I spotted a young lieutenant, Serop Dawood, an Armenian, the only Armenian officer in the entire Iraqi army. He was married to Victoria, the daughter of Khatchig Terzian whose pharmacy many of us frequented, siesta time, to discuss matters of the world and Communism.

9

The IPC and Us

Kirkuk was the commercial center of the whole region, it was far advanced than Erbeel (Arbil) and Suleymania, mainly because of the IPC and partly because of The Second Army Division Headquarters.

Farmers brought grain, ghee, rice, produce, and the rest to Kirkuk for distribution to different towns and villages. The biggest hospitals, educational facilities, and commerce were in Kirkuk, not Suleymania or Erbeel. Transportation was in the hands of Armenians: Alexan Juvelegian, Nerses Der Nersesian, Taveet Hagopian, and the Yeranosian brothers who owned the majority of the trucks that transported grain and rice.

One major retail souk was Qoriya Bazaari, which unlike the bazaars of the Citadel, was not covered and was not organized; a butcher shop could be next to a haberdasher, for instance. Most of the shops sold fresh vegetables, fruits, meats, cheese, huge watermelons, and some were general stores selling everything from ropes to baskets to candles, teakettles, and candy.

There was an ice factory not far from the souk; it produced large blocks of ice; huge tongs pulled the ice out of their molds, like lollipops, and distributed them. The owner's son, Lateef Mohammed Boza, was my classmate. He had taken me to the factory to show me around. I would say, aside from the oil refinery and the electric powerhouse, this was the only other mechanized industry in town.

The IPC was Kirkuk's lifeline, not only because it poured more than half a million sterling pounds a month into the city's economy, a substantial sum at the time, but also because of what it brought to us in other aspects of life. For one it was a window to the outside world and Western lifestyle.

Through IPC, we could sample European life and culture and aspire for a better future for ourselves. IPC fired our imagination about what life could be, which eventually made most of us discontented. Many of us began disliking the country, which had given refuge and a safe haven to our immigrant parents, the survivors of the Armenian Genocide.

The youth of Kirkuk thought that one had to either live like the Europeans or migrate to where he could find it. Western culture had captivated our hearts and minds. Hollywood had done its job. Nouri Qadir, a half-educated son of a Kurdish illiterate shopkeeper, for instance, talked about going to Hollywood to direct movies. This was the thought that motivated but also tortured us, all of us: Armenians, Assyrians, and Turkomans alike.

We had inner conflicts: perhaps my share of it was greater than the rest, or so it seemed. Though Britain, with its colonial culture, was my mental home, Armenian Nationalism was my spiritual base. These clashed with my feelings for my birthplace Kirkuk, which had bound me to its earth like a child to his mother.

Life dictates, and for me life in the West was enchanting and tempting. Migrating to Britain and America, mostly Britain, was a dream to pursue! I preferred Britain for its civility and social structure. Saville Row hand-cut three-piece suits, Churchill or Barrett shoes, Dunhill pipes, Capstan tobacco, Johnny Walker Black, the signet ring on the pinkie, and maybe a gold pocket watch on a gold chain with a fob, all symbols of British lifestyle, had already tailored ours.

I thought America was too wild, too restless, too unconventional, and too riddled with "gun wielding cowboys," and therefore, it was unacceptable to most of us.

Yes, IPC was our lifeline! It had come to town as Turkish Petroleum Company until Caloust Gulbenkian, better known in the industry as "Mr. Five Percent" had put a British-led consortium together and formed the new company. IPC was for Iraq, what General Motors is or was for America, except more.

Since drilling the first oil well in 1924 to the present, oil has shaped the internal and external policies of Iraq and the major powers. It has influenced the balance of power in the Middle East by causing aggression and wars resulting in death and destruction. It has rearranged the demographics and the social structure of the region.

Many considered this discovery a mixed blessing, others God's curse: on one hand, it meant prosperity, and on the other hand a hindrance to political independence. Nationalists were of the opinion that the oil-producing nations would always be victims of a million different plots, schemes by super powers, and never be free to pursue their national dreams, such as United Arabia. Time has proven them right.

During the reign of the Hashimite Family, which lasted for almost four decades, Britain and the oil companies had a relatively easy time. They had an "ally" in King Faisal I who was smart enough to walk a tightrope between the British on one side, and Arab Nationalists, of whom he was one, on the other. Can kings be nationalist? Well, this was one!

He was a purebred Arab, born to nobility in Hijaaz (now part of Saudia), the hub of the Arab nation. His father was King Hussein Ibn Ali El Hashimi, a descendant of Prophet Muhammad. His brothers were King Ali (briefly King of Syria), and King Abdullah of Trans Jordan (the grandfather of King Hussein). With impeccable credentials, he was a fierce Arabist, also a pragmatic realist who had no illusions about political realities; he knew who held the levers of power in the world and avoided antagonizing them. He tried to keep the nationalist zealots, most of the time on leash, yet unleashed them when the British really got out of hand.

He was a wise man, a father figure in the best tribal sense of the word. He had worked with Lawrence of Arabia in the early days of the Arab uprising against the Ottoman Turks. He had even closer ties with Gertrude Bell, the British diplomat-King maker who helped create and shape the Kingdom of Iraq, and who had, by all accounts, a romantic relationship with him.

Gertrude Bell was an ultracolonialist who served her King and country admirably and set the Iraqi State ship in a direction suitable to Britain. In her time, IPC produced and sold oil without a hitch; Iraq was getting, through the generosity of Britain, 50 cents on the barrel.

She was a determined, domineering woman who alienated many people, including the British Embassy diplomats. Her actions also lay the foundation for discontent, opposition, and eventual political unrest in the country. Her influence on the king was so profound that the opposition considered him to be her puppet.

King Faisal was a desert man who was well-educated, spoke fluent English, French, and of course, classical Qur'anic Arabic.

He was keenly aware of the plight of the Armenian people and their suffering in the hands of their common oppressor, the Ottoman Turk. His father, Shereef Hussein Ibn Ali, had fought side by side with the British, against the Ottoman Empire, seeking independence for his people and the Arab nation at large. At one point in his struggle the "Red Sultan," Sultan Abdul Hamid II, exiled him to Istanbul and kept him there for a long time.

Shereef Hussein admired Armenians who had planted a bomb to assassinate the Red Sultan in 1905. He sympathized with the Armenian cause, and considered them comrades in arms: On the eve of the Genocide and massive deportation of Armenians, he issued a directive to all Arabs asking them to help the Armenian refugees, settle them on their land, and treat them kindly, "as if they were one of your own." That signed document still hangs in the rectory of the Armenian Church in Baghdad.

His son King Faisal I had the same kind of sentiments toward the Armenians. He trusted them unequivocally: his car mechanics, his personal chauffeur, and a battery of other technicians were all Armenians. In his memoirs, Dr. Sinderson, his personal physician and the founder of my school, the Royal College of Medicine, Baghdad, mentions that, "His majesty decided to stay overnight at the farm of an Armenian family in Fallujah and attend a banquet in his honor, rather than stay in the mayor's house, very much to the mayor's disappointment."

King Faisal's death in 1933 did not augur well for the British. They lost a partner, though not always an ally. More than losing the King, their concern was about his heir, his only son King Ghazi, who was a pro-Nazi Arab chauvinist.

He disliked the Kurds, the Assyrians, and the British who, with their unique problems and threats, posed a challenge to his authority. He lacked pragmatism and flexibility, the two major requirements in governance and politics. He surrounded himself with like-minded Army officers, who continually bombarded his mind with anti-Jew, anti-British propaganda. He did not need much convincing, anyway.

This kind of orientation spelled disaster for the country as well as the British: The pro-German, pro-Nationalist Arabs were getting the upper hand in the name of ridding Iraq of the Imperialist-colonialist Britain. By then, Balfour had made his Declaration, Hitler was just rising on the scene, and the Jewish influx into Palestine had accelerated. The prevailing Arab thought of the time as, "They are grabbing Arab land; we must do something about it."

In 1937, King Ghazi was involved in a fatal car accident. Official statements presented it as a regular accident, a brake failure or some such thing; however, the Nationalists were convinced that "It was murder, the British killed him!" because he was a fanatic nationalist, and a Nazi sympathizer.

His infant heir Faisal II inherited the throne, but because he was not of age, his pro-British maternal uncle, Prince Abdul Ilaah, became Regent. The new set of circumstances propelled the pro-British Regent and his entourage, headed by Nouri Sa'id (later Knighted by ERII) to the fore. Of course, the British liked this arrangement because their team was now in power replacing the pro-Nazi King Ghazi.

It is uncertain whether King Ghazi would have allowed it, but the new team not only did not object to the Jewish migration from Iraq to the newly formed Israel, but also facilitated it. Recently, in an Aljazeera TV documentary entitled "Arab Jews," many Israeli citizens mentioned that the Iraqi government forcefully deported them, otherwise they would not have left Iraq.

In doing so, they kept a Hashimite family tradition of facilitating Jewish immigration; King Abdullah (King Hussein of Jordan's grandfather, and the uncle of King Ghazi), like some Palestinian prominent influential families, was accommodative to the idea of Jewish settlements in Palestine. Because of this decision, the Iraqi Royal family shared the label of "Traitors" with their cousins in Jordan. In the grand tradition of Arab culture, the Free Officers had to punish the Hashimite, and wipe this shame off their faces.

Regardless of King Ghazi's Germanophile inclinations, the British kept things pretty much under control and were dominant in the battle over Baba Gurgur: IPC kept the oil flowing from Kirkuk, without interruption, through the "K" then "T" lines to Tripoli, Lebanon, and through the "H" line to Haifa on the Mediterranean.

The death of King Ghazi energized the nationalist movement. They vowed to continue their King's plans to rid Iraq of British domination. Some five years had passed since King Ghazi's demise and WWII was already at its peak, and they turned to Hitler and the Nazis for help. However, it was not until 1943 that they managed to arrange for a coup and formed a "National" government headed by Nazi sympathizer, Mr. Rashid Ali al-Geylani, who attempted to tip the balance of power in favor of the Germans.

Under this man's watch, at least one pogrom was committed against the Jewish community in Baghdad and Basra. Mobs looted their shops and homes, terrorizing everyone. Though nothing much happened to the Christian Community in general, the non-Muslims were equally scared; after each Jewish pogrom, they would stay home for a few days and keep their shops closed. They could not do much of that either for fear of being accused of sabotage, a big dilemma indeed.

The coup, named after this prime minister, however, lasted for a few days only. Forces loyal to the British folded the coup very quickly. Once more, the oil fields were safely in the hands of the West, but Kirkuk continued to be in turmoil. It had always been a city of high tensions and high stakes, full of British and governmental agents.

One arena of espionage and secret police activities was Ahmed Agha's chaikhana (teahouse), which stood at the corner of the entrance to Qoriya Bazari, a popular souk for every imaginable item. This was a cavernous structure with floor-to-ceiling art decorated glass windows, a thousand and one chairs, wooden divans, huge samovars, dozens of teapots, and a multitude of coffee jezvehs (oriental coffee pot), brewing Arab coffee, strong and bitter.

A variety of old prints of mosques, Mecca, Kings, Persian Shahs, bordellos, and pretty Shanghai prostitutes looked from the walls at the customers, who were lazing away with nergilas (water pipes), or playing backgammon and dominos. Old Turkish and Um Kalthoum songs were played, by request, on a phonograph box labeled "His Master's Voice."

This teahouse was a landmark and a rendezvous spot. A handful of taxis that took passengers to the train station, about five miles away, parked there. Secret police and IPC agents set anchor in the front seats scrutinizing the human traffic, which had arrived on the train from Baghdad. They reported suspects, subversive elements, known Communists, and other undesirables to the headquarters. They arrested many of them for questioning at the railway station and searched their bodies and belongings for messages intended for their collaborators in the rest of the country. Their mission was to protect Baba Gurgur at all costs.

This chaikhana was also a club of sorts for the Turkomans of Kirkuk, who were still pursuing pan-Turanism, the dream of unifying all the Turkic-speaking nations under Turkey. The idea is alive today and especially after the disintegration of the Soviet Union.

Turkey's alliance with Nazi Germany had converted many a Kirkuki Turkoman into a Nazi of sorts; at least the sentiments were there! It was said that Ahmed Agha himself was a Nazi because the German and Italian pilots who landed in Kirkuk for two or three days in 1941 were looking for him, and his chaikhana became their headquarters for the duration of their stay, some seventy-three hours or so. When the German plot failed and Rashid Ali El-Geylani, the Germanophile Prime Minister fled the country, the British exiled Ahmed Agha for a while.

I remember one day, past midnight, Italian officers accompanied by local police knocked on our door, looking for someone who could translate German. My father called on our neighbor, Singer Vartan (the owner of Singer Sewing

Machine store), whose wife Louisa was an Italian. They talked to her for a few minutes and then left; we did not see them again. To this day, I do not know what transpired in that conversation, or why they came to our door, or who directed them to my father, in the first place. Some decades later I found Vartan's son, my friend Paul, in Manhattan; he confirmed my recollection but could not shed light on the purpose of the Italian Officer's visit to their house. We both were little then.

Arab Nationalists were pro-Nazi, not because they subscribed to Nazism, but because Hitler, the anti-Jew, anti-Zionist, was the enemy of their enemy, therefore a friend; Also because Britain had gained their enmity through the Balfour Declaration and the support of Jewish settlements in Palestine, and their continued neocolonialist policies in Iraq. Defeat of Britain would have restored Arab legitimate rights.

Arabs considered the European Jew as a "Foreign Body," similar to cancer, afflicting their society and threatening their very existence. They had no problems with the Iraqi, or Syrian, or Yemenite Jews, who were considered to be of "Ahlul-Dhimma" (non-Muslim monotheistic minorities living "freely" and "securely" under Muslim overall rule, and enjoying Muslim protection), who were a part of the Arab Islamic world. Their fight was against Zionism, not the Jews.

Arabs looked at Hitler's accomplishments with pride and joy. Though, like the rest of the world, they were unaware of Crystal Nacht, Auschwitz, Dachau, and Triblenka, it is doubtful that, even if they knew, they would have objected to those events, or diminished their admiration of Hitler. This is how bitter the Arabs were! Berlin nurtured these negatives through a propaganda war with BBC to win the hearts and minds of the Arabs. They had the fiery Nazi Younis Bahhri, an Iraqi Arab, who feverishly and enthusiastically broadcasted Nazi counterpropaganda and disinformation to the Arabs on Berlin radio. He had escaped Baghdad after the collapse of Rasheed Ali Gaylani's pro-Nazi government in 1941, and now was living in Berlin.

Younis Bahri's commentary was something else! He knew the Arab psychology, especially that of the Iraqis. His language was fluent and effortless, and designed to fortify Arab patriotism and highlight the evils of British influence in the region. He did not have to belabor much to convince his compatriots of the dangers of that "growing cancer," the Jewish settlements in Palestine. His oratory could easily inspire armies and lead them to battle. He was a pro!

10

The Dawn of the Kurdish Era

After the July 14, 1958 revolution of General Qasim, the Barzanis were "pardoned" and allowed to return from the Soviet Union. Upon their arrival at Baghdad airport via Czechoslovakia, Mala Mustafa Barzani and his entourage were received with open arms, warm feelings, and traditional embraces of "brotherhood," full of promises. General Qasim gave Mala Mustafa, full moral support, a monthly salary, and some light arms, and made promises for immediate reforms in Kurdistan leading to an extensive proportionate power sharing, and possible autonomy. "This country is for the Kurds and Arabs," he said. This was an indication that finally the Kurdish Question was on its way to a just and final solution. It wasn't! Within a few weeks, the entire deal fell apart, and disintegrated. Promises never materialized and once again, the central government faced yet another Barzani armed revolt.

Qasim delegated Baba Ali Sheikh Mahmoud (the son of Sheikh Mahmoud Hafidzadeh, the architect of the Kurdish Republic of Suleymania, which was busted by the British in 1919), a minister in the cabinet, to mediate. Baba Ali took his friend and partner in the Pfizer drug company, Nigoghos Alexandrian (a notable Armenian), and met Mala Mustafa Barzani in his mountain den. Despite their Herculean efforts, the mediation failed; Mala Mustafa demanded more than Qasim was willing to give. Baba Gurgur was but one stumbling block.

The struggle for Kurdistan resumed! Kurds belabored to overcome paramount obstacles created for them by almost all the governments of the region and all the Big Powers, each for its own reasons. Creation of a Kurdistan would have meant:

(1) For Iraq, loss of sovereignty over a big territory of the country including the oilfields of Baba Gurgur in Kirkuk, and Ain Zaala, in Mosul, the two main sources of gross national income.

(2) For Turkey and Iran, the expected negative effects over their own Kurdish population. Iran was especially concerned because she had had the bad experience of losing sovereignty over Mahabaad to the Kurdish Republic of Mahabaad, which Qazi Mohammed had established in 1945.

The situation in Turkey was much more complicated. Unlike Iran and Iraq, Turkey had not recognized its Kurdish population as an ethnic minority, neither had the Treaty of Lausanne. In 1921, after establishing the Republic of Turkey, Ataturk had taken away their identity and called them "Mountain Turks." Regardless of what the others considered them to be, for some 12 million Kurds living in Turkey, a Kurd was a Kurd, a distinct race, which had lived in southeastern Turkey for some 4,000 years. They deserved to gain political and civic rights, including self-rule, a cause, which is worth struggling for. In the Treaty of Lausanne, Kurds and Armenians lost whatever gains they had made in the Treaty of Sevres. Whereas this treaty designated Armenians and Greeks living in Turkey at the time, a minority, Kurds were not. The implications of this denial cost the Kurds dearly, for they were denied Lausanne's protection.

Ataturk tried, through legislation, to erase Kurd's ethnic identity. We will expand on this in the coming chapters.

The British never trusted the Kurds and never wanted them to control Baba Gurgur for obvious reasons: First, they wanted the oil fields for themselves. Second, because the Kurdish society was tribal, and the rivalries and actual armed clashes amongst them was the cause for instability, it was detrimental to operating giant oil operations. The main argument supporting their hypothesis was the Kurds failure to unite and take advantage of the Treaty of Sèvres of 1920, which had provided sovereignty "...should they [Kurds] desire."

Kurds could not put their act together and their aspiration and cause was buried in the postwar arrangements of Sykes-Picot.

During and immediately after WWI, the Middle East, like today, was in turmoil: Mark Sykes and George Picot had divided the Ottoman Empire according to their whim, to serve the interests of Britain and France. Apportionment of different real estate to different groups had created a lot of disputes and enmity in the region. The agreement deranged the Arab political and geographical mosaic: Beirut, which was a Syrian governorate, was amputated from Syria and given to Lebanon, Iskenderoun was cut out of Syria and annexed to Turkey, Trans Jordan was carved out of Palestine, Mosul was given to Iraq despite the protests of Turkey and the Turkomans of Kirkuk. Kurdistan, though not a State, was divided into four factions. Turkey, Iraq, Iran, and Syria, each got a part thus creating a lingering problem until today.

These arrangements were very much to everyone's dissatisfaction and became the genesis of hatred toward the West. It sowed the seeds of quarrels, uprisings, and war. The arrangement has plagued the Middle East ever since. It has also boosted Arab nationalism to a degree rivaled only by that of Gamal Abdul-Nasser who brought anti-British sentiment to its peak. Global anticolonialism, which peaked with India's independence, helped this movement. Kurds were left out of all these arrangements.

Armenians had a more complex situation. Western Armenia, consisting of the six Anatolian vilayets of Kars, Ardahan, Van, Mush Bitlis, and Erzrum, were in the hands of Turkey devoid of Armenian presence. The Turkish Genocide of Armenians had created that situation. Eastern Armenia had already become one of the sixteen Republics of the Soviet Union. Armenians of Diaspora, the post-Genocide Generation, had developed allegiances to the host countries, where they had taken refuge. Armenians of France, for instance, had views similar to the French.

In Iraq, as a group, Armenians had no political influence; however, individual Armenians played some potentially important roles in influencing events in Iraq: Some worked with Mr. Chapman to advance the British views and interests, yet others were Soviet sympathizers worshipping Stalin. There were some Nazi sympathizers too. They were on Hitler's side because Hitler had classified Armenians as Aryans, or just Indo-Europeans, therefore a superior race unlike the Jews and the rest. General Tro, an Armenian military commander, had organized an Armenian battalion to fight on Hitler's side in the Caucasus. Communists and Leftists blamed him for waging a war against the fatherland, yet other Armenians were supportive of his affiliation with the Nazis because, they argued, "one should not put all his eggs in one basket." They considered his actions as an insurance policy in the event of Hitler's victory; "We support the Allies all right, but how about if they lose; where will we be then? At least with Tro we will have some credit with Hitler."

11

The Western Trajectory

Through reading, my curiosity propelled me out of the Arab Galaxy; now in addition to Al-Akhbaar, Akher Saa'a, Al-Mussaawwar, Rose El-Yousif, and other Egyptian weeklies, I also got the Arabic version of *Reader's Digest*, Al-Mukhtaar. A new Egyptian monthly, Kitaabi (*My Book*), competed with *Reader's Digest*. Voltaire, Moliere, Guy de Maupassant, Victor Hugo, T. S. Elliot, W. Somerset Maugham, Shakespeare, Bertrand Russell, Annemarie Selinko, Hemmingway, Bernard Shaw, the Bronte sisters, Khaleel Gibraan, and a million other writers adorned the pages of this publication.

I read Dante, Thaies, Madame Bovary, *The Divine Comedy*, *Desiree*, *Les Miserable*, *The Prophet*, *The Tale of Two Cities*, and many, many other works, in Arabic, in those publications. At age 14 or 15, when I learned to read and understand some English, I loved reading *Look*, *Life*, and *Time* magazines. Occasionally, the *Daily Telegraph*, *The Guardian*, *The London Times*, and the *Observer* were available too. Of course, I couldn't understand all that I read, but I managed to understand what was offered with the aid of a dictionary. I also became aware of Fleet Street, and Lord Beaverbrook, and Churchill, and decided that I liked the Conservative Party better than Labor.

I don't believe that I left a single unread letter in *Look* or *Life*. Ads were my favorites: a little dog biting the pants of a little girl at the beach exposing her tush, for Coppertone. An ad for Nash, Hudson, Willis Jeep, or a station wagon showing the prosperity of the Americans, which we did not have. Ads of an aproned, smiling, housewife, whose hands have not seen a day's housework, standing by a washing machine mounted with a hand-operated wringer. Ads inviting vacationers to Florida, California, and Colorado to fish for salmon, or ski on the mountain slopes. Oh, what a life that must be, I used to think! America! If I only could get there, if I only could!

But how could I go to America? My mother wouldn't allow me to even go to Baghdad. I was stuck in that dump; my mother would never let me get out of Kirkuk! I felt terribly boxed in! She would never let me go!

If printed matter gave me a visual view of the outside world, radio became my companion, my friend who would talk to me all the time; my ears became glued to the set for news of Europe and the war. Radio built and shaped my thoughts and opinions, and boosted my imagination. Through radio, I could visualize the London Blitzes, King George and the Queen visiting the devastated areas, the firefighters, Churchill, and the other events. I knew General Eisenhower, Montgomery, Patten, Romell, Guderian, Goering, and of course Hitler. I knew about El-Alamaine, Dunkirk, and the D-Day. I knew about the meetings of Tehran, Cairo, and finally Yalta.

I owed this experience to a bulb-operated Philips radio set that we had. Transistors were not invented then, and there was no Voice of America, Radio Liberty, or Radio Free Europe, or if there were, I wasn't aware of them. I used to listen to BBC on short wave, twenty-five, or thirty-one meter bands.

"This is London." A jingle followed, then, six high-pitched beeps led to an authoritative voice announcing "BBC World Service. Here is the news read by. . .." That jingle, which remains unchanged to date, is the only direct voice-link to my past, my teen years. I still get excited, several times a day, when I listen to the BBC World Service. And every time I find myself traveling back in time and find myself sitting in front of that magic box which, like a lady having an audience with the Pope, was covered with a small kerchief crocheted by my mother. "BBC London," omnipresent words, exciting and reliable!

Sometimes I used to listen to songs, foxtrots, club music in mono, "Listeners Requests," and a variety of informative programs and propaganda on the British Armed Forces Radio from Cyprus. What a great satisfaction! To me Britain was it and Churchill was definitely my hero. When, in 1946, he lost the election to Laborite Clement Atlee, I cried.

In 1963, I watched, on television, his funeral train pass from station to station with a commentary by Richard Dimbelby. I was in Edinburgh then doing post-graduate training on an IPC scholarship. The event took me back to my childhood and my Philips radio.

12

The Fermenting Coups

This was then the overall picture of Iraq: complex, confusing, unsettling, and anticipatory. The armed forces that were defeated in Palestine were organizing a coup to restore their honor, change the royal regime, and to realize a Pan Arab dream of unification.

For the Iraqi Free Officers this was not an easy task! While the revolution in Cairo was bloodless and had the initial support of the West, such a support was not available to the rest of the Arab world. Especially for Iraq, the Egyptian revolution had failed to become a prototype. While the West was in favor of getting rid of the Egyptian monarch, King Farouq, Britain was solidly behind its creation, the ruling Iraqi monarchy. British support was not because of their affection for the ailing monarch, but because monarchy guaranteed British presence in Iraq, and control over Baba Gurgur. Despite all the difficulties, the Iraqi "Free Officers" movement was making headway. Sharing their objectives were the Kurds, the Ba'athists, the Arab Nationalists, and the disenchanted of every shade and color. These groups operated separately; each had its own agenda and pursued it vehemently. The Kurd's goal was to have some sort of autonomy, and regain what Sevres had allocated them in the past. Their best vehicle to reach their national aspiration was the USSR, so they collaborated with them. In the eyes of the government and the Free Officers, they were Communists, therefore untrustworthy, to be excluded from their real coup plans. Thus, those Kurdish officers were given disinformation about the real plans for a coup.

The Free Officer's opposition to the Communists was partly because of their ideology and partly because they were conduits of the Soviet Union, which amongst other things, supported the creation of Israel in the United Nations. For them Communism and Zionism had a common parentage.

There were additional ideological reasons for the exclusion; the Communists were untrustworthy because they were atheists, and to Islam they were infidels. Additionally they did not want to substitute the English Fox with the Russian Bear. The officers considered the Soviet intentions and geopolitical agenda for Iraq and the Middle East colonialism, of sorts. They had seen what the Soviet Union had done to oppress the Muslims in the great Islamic centers of Tashkent, Samarkand, and the rest of the Soviet Central Asian Republics.

The Iraqi Communist's modus operandi was the same as in other places: hide your identity, cooperate with any dissident faction to change the regime, and then hijack the "Revolution." That is exactly what happened ten years after Free Officers set on changing the Iraqi regime. On July 14, 1958, six years after the Egyptian revolution and inspired by it, two army officers, Colonel Abdul Salaam Arif and Brigadier General Abdul Karim Qasim, led a bloody coup d'etat in Iraq.

These two were unknowns. Everyone thought that Gamal Abdul Nasser had masterminded the coup; however, within a day or two it became apparent that it was not so, the Communists and the Kurds had also participated in pursuit of their own independent inspirations, motivations, and agendas.

The two leaders had led the revolution with diabolically opposite goals in mind. Whether they had communicated their differences to each other beforehand is not clear; however within days, a sharp, heated dispute between them surfaced over a major issue with colossal international implications—that of immediate unification with the United Arab Republic (UAR).

Arif, a mercurial political lightweight, was a dedicated Muslim Arab and a devout follower of Nasser, the "Big Brother," and a firm believer in joining the UAR. He believed in instant unification, a posture, which Nasser endorsed but asked for time. He made this clear to Arif four days after the coup when he visited Nasser's people in Syria, the other partner in UAR. He thought that with the revolution, he had completed his mission, and now he would hand over Iraq to Nasser on a silver platter. Not only Qasim, but also the United States and the West vehemently opposed the idea. For all concerned it meant handing over Baba Gurgur to Nasser, resulting in dire consequences.

Qasim was an Iraqi nationalist whose political conviction was to build a strong Iraq. His agenda excluded immediate union with UAR, or any other Arab country. This unknown duo, especially Qasim, puzzled people. He had seen military training in Britain and, was pro-British in orientation. He was one of the most trusted generals of the Palace and Sir Nouri Sa'id. How could such a man lead a coup against his masters? Sir Nouri Sa'id was the perennial prime minister of Iraq. He was one of the most seasoned Iraqi politicians ever, and was a major player on the international scene. He was an architect of the Baghdad Pact, later CENTO. He was in King Faisal's entourage when he entered Iraq to become King. The British supported him, opposed him, feared him, solicited his advice, and in time, knighted him. The man was respected, feared, loved, and hated by the Palace, and by ordinary people, but his political skills no one underestimated. How is it then that an officer like Qasim, with his kind of a background and credentials would lead a revolution against his masters? That was the question of the day begging answers! For conspiratorial theorists the answer was clear: an unstable kingdom and the fear of losing control over Baba Gurgur.

For a decade after the Arab defeat in Palestine, and partly because of it, enmity toward the Monarchy grew in all dimensions. Unrest by all the dissenting political parties was so strong, official corruption so deep, Nasser's pan-Arabism so awesome, the Soviet threat in the Middle East so destabilizing, and the Royal family's grip on the country (especially the Kurdish north) so weak that some kind of a radical change was in order.

People were convinced of this! The developing situation alarmed the British, who would have lost strategic control over Iraq and Baba Gurgur, had the undesirables deposed the Royal family. That would have meant Nasser's control over the West's lifeline, oil. To prevent such a scenario from happening, a preemptive coup d'etat was thought to be the remedy, and General Qasim, an unsuspected Nouri Sa'id loyalist, the ideal person for the task.

Such an arrangement made sense to people who believed in conspiracies. They believed that he was selected because he was an unsuspected, quiet, and withdrawn patriot who understood the theory behind the plan and appreciated the dangers that might befall Iraq if the situation was not saved.

Was the plan cooked in the kitchens of Whitehall? Nobody knew for sure, but it is reasonable to believe that the British, with their deep intelligence penetration in Iraq, knew of the Free Officers movement and the pending overthrow of the regime; consequently if they did not covertly support it, they looked the other way.

On July 14, 1958, Units of the IIIrd Army Division, specifically Battalion 19, led by Colonel Abdul Salaam Arif, followed by Battalion 20, led by Brigadier General Abdul Karim Qasim, left Ba'qooba via Baghdad, for deployment in troubled Lebanon and Jordan. At dawn, instead of passing through, the convoy stalled in Baghdad and staged a coup: A handful of officers surrounded the Royal Palace. A tank or two overtook the government-run radio station. In a few hours, the whole takeover concluded without resistance, except briefly at the Royal palaces.

The entire Royal Family, including young King Faisal II, was killed. The mob dragged the Regent, Abdul-Ilaah's body for miles; by the time it reached King Faisal Circle it was already in shreds. What was left was mutilated, cut into pieces, and hung from a telephone pole in front of the Ministry of Defense. Young King Faisal II was considered innocent, therefore he was buried, body intact, quietly in some cemetery. Such was the magnitude of ordinary people's anger.

Nouri Sa'id escaped the massacre, though only for a few days, after which he was captured through the deception of the son of the family that was hiding him. He was killed in the street. One of my medical school colleagues, the son of a Minister, showed off a slipper that Nouri Sa'id was wearing during his escape. He had obtained it for some cash.

These tragic events were because of a number of gross logistical "Mistakes" in deploying the armed forces:

a) In violation of the military deployment rules, which called for distribution of ammunition after crossing the capital, Baghdad, the troops left the barracks with both arms and ammunition; and

b) They mobilized the battalions in large units instead of small fractions, one at a time.

The "Free Officers" formed the government assigning important posts for themselves: Qasim became the Commander in Chief, and reserved many other key portfolios for himself. Arif became his deputy and took the Interior Ministry. Rif'at Al-Haj Sirri, the founder of the Free Officers movement, headed the Military Intelligence Service, while Major Nadhim Al-Tabaqchali, another Free Officer, commanded the Second Army Division stationed in the strategic city, Kirkuk. Thus, almost ten years after the "Grand Deception" in Palestine, the Free Officers avenged the humiliation, part of it anyway, which brought them one step closer to liberating Palestine.

The new order brought with it new disorders and problems begging immediate solutions. From minute one the discord between the two leaders surfaced. It became apparent that each had deceitfully kept his real agenda from the other during the planning stages of the coup. Now that they were in power, disputes, deceptions, competition, political plots, and mistrust, set in amongst them. The major fundamental and interrelated disagreements were:

a) Formation of a Revolutionary Council, which Arif demanded, and Qasim opposed, and

b) Instantaneous joining of the United Arab Republic.

Arif and his group accused Qasim of reneging on these pre-coup agreements. They accused him of "working to derail the revolution; he had never intended to join UAR in the first place."

Forming a Revolutionary Council would have meant collective governance by pro-UAR men who would have voted to join UAR immediately. Since Qasim opposed such a union, he refused to create the Council. His action consolidated his power; now he was the "sole leader" of Iraq.

Support for his policy came from the majority of Iraqi Arabs, all the Kurds, the Communist party, Britain, the United States, and by default, Israel. Within hours of the coup, the United States ambassador visited him and threatened him with invasion if he joined UAR. The British ambassador visited him in the Ministry of Defense, one half hour after his taking over, and sought reassurances about their oil interests. Qasim reassured both of them and promised uninterrupted flow of oil at the same prices as before. Both ambassadors went home, happy. The other elements of the ethnic and political spectrum supported him because his stance facilitated their aspirations. The West breathed a sigh of relief!

Union would have meant not only handing Baba Gurgur over to Nasser, but also robbing Iraq of its pride and sovereignty; Syria's bad experience in going to bed with Nasser was a testimony to that. Qasim exploited this support to the fullest by rewarding his backers. He granted the Communists legitimacy, and promised the Kurds to right the wrong that had befallen them under the previous regime. These two sectors formed his power base, and eventually caused his demise. Backing Arif were the Nationalists, the Ba'thists, and the political parties, who saw in him the vehicle to advance, one more step, toward their grand dream of a Unified Arab entity extending from the Ocean to the Gulf. Some of these forces advised him to slow the pace, but he would not listen to them.

Thus, in the first few days of the Revolution, the battle lines were already drawn, the country was sharply divided, and that dictated all the other events that followed.

13

The Morning of July 14, 1958

I witnessed that revolution from the first hour of its inception. At 6 AM on July 14, I left my apartment to go to the barracks at the Al-Rasheed military base. The recent crop of doctors was to receive military orientation there, before joining their assigned posts, and I was one of them. I heard the radio from an adjacent chaikhana (teahouse) blasting the determined voice of a man reading decree after decree in the name of the revolutionary committee. After each decree, he identified himself as Colonel Ahmed Salih Al-'Abdi. Ordinarily, at that hour, the broadcast would have been a recitation of the Holy Qur'an, but not this morning.

The firm voice, exuding confidence and control announced:

- Decree #1: "The Monarchy is abolished."
- Decree #2: "We have revolted in your name and established The Republic of Iraq."
- Decree #3: "The following officers are excused of duty in the armed forces, and are replaced by the following, with promotion..."

Other important decrees followed, asserting the authority of the new regime.

Military music, especially the Egyptian revolutionary song "Allahu Akbar Fouqah Qaid al-Mu'tadeen," laced the announcements. This very effective, inspiring revolutionary song, composed at Nasser's request, served as the battle hymn of the revolutionary Arabs everywhere. These were people and activists who were advancing the Arab Cause defined as ending the neocolonial hegemony, and getting rid of their corrupt rulers.

This march ran the chills down the spines of those who opposed and hated Nasser and his leadership of the Arab Cause. The intent of this song was to do just that and contribute to Nasser's psychological warfare and propaganda.

I was confused and could not comprehend what was going on. What revolution, I asked myself? Who is Ahmed Salih Al-'Abdi? Who actually carried out the coup? What happened to all these intelligence gathering services, the CID, the CIA, and the British Intelligence Service—where were they? Didn't they see what was coming? What happened to CENTO's (Central Treaty Organization) intelligence services? What happened to the "Fox," Sir Nouri Sa'id the Prime Minister? What happened to the King who was to fly to Istanbul to visit his fiancé this morning; did he make it?

I could not believe what I was hearing! I was alarmed, worried, and frightened and did not know what to expect. A coup in Iraq? Unbelievable! No, not in Iraq! Besides who are these people? I never heard of them. But, what difference does it make? There is no royal regime anymore; they have started a republic!

As I headed toward King Faisal II Square to explore, all these thoughts and more crossed my mind at fleeting speed.

The street leading to the Square was quiet, as if nothing was going on some 200 yards away. Lined up against the wall were the usual fast food vendors who were serving breakfast to the workers of Abbakhaana, the largest electric powerhouse in Baghdad, which was just across the street, and quiet.

Workers squatting in front of a wall on the curb were busy eating the favorite Iraqi breakfast, fava beans on torn bread soaked in meat broth, topped with onions. Others munched, as they walked to their jobs, on boiled chickpeas generously spread with oregano and black pepper rolled in flat bread. The workers, like their workplace, were quiet; maybe they had not yet received directives from their Leftist union.

Yes, the street was quiet and its activities ordinary, similar to other mornings when I used to walk the half-mile street, to catch the bus to medical school, or the military truck to Al-Rasheed Training Camp.

The quietness did not last long; some unrecognizable noises coming from afar changed it. As I approached the Square, the cacophony became louder and louder. There were a few hundred people demonstrating.

At first I thought they were Communists, but soon I realized that there were no signs, or posters, or chants, to indicate Communist participation; the crowd was carrying Nasser's pictures. That eased my fears some! Then I thought what difference does that make? One is worse than the other; the stability of the country is destroyed, and I am right in the middle of it.

Soon the crowd became bigger, more vocal and out of control. Demonstrators jumping up and down were waving sticks and machetes, slicing the air in anger, until a bunch of people dragging some unrecognizable body as if it was the side of cattle, arrived. They used their weapons to cut the body into chunks. It was the Regent's body, which they had dragged for miles from the royal palace to the Square, and now were mutilating it. Whoever could, cut a piece of the flesh, kicked the body, spat on it, and stomped on it, until it reached the end of the chic El-Rasheed Street. There, in front of the Ministry of Defense they hung it from a telephone pole to dry.

More mutilated and dragged bodies crossing the Maud Bridge (connecting Karkh, the West Bank, with Rassafa, the east of Tigris) appeared in the Square.

The radio continued blasting revolutionary, military music, and more decrees and announcements. Now, almost an hour had passed since the first radio announcement.

I was witnessing the events with horror, terrified. The uncertainty of the future, and more importantly the immediate present, was shattering my thoughts.

Even though chaos ruled the streets, there was no destruction of property, burning of cars, or looting shops! For instance, trade showrooms of Hafidh Al-Qadhi, a major G M and Carrier agency overlooking the square was not vandalized. Nor did they touch the store, which displayed Omega, Tissot, and Longine watches, across the Square from it. This behavior defined the mob as a politically motivated crowd, not thieves, and looters. The man at the corner shop, across from the Square, was conducting business as usual squeezing Ba'qooba oranges to meet the heavy demand of the shouting, thirsty people.

El-'Assima and Shereef Haddaad restaurants, on the opposite sides of the Bridge, were open for breakfast, but there was no service because the waiters were standing there, jubilantly cheering the mob. Most waiters working in these two restaurants were from Telkeyf, a Christian village in Mosul, which was famous for being a source of cheap labor for the Food and Entertainment industry in Baghdad and Mosul.

Once the proud subjects of the Assyrian Empire of Nineveh, history had committed these people to poverty, disintegration, and irrelevance. Telkeyf was neglected by the government, therefore the youth would leave to make a living elsewhere and to escape surrounding Muslim Kurdish hegemony. For them, like most oppressed people, Communism was the needed change, and now, change was happening, right before their eyes at the King Faisal Square.

The morning was still young. Dawn, like the coup, had given birth to a new day: The sun was out, the sky cerulean blue, the shade cool, and the square white-hot. The passing gentle breeze, and the orange juice were not enough to cool heads and quench thirst, they demanded more corpses, more heads; the first dragged corpse had reached the Square some two hours before.

By now, the crowd had grown much larger, more vocal, and more energized. They were all carrying pictures of Gamal Abdul Nasser and chanting, "Wahda wahda Arabiya, la infissaal wala raj'iyya," the unionist slogan of call for Arab unity and rejection of the reactionaries and the separatists.

Soon the crowd grew even bigger. The distant cacophony reached a crescendo as another wave of demonstrators approached with their Iraqi flags rippling in the air. These too were not Communists, but supporters of Nasser.

Was this a Nasser-revolution? What happened to the other groups? Yes, Kurds' absence was understandable because there were not enough Kurds in Baghdad to demonstrate, but how about the Communists? Why were they absent?

A moment later, a military jeep negotiated its way through the crowds honking its horn, and then sped toward the Ministry of Defense. Another jeep followed, then a third one. The radio still blasting martial music, announcements, and decrees, was instructing the public:

> The public, hereby, is instructed to maintain order. Those who do not obey will face prosecution! The army has revolted on your behalf to return your just rights to you and free you, our valiant people, from the colonial and imperialist oppression. Stay vigilant to the tricks of the enemies of the people who may attempt to abort this holy revolution. Stay tuned for more directives and news.

"Maintain order" was not the intent of this crowd who was competing to reach a corpse and have a chance to stab or spit on whatever was left of its face. The mob was coming from Karkh, the West bank of Tigris, where they had passed the bronze statue of a mounted leader, King Faisal I. I wondered, what would the statue say if he took life again? He had sacrificed so much for his nation, built it from the ashes of the Ottoman oppressor, struggled for independence and sovereignty, fought with the British for a just Anglo-Iraqi treaty, and now his heirs, the entire Hashimite family, was massacred in this brutal fashion. Probably he would have shaken his head in disbelief, held his tears, recited the Al-Fatiha (the Islamic prayer for the dead), and grieved in private, which was the appropriate behavior for an Arab prince from the deserts of Hijaz. Real princes do not cry in public, they mourn in silence!

As in real life, juxtaposing him on the this side of the bridge was the statue of General Stanley Maude at the Square, where all the horror-show was taking place, right there before his eyes. He too was on a bronze horse. I wondered, what this General, who in 1917 "liberated" Iraq, would say if he could talk. Would he admit that it was he and his colonialist government's forty-one years of deceptive policies, which brought the country to this boiling point? Would he admit, "It is that cloud which brought this rain" as the Bedouins would say? He couldn't talk, and I could only guess his response! He probably would have shaken his head in sorrow for the failure of his mission, and the loss of the British era in Iraq. He probably would have said, "I did it for the King and the country."

I stood there, leaning on a pillar, watching people, some excited, some numbed, yet others, like me, consumed in thought. How could this be? How can the big powers allow this to happen? How can the country fall into Nasser's lap like this? How about Baba Gurgur and the rest of the oil fields?

It is all Ike's fault, I concluded; had he not stopped Anthony Eden, in 1956, the Suez Campaign would have succeeded, Nasser would have been finished, and this crap would not have happened! I couldn't understand it, I really couldn't. Why didn't the big powers know about it?

Yes, it was all Ike's fault! That naive Ike! That idiot! How could he hand Khrushchev such a victory? Could he not see what would happen to the entire Middle East? This was where the controls of the entire region were, in Baghdad. Now CENTO would be finished! How and where could they find another ally like Nouri Al-Sa'id? These Americans didn't know foreign policy, they just didn't.

Now Iraq would be Communist, a Soviet territory. God forbid! They would do to the men of the old regime what they did to thousands of nationalist Armenians in 1920 in Yerevan, Armenia; they axed them to death.

Definitely, absolutely, categorically, there was no doubt in my mind that the country would turn scarlet red, as red as the blood that was now flowing.

Maybe Ike was listening to his rather stupid Secretary of State who didn't see what was coming! I thought, in anger.

Poor, King Faisal, he didn't deserve to die like this! He was young and innocent; he did not even have an opportunity to enjoy his fiancé. He paid with his life for his uncle's evil conduct. But, couldn't they have exiled him, in style, same as King Farouq? The Egyptian officers put him in his Royal Yacht and sailed him to Europe, with a twenty-one-gun salute. That was the civilized way, wasn't it? But Iraqis were different; the Arab forces fighting in Palestine had labeled them "wahhshee" (wild) for slaughtering thousands of civilian Jews, in cold blood, in Der Yaseen. What I was seeing now proved all that: they were just plain wahshees, and I was living amongst them. What a pity!

Thoughts, thoughts, thoughts, fleeting thoughts, tore my mind to shreds. The confusion and the uncertainty threatened me, but I was hoping that Nouri Sa'id would be at large, and maybe, just maybe, with CIA's help would wage a countercoup, like it happened six years ago in Iran.

No, Britain would not let Baba Gurgur go, how could they? Oil is their lifeline! If they could not afford to let Baba Gurgur go, then, why did they let this whole thing happen? There must be a good reason, which I don't know yet! Was it possible that the British orchestrated this revolution?

I drifted to other thoughts, all the time feeling sorry for Iraq and myself. Was this the Baghdad that I knew and loved? Baghdad the city of civility, modernity, prosperity, and elegance?

Was this the same bustling Shari'e Al Rasheed where Cafe Brazil and Cafe Swiss provided European ambiance for the writers and the intellectuals, who met there for a chat and a cup of espresso?

Was this the same busy street where one could shop for elegant furs, jewelry, and French perfume?

Was this the same street where seductive girls passed wearing the latest Parisian dresses, as if on a fashion show ramp?

No, it was not! The street was full of corpses and blood, and God knew when the carnage would end! I didn't like what I saw and felt. Iraq was going to the dogs, I thought.

I left the scene to the mob, and returned home in despair, still hoping for Nouri Sa'id's salvation efforts. That was not to be; two or three days after the coup, the authorities captured him while trying to change venue, disguised in a veil. The son of his host had deceived him for money. One of my classmates had purchased his slippers, which was left on the street while escaping, for posterity and was proudly showing it off. Two decades later he became the victim of a deception and on Saddam's orders, was executed.

During all this, one question never left my mind. Where were the British, where was their countercoup? Each time, the answer was the same: They instigated, planned, and executed this coup as a preemptive strike to prevent the country from falling into the hands of Nasser, or the Communists. The Royal family had lost control over the political termites, which had eroded the country's structure; it was time for change.

The psychological effects of this coup on me were overwhelming; to compound it, the school cancelled our graduation ceremony. I, together with some 140 men and women, were not to be capped and gowned to receive our medical diploma. We were terribly disappointed. We were to go to the Dean's office, and pick up our diplomas, unceremoniously. To add insult to injury, they had crossed "Royal" from the heading "Royal College of Medicine" and had handwritten "Republic" instead.

"Graduation" was a sad event for me, and the future a big "unknown." Revenge came much later in life when I was appointed Associate Clinical Professor in Neurology at Tufts, Boston

In April 1976 I received a call from Tufts School of Medicine asking me whether I would be joining the graduation procession that year. I was jumping with joy. I answered in the affirmative. She asked me about the colors of my school in Baghdad. I did not know I had not seen one before. They found the colors, and I joined the graduation of a new crop of doctors with tears in my eyes and memories of the "Royal" College of Medicine in Baghdad. I was at the procession, but I wasn't; my thoughts were completely absorbed by my past. I murmured to myself "Only in America." It was an equalizer. I had scored a home run, I thought.

14

The Turmoil of the 1940s

The decade of the 1940s did not augur well for Iraq. She was plagued by Iraqi-Nazi attempts to come to power, and there were numerous uprisings by the Kurds, especially the Barzanis, from 1943 to 1945.

There was defeat of the Iraqi Army in the war against the newly born Jewish State, and there was unrest in the armed forces, threatening to take it out on the "Traitors of the Arab Cause," the Royal family.

Adjustments of the Anglo-Iraqi Treaty were very much in the air and the Treaty of Portsmouth had just failed. The Communist Party was creating havoc in the country organizing strikes and undermining the government's authority.

There was a brain drain in the country: Jews who were doctors and scientists had migrated to Israel. The British were still dictating terms, paying $1.5 a barrel net to Iraq, robbing the country of its wealth.

The regime was on shaky grounds, for many reasons; not the least because of regional instability:

> There was tremendous turmoil in Syria; one coup after another was the norm.
> Michel Aflaq and Akram El Horani were laying the foundations of the Ba'ath Party, which eventually came to power in both Syria and Iraq.
> Khalid Bektash, the biggest and the most virulent Communist in the Middle East, and a Kurd at that, was rocking the traditional regimes in the region.
> Iraq's relations with Turkey were not the best; there were disputes and bad feelings between the two countries over Mosul, which was given to the newly formed Iraq, in a plebiscite, by the League of Nations. There was the question of Colonel Salahaddin El-Sabbagh (one of the "Golden Four" military officers who implemented the Nazi oriented "Nationalist" Coup

of Rashid Ali El-Gaylani in 1941), a wanted man by Iraq, who was given refuge in Turkey, albeit in a comfortable jail. Iraq considered that as an unfriendly act.

There was the dispute over Shatt-el-Arab and Khozestan (Arabistan) between Iraq and Iran. And there was the question of Kuwait, which King Faisal I had already claimed to be an Iraqi territory.

The powerful Iranian Communist Tudeh Party, commissioned and financed by the Soviet Union, was exporting its ideology, via the clergy, to South-Western Iraqi Holy cities of Karbala and Najaf where the shrines of Hassan and Hussein (Prophet Mohammed's grandchildren) were. These are the cities where Ayatollah Ruhallah Khomeini took refuge, while escaping from the Shah before being expelled to Noufle Le Chateau by Saddam Hussein.

Other global situations gave Iraq indigestion:

In Egypt, the humiliating defeat of the armed forces on the Israeli front was fermenting dissent and bringing suppressed discontent to a peak. Ideas of pan-Arabism were crystallizing all over the Arab land bringing discomfort to the ruling monarchy of Iraq and Britain.

Globally: Hitler had lost the war, and the Arab Nationalists had lost Hitler, their spiritual ally. Now they were under the mercy of Britain, the colonialist, the Imperialist, who was trying to choke Arab nationalist movements to death by creating "Illegitimate Israel."

For the Arabs, this situation generated hopelessness, which, in turn, evolved into hatred.

For the ruling class there was no alternative; they couldn't and wouldn't go with the atheist Communists for reasons of religion, cultural disorientation, and historic political dichotomy, so they had to swallow their pride and settle for getting the best deal out of their previous colonial masters, the British.

Ordinary people however, had several choices; they could either join the ranks of the Communist Party, which some did, join some other nationalistic political party, or join a covert movement which was taking shape in the country.

For the Kurds the lines were clearer: either Barzani's Group, which meant a tribal type of a setup, or some other secular political party such as the Communists. Communists attracted the Kurds to their ranks and exploited them to the fullest in the name of helping the oppressed people of the world to free themselves from the evil of imperialist West.

In the decade of the 1940s, the Communists, pursuing that line of logic, were gaining greater prestige and popularity amongst the poor, especially the Shiites in the south and Kurds in the north.

The default lines between the pro-British rulers and Leftist Kurds backed by the Soviet Union was well established. The Soviet backing of the Kurds was not motivated by admiration for the Kurds, rather it was an attempt to control the "Two Liquids," which they had in abundance: Oil and Water. Oil in Kirkuk and Mosul, and the waters of the Tigris and the Euphrates in Turkish Kurdistan.

Most Arabs had no use for this kind of a game; they equated Zionism with Communism and considered them one and the same. "Jews created Communism." They had grounds for this belief: Carl Marx was a Jew, and the Communist hierarchy was full of Jews. Furthermore, the Iraqi Communist Party leadership had at least one Jew amongst them.

Britain was no longer the empire that it was. She had divested its Crown Jewel, India, in 1948. The Arabs admired the hero of Indian independence, Gandhi, for defeating Britain. His assassination was, rightly or wrongly, blamed on the British: "They wouldn't let him digest it [Indian Independence], they killed him. The British never forget," they would say.

With Nehru's succession, a new "ideology" was jelling, that of "positive neutrality." Nasser and Tito joined Nehru, and Sukarno of Indonesia; between them, they controlled vast strategic territory, and forced the world to become tripolar instead of bipolar.

In 1945 after Roosevelt's meeting with King Abdul 'Azeez Bin Saoud, the Americans had virtually taken over oil rich Saudi Arabia and were competing with the old masters, the British; now, ARAMCO was giving IPC a stiff competition.

Though the governments did not say much, Arab intelligentsia also did not like America because, "It was Truman's vote in the U.N. which created Israel." Rightly or wrongly, they considered America as another Imperialist country, which was set up by Israel to hurt the Arabs. This thought has now grown to become a firm belief of the Arab street and the leadership; the Israeli lobby in the United States is directing the country in favor of Israel, against the Arab countries.

The turn of the decade brought new sets of opportunities, challenges, and problems for Iraq and the region.

Baghdad International Trade Fair, a very big event, was held and we saw television for the first time in 1953; the British firm PYE, had exhibited television technology in the Trade Fair, then sold it to the government. I recall being amazed and amused at seeing my image on the TV screen when I passed in front of the camera set at the showroom of Hafidh-el-Qadhi. They were asking people to pass in front of the camera and experience the miracle of PYE. I had seen TV before but only in the pages of *Look* and *LIFE* magazines, and they were Philco and Marconi products. PYE was British, therefore it did not advertise in American magazines.

Hafidh-el-Qadhi showrooms were elegant and centrally located on King Faisal II Square at the entrance of "Jisr Maude" (the bridge named after the conquering British General Stanley Maude of WWI). This was a very big merchant. He was agent to big American giants including General Motors, and Carrier.

Hafidh-el-Qadhi had bought the business from Bait (The House) Lawi, a Jewish family, who had owned the agency before their migration from Iraq in 1948.

In Gruner Baum, an Alpine Hotel in Bad Gastein, Austria, I had the good fortune of meeting an Iraqi Jewess, Mitzi Daniel, the daughter of Menachim Daniel, who was eighty-three at the time. We shared memories of Baghdad. I praised her father and uncle's efforts in educating a generation of Iraqis. He had established the Menachim Daniel School, an exclusive learning institution where Muslim aristocracy used to send their daughters for a proper education. Mitzi had not attended that school. With her usual wit, she crossed her lips with her finger and said, "Shuuush, don't tell anybody I went to Catholic schools in Vienna."

This lady had a real aristocratic demeanor, which became more obvious when she was our houseguest in New Hampshire. She was with us for a few days. Given her background and experiences, I believe she had taken a courageous step in accepting the invitation of relative strangers. She was totally relaxed and happy except for one day when I took her for a spin in the car to show her our beautiful village. She felt insecure and kept asking the direction in which we were traveling and why we were going in that direction. I got the message, knowing the source of her insecurity and anxiety. After all, in her eyes, I was still an Iraqi. I addressed the issue openly, after which she relaxed, admitting her fears to me.

In the 1950s, aside from Hafidh-el-Qadhi and thousands of other Iraqi companies doing business with the West, there were an estimated 1,500 foreign companies doing business in Iraq. Armenians staffed most of these companies because they knew English and were skilled in running offices and businesses.

Iraq was on the go: the Iraqi State Railway running from Baghdad to Kirkuk was extended to Erbil, now the Capital of Iraqi Kurdistan. It was the second longest railway of the country and it was narrow-gauged. The wide-gauge railway, part of the Berlin-Istanbul-Baghdad line, was now extended to Basra, on the Gulf, thus connecting the heart of Europe with the riches of the Gulf. This was an important strategic pathway indeed!

The cold war was at its peak. Nouri Sa'id, in an effort to implement Western policies to contain the Soviet Union, worked hard to materialize and formalize an alliance with Britain, Turkey, and Pakistan. So, he collaborated in forming CENTO in 1958. The Nationalists considered this yet another attempt by Britain to keep her hands in the region's affairs. The pact faced tremendous opposition by the Iraqi street. The organization was short-lived.

In this decade, eight short years after its defeat in Palestine, the Iraqi Army got reequipped with modern arsenal, and its standard of living improved. More and more officers were given additional schooling and military training abroad. In addition to Sandhurst and other British Military training institutions, the Iraqi officers were now also being sent to the United States. This indicated a landmark change in the Iraqi government's orientation. It also indicated America's efforts to take Iraq away from the British sphere.

The United States was making progress in the region, while British influence was dwindling. France was almost totally out of the political game even in her previous territories, like Syria and Lebanon. Iraq, having never been a French territory, knew France only through Coco Channel perfume, and the ill-fated, despised, disastrous Sykes-Picot Treaty.

The decade of the 1950s was special for Iraq: British neocolonial influence on her was neither palpable nor visible by the ordinary citizen; it was modified to obscurity in a covert manner. Colonial micromanagement had given way to other ploys designed to keep Iraq within the galaxy of the West, thus assuring control over Baba Gurgur.

In this decade new winds were blowing over Iraq: that of American cultural influence over the youth; Hollywood had invaded and taken over the hearts and minds of the Iraqi youth, so had Coca-Cola, Chesterfield, Lucky Strike, and Camel cigarettes. There was no Marlboro then, or if there was, it was not popular, neither were the English cigarettes, Players, Craven A, Gold Flake, and Marcovitch. Also out of style was pipe smoking like the British, which I had taken up since medical school. The habit has stuck with me to date. To be suave was to be American, not English. Hollywood actors and actresses like Eva Gardner, Doris Day, Jane Russell, Katherine Hepburn, June Alison, Clark Gable, Gregory Peck, and the rest had set the standard for girl-boy behavior in Baghdad.

The glorious Arab culture and tradition were now considered to be reactionary and passé. Even the English way of life, as propagated by the British Institute in Baghdad, (established by Doctor Sinderson "Pasha," the founder of the Royal College of Medicine, and the physician to the Court), was considered to be old-fashioned. The youth were attracted to USIS (United States Information Service), while the older generation clung to Alwiyah Club (the social-athletic club in Baghdad akin to El-Gazira Club in Cairo), where they drank scotch, chased each other's wives, and loyally served their Free Mason Lodge.

15

Kirkuk, the Jerusalem of Iraq

Soon after graduation I was assigned to a military post in Qalah Dize (Qal'at Diza = Fortress of Thieves) in Iraqi Kurdistan, where I met an officer, Colonel Abdullah Mustafa, a Kurdish Nationalist; who was just transferred to that unit. He claimed to have led the attack on Qasr El-Rihhaab, the Royal Palace, on the morning of July 14, the day of the coup.

He boasted that he was the first who opened fire on the Royal Family, as they came out of their Palace, single file, holding the Holy Qur'an high above their heads for protection.

According to published books by reliable authors, such as Khalil Ibrahim Hussein, Mustafa's story appears to be accurate, except that he was not that hero, Khalil himself was.

Khalil, the author of many authentic books regarding the Revolutions in Iraq, swears to God and the Holy Qur'an, that he was the person who killed the Royal family. I tend to believe him rather than Mustafa, because his credibility was established through his writings, whereas Mustafa was totally unknown until then.

Over a glass of arak, he told me that he was a Free Officer in a secret cell, and he was supposed to know the coup plans and the zero hour, but the Arab coconspirators deceived him. They left him behind because "I was a Kurd." That might very well be the truth, because they did not want Kurdish participation in the actual revolt so as not to legitimize Kurdish demands for autonomy. It is also possible that the officers panicked at the last minute and could not get in touch with all the officers, including Mustafa. Regardless, Mustafa saw conspiracy in their action.

The rest of his story was that he got the whiff of the imminent attack, took his submachine gun, and went directly to the Royal Palace. There he saw a tank or two, which fired some three rounds, demolishing part of the Palace. The Palace Guard surrendered immediately, which forced the Royal family to come out. Mustafa thought the Arab officers would arrest the royal family and exile them, the way their Egyptian counterparts did to their King. This was unacceptable to him because the plotters were Arabs, therefore "unreliable." He rationalized that if they were exiled, the British would somehow restore them to the Hashimite throne after a period. His fears were backed by precedence: Americans, facing a similar dilemma with Musaddegh's coup in Iran, had reinstated the Shah to the Peacock Throne in 1952. If that happened here, it "Would kill the Kurdish cause." So, in a "split-second judgment, I decided to finish them off, and opened fire and killed the family."

Regardless of who did what, two things were apparent:

(a) The Royal family was dead, and
(b) The Arab Officers had deceived their Kurdish ally by denying them participation in the coup.

Colonel Mustafa was in "internal exile" of sorts, in Qalah Dize (The Fortress of Thieves). The army had attached him to our garrison in this north easternmost Kurdish town bordering Iran. The political developments in Baghdad had disfavored him, not in the least because he was a Kurd therefore a persona non-grata.

I am not sure whether Colonel Mustafa had fought in Palestine, but he had a chip on his shoulder similar to the Arab officers who also suffered from it; he looked and sounded angry, bitter, and defeated. Now his anger and bitterness compounded because the revolution did not recognize him as a hero; he felt ostracized.

Kurds did not get their share of the spoils promised them before the revolution, and there was no Kurdish participation in the newly created power structure. To him this was a betrayal of Kurdistan, reflecting inherent deceitful Arab behavior. Now the Kurdish national hopes and aspirations were seriously set back.

Colonel Mustafa's skepticism ran even deeper than that and had basis in history. It, in a sense, echoed the feelings of the entire Kurdish population, which called parts of Turkey, Iran, Syria, and Iraq, home. It echoed the Kurdish peoples' anger toward the big powers who had repeatedly betrayed them through local and international conspiracies, handing them a string of defeats, the latest of which being the dismantling of the Kurdish Republic of Mahabad (1945–1946, Iran) where Mala Mustafa Barzani (father of Mas'oud Barzani) was the Minister of Defense.

Throughout history, Kurds have never had independence and sovereignty. The governments, under which they lived, indeed the big powers, have always belittled and shortchanged them, and denied them their national rights; consequently, they have lost land, population, self-respect, and opportunities for independence or autonomy.

Additionally, under the best of circumstances, the governments have treated them as second-class citizens, and at the birth of the Republic of Turkey, Kemal Ataturk officially erased their ethnic identity and labeled them as "Mountain Turks."

True, the Iraqi regime also neglected the Kurds but not any more than their neglect of the Arabs of the South.

Unlike their kin in Turkey, the Iraqi Kurds had the right to speak, teach, publish, in Kurdish, and enjoy their culture without restrictions. The government told them, you are Kurds and we are Arabs, but we both are Iraqis. Baghdad radio, the only broadcasting station in the country, had a Kurdish news and culture program. I used to listen to it often, especially when Shamal Sa'ib, my classmate, was on. He was a folk singer and therefore loved by the Kurds, who cherished his performances on Bashi Kurdi (the Kurdish part of the broadcast). He was a lyricist and a composer. One of his songs, "Halsa-Halsa," was a classic, in which he was awakening his lover: "Wake up, wake up my love, enough of sleeping." At the time, no one predicted that the "Love" he was trying to awaken was the Kurdish nation. "Wake-up my love wake up"!

For over forty years, those songs and Shamal Sa'ib were only pleasant memories of my distant past. I had missed his singing. A few years ago, I met Omar in a San Francisco convention, who told me that he not only knew Shamal but they were roommates in Maryland for five years. He had died a few years before. I asked for, and got a tape of Shamal's "Halsa, Halsa," to which I listen often.

Kurds, individually and collectively, participated in government. There were Kurdish ministers in the cabinet such as Baba Ali Sheikh Mahmoud, Ahmed Mukhtar Baabaan, and Sa'id Qazzaaz. However, these people had no credibility with the Kurdish political movements who considered them a part of the establishment, therefore, conduits of Britain.

The Parliament had Kurdish representatives proportionate to their population. These perennial representatives had no political influence; they served their own interests and that of the Crown, sometimes only theirs, neglecting the people. Thus, Kurdistan remained neglected and underdeveloped.

The system, however, was universally corrupt: bribery, theft, favoritism, dishonesty, and outright embezzlement, characterized the regime. This was not surprising since modern Iraq was a continuum of the old Ottoman rule, and the vast majority of the civil servants were carry-overs from that corrupt regime.

The feudal system, in operation for centuries, formed the matrix of society. A tribal Sheikh in the south or a Kurdish Agha in the north held the strings of ones very existence: he owned the land, provided seeds, mules, and later tractors, to their tribesmen. He advanced the money one needed to get married, and owned the shack one lived in. The chieftain administered justice according to local tradition and the Islamic law tailored to their liking.

The British and the Royal family exploited this system to the fullest! Through enticements and favors, they controlled the chieftains who in turn controlled the tribes, which formed almost the entire population of the country. This decay radicalized the Kurdish political orientation and advanced their search for some sort of a new radical solution.

Search for a solution to the Kurdish Question was not new. They had been repeatedly deceived in the past by the big powers.

The grandest deception happened upon the conclusion of WWI when The Peace Treaty (1919) and the Treaty of Sèvres (August 10, 1920) dealt with this issue. Britain had assumed mandate over the newly formed Iraq with ill-defined borders, which needed adjustment and permanency. The southern borders were easy; a junior British military officer, sitting in a tent, using a ruler, drew lines, arbitrarily carving out Kuwait and the adjacent desert from the Iraqi land. Iraq objected but to no avail, the issue remained alive: successive Iraqi regimes demanded Kuwait's re-annexation to the mother country. King Faisal I was the initial claimer, but his political maneuvering did not succeed. After the revolution, in 1961, General Qasim lay claim to Kuwait, mobilized his forces to invade it, but the British prevented his action. This issue, together with other reasons, led Saddam to invade Kuwait in 1990.

The northern borders of Iraq were not as simple as drawing lines in the sand in the South! The Treaty of Peace had left newly created Iraq in a major dispute with Turkey over vilayet of Mosul, a vast province bordering Turkey, which is now, Iraqi Kurdistan.

Much to the opposition of Kemalist Turkey, Britain maneuvered at the negotiating table to assign Mosul to the newly formed Kingdom of Iraq. Britain's insistence was not because of her love for Iraq, but because of the vilayet's oil riches. British mandated Iraq would have guaranteed British control over the riches, which otherwise would have been Turkey's.

Mustafa Kemal Attaturk contested the League of Nation's decision. Both sides vehemently defended their positions. To break the stalemate the League decided to hold a plebiscite in Mosul on the issue. A committee of seventeen came to Mosul and met with the representatives of Turkomans of Kirkuk, the Kurds of Mosul, and the Arabs. Turkomans were overwhelmingly in favor of rejoining their mother country, Turkey, but not the Arabs or the Kurds. Naturally, Arabs were in favor of Iraq, but the Kurds needed persuasion.

My Uncle Krikor, who was a prominent physician in Mosul, and who knew all the Kurdish Aghas (Chieftains), played a significant role in persuading them to vote against joining Ataturk's Turkey. He went from mosque to mosque telling the audience that if they joined Turkey, Ataturk will force them to change their way of life; would force their daughters to attend co-ed schools, give freedom to women who would dress Western style, short sleeves and all, and be a man's equal. "Then you would lose your control over your wife and daughters," he said. "If you like to have that kind of a social arrangement, which is against the teachings of Prophet Mohammed (peace be upon him), then vote to join Turkey."

This approach echoed favorably in the Kurdish community and they responded. Turkey lost. The plebiscite favored keeping vilayet of Mosul within the borders of young Iraq. Turkomans of Kirkuk were livid! The immediate fall-out of this arrangement was the ethnic polarization that entrenched itself in society and multiplied until now, when Iraq is paying for the mistakes committed by its founders, the Big Powers, almost a century ago.

The irony of this victory for the Kurds was that it not only changed geography, but also the destiny of the Kurdish Nation: it divided Kurdistan.

Kurdistan, consisting mainly of tribes inhabiting Turkey, Iraq, Syria, and Iran did not have, at the time, the collective political maturity to foresee the effects of their decision. Each tribe, following its agha, pursued its local interests: mainly control of their tribal territory. Thus, Kurds lost an excellent opportunity provided them by Article 62 of the Sevres Treaty, which read:

> Britain, France and Italy...shall draft...a scheme of local autonomy for the predominantly Kurdish areas lying east of the Euphrates, south of the southern boundary of Armenia as it may be hereafter determined, and north of the frontier of Turkey with Syria and Mesopotamia, as defined in Article 27."

Furthermore, Article 63 stated, "The Turkish Government hereby agrees to accept and execute the decisions of both the Commissions mentioned in Article 62." However, Article 64 provided:

> If within one year from the coming into force of the present Treaty, the Kurdish peoples within the areas defined in Article 62 shall address themselves to the Council of the League of Nations in such a manner as to show that a majority of the population of these areas desires independence from Turkey. And if the Council then considers that these peoples are capable of such independence and recommends that it should be granted to them, Turkey hereby agrees to execute such a recommendation, and to renounce all rights and title over these areas.

In Iraqi Kurdistan (Southern Kurdistan), the Kurds were divided demographically. Two major tribal conglomerates; the Bahtinan (which includes the Barzanis), who lived in northern Iraq, abutting Turkey, and Soranis (which includes the Talabanis), who lived in northeastern Iraq abutting Iran, spoke different Kurdish dialects, and had different cultural and tribal traditions, a dividing rather than a unifying factor. It was, therefore, natural for these factions to have closer rapport with their kin living just across the border, than with each other. From the social, political, and ideological make-up of the Kurdish "Nation" of the time, it is fair to conclude that the Kurds themselves had not yet developed the idea of a sovereign united Kurdistan. In Iraq, they had no history of organized political movement resembling a revolution, except for the local uprising of Sheikh Mahmoud Hafidzadeh, in Suleymania in 1919, which the British forces quashed. In Turkey, they had a history of three: of Prince Badrkhan of Bohtan, in the 1830s; of Sheikh Obeydullah in the 1880s; and of Sheikh Sa'id in 1929. These uprisings, although unsuccessful in their intent to self-rule, metamorphosed the idea of the

Kurdish Cause into the goal of Independent United Kurdistan, and this became the quest of all Kurds, even to date.

After the demise of the Mahabaad Kurdish Republic in 1946, and Mala Mustafa Barzani's retreat to the Soviet Union, there was a political power vacuum in Iraqi Kurdistan; the Iraqi Kurdish movement and Mala Mustafa were synonymous, a rather anachronistic situation for the twentieth-century liberation movements. The political thoughts had not transformed into organizational structures capable of mobilizing the masses into political action; tribal setups, and agha-led revolts were still the Kurdish modus operandi.

Mala's asylum in the Soviet Union and the political vacuum, which his absence created, was an excellent opportunity for Communist penetration into the Kurdish community. Soviet propaganda portrayed Moscow as the defender of the Kurdish people against the colonialists-Imperialists, and their puppet, the Iraqi government. Thus, within a short period, the Communists hijacked the Kurdish national movement, which was primarily based on ethnicity, not internationalism. The Iraqi government, now, had a legitimate reason to persecute the Kurds with the false pretense that they were not fighting the Kurds, but Communism!

In the mid-1950s, young, educated, and sophisticated Kurdish leaders emerged on the political scene, amongst whom Jalal Talabani, a lawyer, was the most prominent and promising. His prominence heralded the emergence of a new cadre of politicians, which would challenge the Kurdish tribal, feudal, and reactionary establishment. I knew him; he was both a neighbor and a schoolmate. The government constantly persecuted him for his political activities.

With these factors in force, the center of power shifted from the militarily oriented Barzan to the cultural center of Iraqi Kurdistan, Suleymania, home of the Talabanis.

The idea of "Kurdistan for the Kurds" was budding amongst the Kurds, but had not yet fully developed, not only because of tribal and linguistic differences, but also because of how they viewed each other. For the Talabani faction the Barzanis were just a bunch of trigger-happy provincial, tribal, feudal, and reactionary warriors who have continuously failed to secure gains for the Kurdish Cause, while Barzanis viewed the Talabanis as a group of unreliable, ineffective, and white-collared intellectuals who couldn't fight.

Until Mala's repatriation in 1958, the Kurdish Cause in Iraq, now under the leadership of the intellectuals, was confined mostly to vague nationalistic statements, and requests for improvements in Kurdish economic and civil rights. The primary political ideology was blurred and transformed into an odd form of nationalism laced with Marxism, perhaps Socialism. But that did not matter; what mattered was reform to improve the life of an individual Kurd.

This new posture put the Kurdish leadership at odds with their allies, primarily the ICP. Even though the Soviet Union was their godfather, there was a distinct rivalry, even enmity between the ICP consisting of all ethnic groups, and the Kurdish nationalist intellectuals. The ICP, by doctrine, rejected nationalism, whereas the entire Kurdish movement was based on it.

Now there were three dominant political forces swaying the Kurdish ship, all secular: Feudalism, Nationalism, and Communism, each working separately, within their own conviction. It is important to mention here that unlike the case with their cousins in Turkey, Islam or any other religion has never been a factor in Iraqi Kurdish political life until after Saddam's demise in 2003.

This fragmentation of political forces could not have continued! Neither faction could reach its goals working separately. With Mala's return, there evolved an uneasy and unharmonious merger between the intelligentsia and the tribal chiefs, mainly Mala Mustafa. They were to adopt the Iraqi Kurdish Cause, and work together despite their differences and hatred, which defined their relationship! They were to operate under one umbrella to display unity, political sophistication, and a fresh mature image to the world, which had always belittled them and dismissed their cause as being the fantasy of a bunch of nationalist lightweights.

By creating this entity, they combined the best of what each side could offer: guns and political skills. They realized that without this accommodation and unity it would be impossible to achieve their goals. This conviction, though shaky on occasion, remained the driving force behind the endurance of the Kurdish struggle, until today.

After Mala's return and telling about their mistreatment in exile, the Kurds turned away from Communism and the Soviet Union, the two vehicles, which they had used in a bipolar world, and with which they had a symbiotic relationship for decades.

In practical terms, this rapprochement resulted in the formation of a political party, The Kurdistan Democratic Party (KDP), an umbrella organization, which was to embrace the entire Kurdish political spectrum in Iraq, and lead the struggle for a form of self-rule.

In this delicate balance between the two factions, which constituted the Party, the intelligentsia were hoping for the upper hand in running the Party and blunting the tribal influences, especially that of Mala Mustafa, whereas the Barzanis who had the guns, strived for total control.

From the beginning, however, KDP was transformed into an organization controlled by Barzani, a fact that led the more pragmatic Jalal Talabani to exit in protest, and form a party to his liking, the Patriotic Union of Kurdistan (PUK). Thus, Iraqi Kurds were again divided along tribal lines; KDP was the political party in Barzan (also Zakho, Dhok, 'Aqra, 'Amadiya, and Sinjar etc.,) abutting southeastern border of Turkey, while the PUK had its stronghold in northeastern Iraq (Suleymania, Halabja etc.,) abutting Iran.

The separation was natural and expected, since both sides were not mature enough to set aside their inherent differences. All these discrepancies lay the foundation for covert enmity between the sides when Mala Mustafa was alive; however, years after his death, and after Desert Storm, the polite considerations gave way to armed clashes between the KDP and the PUK, which prompted Mas'oud Barzani to ask for Saddam's military help. Thousands died in this fratricide, which was finally brought to a halt through U.S. mediation; the parties signed a reconciliation pact, The Washington Accord, in Washington, only to break it within months of its signing.

After Desert Storm and the implementation of the No Flight Zone, these two main Kurdish factions control the vast majority of the old Vilayet of Mosul.

This huge territory consisted of four subprovinces, now provinces: Mosul, Erbil, Kirkuk, and Suleymania.

Demographically, vilayet of Mosul was a microcosm of Iraq: it consisted of urbanized Sunni Arabs of Mosul, provincial Kurds of Mosul, and a small community of Turkomans in the town of Tela'far, some Assyrians, Chaldians, Yezidis, and a few thousand Armenian émigrés who had survived the Turkish Genocide.

In Erbil and Suleymania, Kurds were a majority, whereas Kirkuk was what it was, a demographic uncertainty; the Turkomani language was predominant; however that did not mean that Kirkuk was ethnically Turkomani. Kurds bowing to the Ottoman hegemony spoke the language, giving the false impression that Kirkuk was ethnically Turkoman. Regardless of this chaos, official transactions, and teachings in schools and mosques was in Arabic.

The vilayet was predominantly Sunni, though there were some pockets of Shiite Turkomans in the villages of Kirkuk, such as Tiseen, Taza Khurmatou, and Tuz-Khurmatou. Shiite Kurds lived further south in Khanaqin and Mandali, but these were not within the borders of vilayet of Mosul.

This ethnic, but not religious, diversity in Kirkuk was a recipe for disputes, dissents, passive resistances, pogroms, and even armed clashes. It is no surprise, then, that one of the major goals of Iraq's rulers was to remove the negative implications of this diversity, by Arabizing Kirkuk. They justified their conviction by the fact that they were the ones who started the Great Arab Revolution from Hijaaz, they were the ones who fought the Ottoman Empire, and they were the ones who liberated the Arab land, not the Kurds, and certainly not the Turkomans. Iraq was and should remain Arab, they decided.

But did it?

To day, Kirkuk's ethnic makeup is a major obstacle to writing a final constitution acceptable to all. The obstacle is Kirkuk's future, whether it should:

(a) Be a part of Iraqi Kurdistan.
(b) Continue the status quo under the central government.
(c) Be internationalized.

In view of the irreconcilable differences, it is unimaginable that any solution is bound to satisfy the competing parties. Kirkuk will remain a source of discord and challenges, if not war. In this sense, Kirkuk is the Jerusalem of Iraq.

Other major international conspiracies stripped the Kurds of their future: In 1923, Britain's Lord Curzon and Turkey's Ismet Inonu, in an unholy alliance managed to sign a new treaty in Lausanne, which nullified the Sevres treaty, thus robbing the Kurds and the Armenians of their rights for land and statehood. The treaty divided Kurdistan between Turkey, Syria, Iraq, and Iran.

What did the future hold for the Kurds? Nobody knew, least of all Colonel Mustafa, whose conversations with me, indeed his mere presence, provoked anxiety day after day.

16

Kurdistan

On my first assignment as a medical officer, I joined the Army garrison in Qalah Dize. At present, Qalah Dize is no longer there; Kurdish intertribal wars destroyed it. In its heyday, it was a natural fortress for the Kurdish rebels who fought against the central government. It was the only town of Puzhder, and as such the commercial center of the region. The area was vast, rugged, and mountainous, which spanned the northeast border of Iraq. It is a truly magnificent country marked with steep gorges, deep valleys, and high snow-covered peaks. If you have been to Innsbruck, Interlaken, Garmish, or any other part of the Alps, you have been to Qalah Dize.

Unlike the Alps, Zagros Mountains are totally undeveloped, unspoiled, and primitive. The mountaintops, capped with snow even in the summer, rise from the deepest gorges to provide diving platforms for the melting snow, creating breathtaking waterfalls, white streams, and brooks.

On lower elevations, walnut, mulberry, and wild fig trees, heavy with fruits, bow their heads to the beauty that surrounds them. One could spot an occasional wild goat hiding behind a rock to elude a hunter. A light brown serpentine trail, bobbing and weaving, threads the green mountainside stretching one's gaze to faraway places, and imagination to infinity.

Somewhere, out there is Iran, where the other half of the Puzhder tribe lives.

This way, about two hours ride to the south, is Suleymania, the cultural berth of Iraqi Kurdistan, and the capital of the province. But, one cannot go that way to reach Suleymania, there are no roads; Puzhder, by decision, had to remain isolated so as not to strengthen Kurds' hand. The plan was to keep Babakr Agha on one mountain, in Puzhder, and Sheikh Mahmoud on another in Suleymania, thus allowing Mr. Allen Chapman, the British Political Officer to control both sides with ease.

The town itself is perched on a decapitated mountain. I never knew the elevation, but it was high. The snow-capped mountains looked like old women's lace shawls covering their heads and shoulders, watching over the children at play. They provided a backdrop to one-story mud houses and huts that cascaded down the mountainside, as if rolled out of the horn of plenty.

The roof of one house made the front yard of the one above it, forming a stage where the drama of life began every day, with the rooster's crow. By then the woman of the house had already started her day by searching the chicken coop for eggs. She then, prepared breakfast of homemade bread, yogurt, milk, honey, tea, and eggs. She hauled water for the family's daily needs, did the washing, and hung them on lines to dry, and lock-in the scents of wild flowers. In the summer months, one could see women bathing their children out in the open, and then spending the day with other household chores. Almost universally, they were illiterate; however, of late education had begun to reach their children in primary schools.

Qalah Dize had a no-name main street, which was punctuated with sporadic telephone poles and plenty of potholes. There might have been a few streetlights, but I do not remember seeing one, except at the entrance of the Army barracks.

Walking down the main street, one would come across the usual: a tailor working on his Singer Sewing Machine, a small jewelry shop, a butcher shop, a bazergaan (cloth and material merchant), a carpenter, and a haberdasher who sold, amongst other things, "kalashes" (hand woven wool, sometimes silk, footwear with leather or rubber sole made out of Good Year tire cuttings). There was the blacksmith who made horseshoes, daggers, and doubled as a gunsmith, of sorts.

A donkey-drawn flat bed cart displayed produce: radishes the size of a cantaloupe, watermelon, Persian and honeydew melons, okra, eggplants, lettuce, cucumbers, scallions, tomatoes, and more, all local products.

Kurdistan had some of the choicest tobaccos in the world, including a naturally aromatic one, rivaling Latakia. I am not sure what its scientific name is, but the locals called it "bondar," aromatic. This was a major source of income for the region and the government, who controlled its trade and export to the world through the Office of Tobacco Control. Probably Balkan Sobranie contains some of that tobacco, which was not available for local consumption.

A peddler, carrying a Persian rug, which had been smuggled the night before from across the border, was trying to make a sale. Qalah Dize truly deserved its name.

Hundreds of numb people walked the main street aimlessly, as if sleepwalking. Some sat in a "chaikhana" to sip sweet tea and watch the passersby; others smoked their clay pipes filled with unprocessed, unadulterated tobacco.

Men wore traditional Kurdish clothes: shalvar (baggy pants tight at the ankles) and shapek (shirt), with many yards long cummerbund wrapped around their bellies and a shorter version wrapped around their heads. There were a few who wore two-sizes-too-big Western style suits, with its sleeves reaching the fingertips, and a tie that had a long way to go to reach the waist. These were the educated, the teachers, and the government employees. Women walked around bra-less, in colorful baggy ankle length dresses. People were generally thin and sturdy. They had light complexions, blue eyes, and cheekbones as high as their pride and their mountains.

It was indeed a colorful scene: purples, yellows, reds, and oranges mixed with blue, gave Kurds a different hue than the Arabs or the Turkomans. Here one did not see the Arab woman's black aba. A Kurd's garb was a distinct hallmark of his race. Indeed, his headdress identified his tribe, and together with his mustache gave him dignity and honor.

Women's attire was what the original Muslim women wore. Muslim scholars argue that during the time of Prophet Mohammed and much later, Muslim women dressed very conservatively, covering the head, the arms to the wrists, and the legs to the ankles, but never used the "chador," the aba, and the veil; those were introduced later on.

Women of Qalah Dize, like Kurdish women everywhere, were "Never to stay empty, the more babies they delivered the better it was for the nation." This was a serious conviction tantamount to a national policy. They all wanted boys, as many of them as possible. Kurds believed that a "Male Kurd is destined to die before his time: in battle." Therefore, there should be "One son for Kurdistan, and the rest for me." This is sad and fatalistic but not an entirely unrealistic attitude; Kurds have always needed fighters to wage battles for their Cause. These young men however were subject to conscription by the Iraqi army and had to serve at least two years. Fathers did not object to that, because they rationalized that their sons will get "advanced military training then come home experienced in modern warfare, to join the rest of Kurdish fighters."

Arabs also wished for male children but for different reasons; families with large numbers of males could cultivate more land and provide more support for the family.

Life in Qalah Dize was complex compared to life in the surrounding villages and hamlets. The government's presence was evident by the flag flying over government buildings. There were not many; there was a school, a deficient civilian hospital, and a few other governmental agencies serving a population of 25,000. Governmental neglect was evident everywhere. The road leading to the town was in utter disrepair, and almost impassable in the winter.

During the days the garrison appeared to be in control; however, nights were a different matter: at night, horror ruled. Disenchanted Kurds, rebels, freedom fighters, even Iranian smugglers who were also Puzhderis, would cross the border to destabilize the region and remind the central government in Baghdad of their Kurdish National Cause In the late 1950s, this was the extent of Baghdad's control over Puzhder.

Before WWII, Babakr Agha, the head of the Puzhder tribe controlled the region completely, the way Barzanis controlled theirs. He even had his own currency using the Iraqi coin, anna, worth four fils; he valued it at five. When I arrived in

Qalah Dize in the summer of 1958, his influence had diminished, and his aura tarnished. He was ailing and bedridden, but still people remembered him with fear and disdain. His patched blind eye, short stature, sculpted emotionless face, and cold brutality had created his negative public image, and the sheer mention of his name, ran the shivers down people's spines.

I had the same feelings when his men stood at my desk asking me to make a trip to his house to treat him. Out of curiosity and duty I agreed; after all it was a rare opportunity to tend to a man of his stature.

He was one of Mr. Chapman's collaborators, and used to trade favors with the British government via this channel. He was a British asset and his value oscillated with Baghdad's compliance with the British demands. Alan Chapman played the Babaker card at will.

Four of his armed men came to pick me up in an open American military jeep and drove me away. With their semiautomatics pointed outward, we drove for over two hours on a dirt road.

When the arms finally relaxed and the barrels pointed downward, it was clear that we were close to his nest. Armed men were scattered here and there on the heights surrounding his house.

Decades later when I had an opportunity to visit the real "Eagles Nest" in Berchtesgaten, it reminded me of this tyrant's "fortress" in the "Kurdish Alps"; I thought tyrants always feared the people who they pretended to defend.

His men received me with utmost respect and tended to my comfort by adding extra cushions on the rug-covered mattress on which I sat. That kind of behavior is cultural and comes naturally to the Kurd: they respect their guests immensely!

The examination was short; it took all of ten minutes. I spent more time telling key tribal men about the seriousness and hopelessness of his condition and that his survival was in the hands of Allah.

They expected that kind of prognosis, but wanted to try this new military doctor, just in case he had some cure.

They insisted that I stay for dinner otherwise "Agha would be offended." I did!

A man poured warm water from a brass ibreeq (gooseneck-shaped water pitcher) to wash my hands before eating, while the other followed holding Turkish towels.

One is to start eating by whispering "Bismillah" (in the name of Allah) loud enough for everyone to hear, then, begin eating using three fingers. They did provide a wooden spoon, but those who know the tribal protocol will score big by eating like one of them, with his fingers, which is a sign of respect to the host. Once finished, the hand-washing ritual is repeated, strong dark tea is served, and then, one would be free to leave.

I ended my visit by raising hope for a speedy recovery, Inshallah (God-willing) even though everyone knew the gravity of his illness, and that he stood no chance to recover.

The men calculated that by the time they returned from delivering me, it would be dark. So, better hurry; we left.

On my way home, I kept thinking; God knows what this man had done to get where he was! How many battles had he waged? How had he blocked total governmental sovereignty over Puzhder? What effects has he had over the Kurdish Cause? What plots had he implemented with Mr. Chapman to keep the Barzani Kurds and other Aghas under control? How effective had he been to keep British control over Baba Gurgur? How much had he cost the British treasury?

So far, what I had seen in Qalah Dize pleased me. I felt that I had made the right choice by accepting this post: beautiful high mountains, waterfalls, brooks, white waters, and a primitive life. It was a kind of paid vacation for me, and I enjoyed it.

Accommodating to military life was easy. The garrison hospital was under my command, all six beds of it, which were scattered across the walls. There was one nurse-medic and one medicine cabinet with some Morphine and essentials in it.

Nurse-Medic Akram was a Turkoman from my hometown Kirkuk. He spoke fractured Arabic, and equally despised the Kurds and their language, which is why he did not learn it. The patient roster was scanty, so, we spent the days socializing.

Within a few days, I discovered that Akram was drinking on the job. I never caught him drinking, but he was drunk, all the time. I was infuriated. Efforts to discipline him, but no proscribed punishments helped.

On one occasion, I slapped him in the face (I had not heard of General Patten then), but that did not help either, so I gave up.

A few months later, this man taught me a lesson, which I have not forgotten, and abided by it until now: I learned to never underestimate a human being, never demean anyone, and never let power get to my head.

Parts of my daily life were personalities who constituted the hierarchy of this town. Colonel Abdul Hameed, the commander of the battalion, Khalo Rasheed of the Tobacco Control Office, Hakim (Judge) Mustafa, Colonel Mustafa, the uncelebrated hero of the Revolution, and Rushdi Awtchi, the Administrator of the town. All were Kurds except for Rushdi who was a Turkoman from my hometown, and knew my father. Rushdi and I shared worries about the political situation and our future as minorities. We both hated Communists; the revolution did not sit well with either of us. However, that is where our agreements ended: he was a Turkoman, therefore a Turani (a Pan Turkic), and I was an Armenian, a victim of Turanism. I believe we mistrusted each other, except in the social sphere.

Colonel Abdul Hameed was a Kurd. He was gentle, kind, and honorable, but lacked charisma. He never participated in risky conversations, and never divulged his real feelings. I suppose he had to; he was the commander and had to maintain a certain image.

Khalo Rasheed was from Suleymania, spoke in the Sorani dialect, and advocated, in his gentle manner, the concept of free Kurdistan. "There is no reason," he would say, "for the Kurds not to have their rights, and govern themselves. There is no reason why school could not be taught in Kurdish." I doubt that he had any idea about how to achieve all that. Autonomy, federation, or confederation with Arab Iraq meant very little to him. He was a nationalist Kurd advocating Kurdish rights.

Khalo had no children, was a heavy smoker, had a drinking problem, and sighed frequently to ventilate his lungs and his worries. He coughed frequently and coughed long. The Kurdish Cause was the reason for his worries, and an excuse to bury them in alcohol. Furthermore, he felt unlucky for not having children, especially boys, to give one to Kurdistan and to keep the rest for himself. That would have bestowed upon him an honor enjoyed by Kurds who were lucky to make that contribution. Khalo was a fierce nationalist, a "Real Kurd."

The disturbed political and security atmospherics, fed by rumors of all kinds about robberies, assault, and other crimes, made me feel insecure and vulnerable. I felt the need to own a firearm.

Through an acquaintance, I bought a Parabellum, and a pack or two of ammunition and went to a remote valley to try. The first shot, my first ever, echoed as if saying "Protecteeeed," and it gave me confidence. That night I slept well, with my security under my pillow. It never occurred to me that one day the purchase of a handgun would come to haunt me and cause me tremendous problems.

17

A Disastrous Task

On March 6, 1959, I received two separate telegrams from the Headquarters of the Ministry of Health as well as the Army Medical Corps in Baghdad, directing me to inspect four remote villages on the Iraqi-Iranian border for outbreak of meningitis and typhus. A copy was given to the commander of the battalion who arranged for my trip the following day. He provided two mounted police officers for protection and guidance.

This trip was quite unexpected, but for the commander, who had received such orders before, it was routine. I welcomed the opportunity to see what was beyond Qal'ah Dize.

Early in the morning, we mounted horse and were on our way. It was early spring, and the skies were clear and blue. A gentle breeze cooled off the horses and their riders. The landscape was studded with a hamlet here, and a hamlet there, strung together with a narrow trail, allowing passage to one horse at a time. What we saw was a magnificent arabesque panorama and spectacular views, as we ascended the Zagros chain. The climb was steep. One had to lean foreword and hold on to the animal to prevent sliding backward, and falling.

The higher we climbed, the thinner the air got. The animals started heaving and stalling. My experienced companions assured me that the animals were not tired, but it was the elevation, which made them short of breath. Whatever the reason, we had no choice but to continue riding single file; we couldn't dismount to give the animals some relief; the trail was too narrow, and the gorges too steep. We couldn't rush them either; the slightest jolt would have plunged us into the gorges. Our lives depended entirely on these "friends." I was nervous. To add to it, my companions were telling me stories about mules throwing their riders off their backs, without warning, if the rider could not control them. That didn't help this novice.

The trails skirted the mountainside, always exposing one side toward the gorge. On occasion, we had to halt so that one of the men could chop an overgrown bush blocking our path. A misstep by the animal would have sent us to face our creator.

Oh, God, I thought is this any way to die? Is this how one's end should be? What if the mule tripped or skidded? How about Vatche, my son? Did he deserve to grow up without his father? How about my parents, who had lost four children before me, could they afford to lose another one? Oh, please God spare me!

I had never recited the Lords Prayer so often in my life. I remembered the church, which I had abandoned; I remembered our parish priest, Khoren Kassabian, and the protestant preacher of the Christian Science Reading Room, Iliyya. Then I attempted to regain my composure; after all, I was still in the saddle.

"Look at those clouds," I said to myself, "you could catch them if you tried." "Don't be stupid, and don't try," a voice answered from within, "Don't shift your balance!" I didn't. I kept looking down to follow the animals' footsteps.

Matchbox-size huts caught my attention as I looked. Blue smoke was spewing from the chimneys, a sign of life, and a sign that they are inhabited. I wondered how daily life would be in a remote hamlet like this. Wake up in the morning, have a rich breakfast of organic and homegrown food, tend to the goats and other animals, light up your clay pipe, and stretch on a mattress until evening, then at night try to procreate one boy for Kurdistan and the rest for you.

What the hell people do living down there? What the hell am I doing up here? Those friggin bastards, sitting in Baghdad, ordering people around, do this, do that! How the hell do they know if there is an outbreak of disease? There are no reported cases! Acting on rumor? That's it. Acting on rumor just to show that they are doing something! Hey, hey, control yourself, you can't afford to get upset, you might lose your balance!

For several hours things didn't change except that I became somewhat light-headed, which led to relaxation; my adrenalin must have been depleted; I noted that my fears had dissipated and I was sitting erect in the saddle. We had reached a plateau where we could disembark for rest. Thank God!

The plateau was vast. Around us, the field was covered with patches of snow and some wild budding flowers, all colorful and delicate. It was early spring. The men told me that the locals boiled the flowers and drank the brew, some for coughs and colds, and some for belly aches and diarrhea. I wished I knew their names, but then that didn't matter. I didn't know a million other things.

After some rest, we continued. The melting snow formed little waterfalls, and the trail snaked itself through the landscape. We sighted two officials on our way; they were measuring the depth of the snow with a pole to report to Baghdad. That would have allowed the Irrigation Department to guestimate the volume of water, which would pour into Tigris, via the Greater Zab.

By the day's end, we had met only a dozen or so people in several hamlets. Men, mostly elderly, and old women with toothless mouths talked to us. Beautiful young women, wearing long colorful Kurdish dresses, with long sleeves rolled up and tied behind their necks, stood there in silence. They had wrapped colorful cloth around their thin waists, to separate their belly from their chests. Their heads were covered with thin veils, which fell gracefully on their shoulders. One of my men asked:

> Hey kaka (brother), is there anybody sick in here?
> Nah.
> Do you know if anybody is sick or has died recently in the nearby hamlets?
> Wallah na zanm (by God, I don't know).
> No matter what we asked, they would reply, "Wallah na zanim."

Not that they didn't know! May be they didn't, but even if they knew, they wouldn't say, in case what they say might hurt them later. They had become so suspicious of strangers that they kept things to themselves. They didn't talk in case the strangers turn out to be government agents. In this case we were government officials.

"Nah zanm, rahat e Jaanm" (my mind is at peace [if I say] I don't know," is a common Kurdish saying.

They probably would have been more cooperative, if we were not uniformed. They resented police, even if they were Kurds, because police made their lives miserable, took bribes, arrested people, and were instruments of government brutality.

Despite all that, the Kurds were hospitable. Wherever we went, we were offered their famous yogurt, tea, and freshly baked bread. In this generosity, they are similar to the Bedouins and the Arab villagers. But unlike them, the Kurds are very clean; their utensils shine, their personal hygiene is better than that of an Arab peasant because of abundance of water in the mountains.

We had another few miles to go to reach our first major stop to spend the night in a village of some one hundred people. We rushed to get there before dark. I don't remember the name of the village. I probably would have if an event of colossal proportions did not happen: All three of us were tired from a trying journey. My legs were bowed, and the derriere ached from riding. We stayed in the home of the village chieftain. The man felt honored to play host to a dignitary, an army officer, and a doctor at that. His men slaughtered a couple of chickens, and the women got busy preparing food. We ate with gusto, sitting on a rug on the floor, then had istikans of sweetened black tea. The mud walls of the room were bare, except for one framed Qur'anic writing that said, "Allah," and a rifle hanging from a long nail. A flickering kerosene lamp provided some soothing light and a tempo, blp-blp, blp-blp, which added to the tranquility of the night and induced sleep. There wasn't much conversation going on; everybody had rolled up and lit up a cigarette and mounted it on a foot-long holder; I was enjoying my pipe and reliving the beauty of nature, which had displayed itself during this trip. I slept right where I was sitting. When I woke up in the morning, I felt refreshed and ready to go to the next village. The boss of this hamlet had reported no illnesses.

I had barely washed my face with cold spring water when my guard approached me and ordered me to give him my wrists. He looked angry and disturbed. He handcuffed me "on orders from the Headquarters." I couldn't understand why, neither did they. They told me that the border guard had received a telegram ordering my immediate arrest, and transfer to Qalah Dize. I was shocked, dumbfounded, and worried, I thought there must be some misunderstanding, otherwise why this? What had I done to be handcuffed?

Well, can I see the telegram? I asked!
No you can't!
Isn't it my right to know who has signed the order?
No, it isn't.

My guards, who were so subservient and obedient the day before, were now playing hardball; they were curt and unyielding partly because they were puzzled, but also scared to handle such a big task, arresting an Army doctor.

We mounted horse and proceeded at an ordinary walking pace. The ride back displayed no scenery. I did not see mountains, gurgling brooks, waterfalls, or budding flowers peeking through the melting snow. The mountains seemed to have melted into hot black lava on that early spring day. It was March 12!

By dusk I knew that we were approaching Qalah Dize because rhythmic human sounds, at first in tempo, became audible. Soon they converted to unsettling noises of a crowd, which became louder and louder, as my heart began to beat faster and faster.

From a distance, first heads, then bodies, and then legs, became visible, as they climbed the hill in front of us. A mob of a few thousand, chanting, "Maaku Za'eem illa Kareem, guwaaweed Ba'thiya" (there is no leader but Karim [Qasim], you bastard Ba'this), approached us demonstrating their support of the "Sole leader," and against Nasser and his surrogates, "the Unionists, the traitors, the reactionaries and the enemies of the Revolution."

It was, undoubtedly, a hostile crowd, gesturing and wielding sticks, clubs, daggers, and handguns. They spat at me, grabbed my foot in an attempt to get me down, and poured all their anger on me, as if I was the cause of their misery, as if I was the Regent, or Nouri Sa'id. They continued yelling, "traitor, traitor."

I was scared. My tongue was stuck to the roof of my mouth. I was mum, and couldn't say a word. How could I and to whom? Who would listen to what I said? Who would reason with me? This was a possessed crowd, white hot, ready to avenge their aghas, the Imperialists, the reactionaries, and the remnants of the old regime, and I was there as an embodiment of all that.

All I could see, before my eyes, was the mutilated body of the Regent being dragged; Iraqis had learned a new technique of expressing their anger: bringing death to living humans by dragging them. I thought the same fate was about to befall me.

Questions crossed my mind, repeatedly, fleetingly, each time weighing heavier and heavier:

Did the Regent die before he was mutilated, or after?
What did he feel other than pain?
Was he yelling for help or begging for mercy?
Naah, the Regent could not have begged for mercy! It's hard to imagine that!
How long did it take him to die?

My inside was melting with fear, but externally I kept my composure. I think, if one shows composure, bravery, and defiance even though he is disintegrating inside, it may have some psychological impact on the mob; it may discourage them from attacking. Under these circumstances, it is just plain wrong to roll over and play dead. I didn't!

This was all bullshit, all theoretical bullshit! In reality, how I looked and behaved didn't make one bit of a difference; they were attacking me, and wanted to drag me, and they almost succeeded if it were not for one of my guard's intervention. He yelled, catching everybody's attention: "We have caught a man, we don't know yet if he is a traitor, though he has been accused of being one. He may not be! But, he must be an important man otherwise they would not have wanted him, they want him alive to interrogate him, if you kill him now, valuable information will be lost! Let me hand him over to the authorities, they know how to deal with him properly. You trust your new leaders, don't you? They all are revolutionaries; they will do the right thing."

That speech gave us safe passage, although the mob never disbursed; they kept following us with their usual chants and threats. Within ten to fifteen minutes, we were at the gates of the garrison. The guards took me in, and kept the still demonstrating, still chanting, still threatening crowd out, I felt safe!

18

A Long Journey

"Dr. Astarjian, this is Comrade Shafiq of the "Muqawama El- Sha'biya" (Communist militia that supported Qasim). With these words Colonel Abdul Hamid opened the Official Inquiry that night.

"You know Colonel Mustafa. Of course, you know Haakm Mustafa (Judge Mustafa). The Headquarters has appointed us to conduct a preliminary inquiry in your matter. I know our questions will be simple. I know of your trip to the Iranian border, I arranged it, I signed the papers for your mission, and I provided you with security, and I know the purpose of your trip. Informants told us you were attempting to escape to Iran. Is that true?"

"Sir, I went to the border to inspect the villages for communicable diseases, you saw the orders from Baghdad, and you arranged for my transportation and security. Why would I escape to Iran? My wife and son are here! Here are the copies of the telegrams you gave me."

"Yes, yes I have them too, I just don't understand, I can't understand! You have gone there on official duty. I provided for your trip, I just can't understand!" He said, looking at comrade Shafiq who was sitting in a commanding position looking like a rabid dog, a vengeful son of a bitch, who appeared to be breathing fire.

Do you belong to the Ba'th party? The comrade asked commandingly, and in a stern voice.
No, I don't.
Do you know Colonel Shawwaaf?
Colonel who? No, never heard of him!
You mean you don't know that traitor?
No, I am sorry, I mean, no I do not.

You mean you are unaware of the events in Mosul?"
No, I don't; what events?
Colonel Mustafa, do you have any questions?" interjected Colonel Abdul Hameed.
No I don't."

I looked at Colonel Mustafa and visualized his spraying of the Royal Family with bullets "lest these Arab Traitors change their minds under pressure from the British or the CIA and reinstate them." I thought this "Hero of the Revolution" who had befriended me, in his own internal exile, cried on my shoulders and told me about his innermost feelings about the Arabs and their deception of the Kurdish cause, would come to my rescue. He didn't! Yet again, he didn't say anything to hurt me either.

The questions were straightforward enough. I thought, Colonel Abdul Hamid's testimony, and the rather relaxed atmosphere that prevailed the inquiry, bode well. They had already removed the handcuffs, so, I felt hopeful.

Colonel Abdul Hamid was gentle and kind. He concluded the inquiry by saying, "I am sure there is some kind of a misunderstanding; it will be sorted out in the morning. You are tired, Dktore, You have gone through a lot, why don't you rest? For your own protection you will stay in the barracks and there will be soldiers to guard you; don't worry about your wife and son. My wife and Haakm Mustafa's wife will take care of them."

The situation now was a little clearer. It had something to do with an uprising in Mosul, and somehow these people were associating me with that movement. What do I have to do with those people? I don't even know who they are, or who Shawwaaf is! I could not make sense out of all these happenings. Not much else crossed my mind; I was innocent, trusting, even naïve!

My sanctuary for the night was a tent pitched especially for the event, near the offices of Colonel Abdul Hamid. I had barely sat down on the portable cot when a soldier walked in and gave me a military salute. Standing in attention, he said, with a good measure of emotion:

"Sayyidi, I am here as your guard, feel safe! Sir, do you see this gun? I will shove it up the ass of anyone who attempts to hurt you. Don't worry, rest." He took a deep breath and said, "Now you must be hungry, I bet you haven't eaten all day. These motherfuckers. . .do you want me to get you some kebab? I'll bring you some kebab!"

I was dumfounded; it was corporal Akram, the alcoholic orderly of mine, whom I had punished mercilessly, and now at the time of my dilemma, he was responding to my cruelty with self-sacrifice, generosity, and kindness. I felt like a jackass for punishing this kind-hearted, considerate man. I felt small and humiliated. My vision, melted into tears like the snow I had just admired in the mountains, except there were no beautiful flowers raising their heads through it all.

This gesture made me grow a decade or two, and right there and then I promised to myself to never again look down at another human being. I have kept that promise for over four decades now.

Just barely holding my tears, I accepted his offer convinced that it could be my last meal for sometime. Kebab never tasted so good. I felt drained; I pulled the blanket over my head, as if for protection, and slept.

In the early hours of the morning, a voice awakened me: "Seyyidi, seyyidi (sir, sir) wake up," I opened my eyes, it was Sergeant Akram, my orderly, I had slept a total of three hours. "Wake up, we are getting out of here, the commander thinks that he will not be able to protect you from the mob tomorrow morning, so he decided to get you out of here and send you to the headquarters in Suleymania".

I had already slept in my army uniform. I had nothing to pack except for my old-fashioned doctor's bag, which contained some medical paraphernalia, and the two telegrams, which delineated my mission to the border villages. I put my shoes on!

Within minutes, we were in the military ambulance, on our way out of town. The driver zipped through town with no headlights on. As soon as we crossed the bridge, in the outskirts of town, we breathed a sigh of relief. Now, they could not catch us, even if they knew about our escape.

By the time we cleared Qalah Dize, it was dawn. Akram was sitting in the back, still holding his submachine gun, and there was another armed soldier sitting with the driver. I thought I was out of danger for now, and I was! It was too early to think about serious matters, regardless; solving this puzzle was very much on my mind. I couldn't concentrate; my mind was drifting from appreciating the nature and the scenery one moment, to feeling a false sense of security, to imminent danger, to life and death the next. Regardless I couldn't dismiss the indescribably beautiful mountain vistas of Kurdistan. Oh, what a joy!

By mid-morning, we were at the army barracks in Suleymania. My handcuffs were off. The military officer who received me asked some routine questions. The doctor's bag, with its contents of stethoscope, medical tools, and the telegrams, were already confiscated and sealed, as exhibits.

The bag was my strongest defense, I thought, but it was not in my possession, and that worried me! If they destroyed the evidence, or lost it, then they could accuse me of anything; these are Communists, they could fabricate anything to convict me. What would I do, then? Naah, I concluded this whole thing is a misunderstanding anyway, they are not going to destroy anything. It is just that they had to bring me here; it is the chain of command. The civility with which I was treated raised my hopes of release. After reading the transfer papers the officer on duty said: "Dktore, I am afraid we can't let you go free, and can't solve this problem, here. We do not understand it in the first place! There must be some other reason that they want you. We talked to the headquarters in Kirkuk; they want to question you themselves. They will decide what to do with you."

But what is it that they want, can't you tell me?
If we knew, we will tell you, but we don't. They want you down there!

I said goodbye to Akram, thanking him for his kindness, and got into the jeep, this time handcuffed, and headed to Kirkuk, the headquarters of the Second Army Division.

The place was known by its Ottoman name "Qishla," the very Qishla that I had passed for years going to Markaziyya school or to the bookstore of Sayyid Abbass. The Christian Science reading room was in front of it, and not far from it were the provision stores owned by Armenians: Karekin Dulgerian, Krikor Yaghljian, Vahan Dulgarian, and Stepan.

The place was very familiar and reassuring at first; however, this time Qishla looked different, it was extraordinarily busy: there were jeeps, generals, and gendarmes getting in and out. Trucks carrying soldiers moved in either direction. The soldiers carried automatic weapons. Military Police stood guard on either side of this huge arcade fully armed with submachine guns, instead of the usual ceremonial rifles. No, this time it was not the same, it was different this time; this place did not look ordinary, sleepy, or tranquil, the way I had known it to be.

We entered a room under the arcade where an army officer, without as much as glancing at me, ordered the guards to lock me up. When I left the room I saw Garabed (not real name), an employee of the Armenian high school in Baghdad, about whom I had written a negative report on one of my evaluations of his classes, a few years before.

There were rumors that he was a Communist, but this sighting proved to me that he indeed was, or at least, he was a collaborator. He spotted me, undoubtedly recognized me, and then, exchanged a few words with the officers who were standing nearby. His body language sent a hostile message to me.

It was, now, a fact that I was a detainee. The soldiers, one on each side of me, opened a solid metal door, and walked me in. It was a dark corridor, damp and dreary. We passed a few occupied cells to the last one. They opened the door to a cage, and threw me in and locked the door. It was now clear that I was in a death row cell, a four by seven space with a very high ceiling, from which hung an unreachable, dim, bare lamp. The cage door allowed a view of the dim passageway, which led to a door with a tiny window allowing a beam of daylight, at the far end of it. There was a feeble light emanating from a bulb hanging from a very high ceiling of the corridor.

The only furnishing the cell had was a thin, dirty, filthy, smelly mattress spread on a compact damp dirt floor. It was full of dried stains of shit, urine, ejaculate, other body fluids, and blood.

The walls were full of writings, using excrement for chalk:

"My last will and testament. . ." signed Mustafa Ahmed of Shaterloo.
"To my son Ahmed: I am gone, take care of your mother and little sister," signed Jaasim.
"I am innocent; I want you to avenge my hanging. . ." Muhammad.
"I did not kill, there is no justice in this country, I don't want to die," Shukri.

"To my mother Khadeeja: Salaam wa al-widaa' until we meet again in Aakhira" (the day of reckoning).

"To my brother Ali: I am innocent, they don't believe me, I haven't killed!"

"Ash hadu an la Ilaaha illa Allaah, Muhammada-ar-Rasoul Allaah" (there is no god but God, and Muhammed is his messenger).

A pair of large breasts decorated a wall in brown, with a penis next to it for counterbalance. I was sure I was in a death row cell.

Cockroaches and a baby mouse were having a field day running around, celebrating the arrival of a new guest, and a new source for their survival. I didn't kill them, I couldn't; they were my live companions. I wondered if I could train them! Could I train them to race? That would be a lot of fun to watch! I suppose I could, but that needs a lot of time, I won't be here for long to train them! May be I should kill them, they are dirty! But, kill them for what? What have they done to me? Here you are asking for justice for yourself, and denying the roaches their right to live? What kind of logic is that? Are you a killer? Just because you can kill them, is that a reason to kill them? God may have created them for a reason, which we don't know! I am sure they don't want to die; I don't either. Yes, of course there is God! I don't care what Aunt Victoria said, I am sure there is God, yes, there is! God! Will you help me? I know I haven't gone to church to praise you for a long time, but you see that is not my fault. I broke up with the church because Der Khoren, the priest, couldn't come up with an answer to my questions, and said some stupid things about my brain liquefying and all that if I practiced what puberty had brought to me. You know what I mean!

All right, if there is God, why am I in this place? Why doesn't he come to my rescue? He didn't rescue a million and a half Armenians during the Genocide either! What kind of a God is he, or she? How about my son and wife? I guess they should be OK; my family will take care of them!

May be he is a good guy, this God, and no, definitely it is not a she! He must be an artist, remember how beautiful the mountains and the waterfalls of Kurdistan were? Only God could create something like that! Oh, if I only were there right now. The delicious hot bread and the warm, fresh, thick yogurt we had in that hamlet! I should have been born to that kind of a peasant family; life would have been simpler and more fun. Do you remember those young Kurdish girls walking around, bra-less, boobs bobbing like the heads of newborn lambs? Oh, how I wish I were a shepherd boy, tending to my flock, in the mountains of Kurdistan!

But, wait a minute! You are an Armenian, not a Kurd, and those mountains are Kurdish, not Armenian. Well, we have mountains too, mountains of Cilicia, and Mount Ararat! All right, I wish I were a shepherd boy, tending to my flock, in the mountains of Armenia. They must be just as beautiful, if not more. I imagine they are more beautiful because they are mine, yes! Mounts Ararat and Cilicia are mine, even though they are empty of Armenians now. Those bastard Turks, they killed what they killed, then deported over a million of us to the Syrian desert of

Der El-Zore to die, but did we really die? No, we are alive! But are we? Am I? And for how long am I going to stay alive?

Oops, here is another baby mouse.
How do I get out of here? Guaaard! Guaard! Guard!
There is no answer.

All of a sudden, I felt the tightness of the place like a jacket that fit me a decade ago, but did not now. The air smelled of dampness, urine, and feces, even with that there wasn't enough air to breathe easily.

I do not recall much of the rest of the day. I do not recall if they gave me anything to eat either. Who had appetite, anyway? I just wanted to get out of that rat hole!

I was desperate to get word out to my father. He had many contacts, may be he could help me. If only I could get word out to him, but how?

I kept shouting and making noises to have the guards come over. I thought if they did, I'd be able to bribe them, but then I had no money. Then I thought if they went to my father with my news, he would pay them something. Then I concluded that these soldiers were indoctrinated ideologues, not your ordinary, uneducated soldiers who would accept bribes. They were a part of the Communist organization implementing a revolutionary plan.

The clanking noise of the metal door woke me up from a snooze. The cell door was similar to those of Sing Sing, with an angle-iron bar at its base. A sergeant opened my cell and ordered me to take off my shoes. I did. He tied my wrists and bare feet, eagle spread, standing on the angle-iron base bar like an X on a vertical plane. Decades later when I saw Richard Nixon, after his resignation, at the helicopter door, victoriously raising both arms, it reminded me of my position on that cell door; I couldn't help but feel his agony which, unlike mine, was not physical but psychological.

Standing on an angle-iron bar bare foot is terribly painful, it doesn't slice the flesh, but it inflicts tremendous, unbearable pain. To stand on a thin metal bar, bare feet, with wrists tied high up, and the body on a vertical plain, is even more painful, just intolerable. No thoughts crossed my mind. I went crazy; I really lost my nerves. How could I sustain this posture, and for how long? My jailers were leaving. My pleas to free me from that position did not help. I asked for mercy to which one of them replied, "You bastard Ba'thi conspirators, you wanted to derail the people's revolution, you are the enemies of the people, you deserve no mercy!"

In that position, my head could not stay upright, it had to fall back. The handcuffs were cutting my wrists, and my feet were hurting just as much. I noted cockroaches and spiders crawling up the wall. Why can they be in a vertical position and sustain it and I can't? I thought fleetingly.

Aside from the unbearable pain, being restricted like that and in a solitary cell is double imprisonment: that of your body, and that of your spirit and soul.

I really don't know for how long I was kept in that position, but it felt like eternity.

After a while, the sergeant came back. I thought in response to my yelling and pleas; it wasn't! He untied me and ordered me to wear my shoes and then he took me out of the building into blinding sunshine, and walked me across the courtyard to the building, which was above the entrance archway.

I could hardly climb the stairs; my feet were hurting. Regardless, I was somewhat relieved for breathing fresh air, and seeing the light. A heavy wooden double door swung open and I walked into a large hallway, which led to several rooms. I was taken to the left hand side corner room, which overlooked the Christian Science Reading Room. Immediately I recognized the officer in charge.

"Oh, Adnaan, how nice to see you, I haven't seen you in several years. How is Kanaan?" (his brother)" I uttered with some encouragement.

It was Adnaan Azzawi, my teenage-era friend. He was one of the attendees of the Iraq pharmacy noon meetings, one of the Communist elites who had tried to indoctrinate me into Communism. A flicker of hope passed my heart, and I thought he would be able to set me free.

"Huh, I see you're one of them, Henry! I am sorry, Henry, this is your party; I have no say in the matter, I can't help you, and I won't preside over this interrogation. I wash my hands off your case, just for old time's sake."

With these words, Major Adnaan Azzawi, my childhood pal from the Iraq pharmacy, left the salon of the second floor of the Qishla where Communists held "torture parties" to extract confessions from the "Enemies of the Revolution."

With some kind of an unexplainable expression on his face, Adnaan told me, "Friendship is something, ideology is something else," it sounded like a statement from Kremlin's, *How to Interrogate a Comrade* guide books.

Much later, when I had time to sort out things in my mind, I realized that he was in a dilemma: he couldn't have presided over my interrogation, because of childhood memories, and a lot of guilt; also, he could not have set me free, because it was beyond his jurisdiction. So, in his mind, washing his hands off my case solved his dilemma. He could have conducted my interrogation in a civilized manner, but he could not because torture was the order of the day, and his ideology had proscribed it. If he was not genuinely intent on avenging the past, he could have held a mock torture, or a light torture, and satisfied the requirements of interrogation, rather than leaving me in the hands of savages.

My head spun! I remembered his words that, "Communism, one day, will prevail," and "One day the oppressed people will rise to overthrow the bloodsuckers who have crushed their chests with their weights for so long."

I thought that day was today; I thought today was his day, but also mine, in a different way.

"You son of a bitch," I thought, "you proved my point, I was right, I am right; this is the Communism I was telling you about, now you can take it and shove it up your ass."

Soon after Adnaan left and the party began:

"Here are some papers, I want you to write everything you know."

"Everything I know about what? I do not even know why I am here! What is it that I have done, what are the charges?"

"Everything about smuggling guns from Iran, your role and position in the Tashnaq Party, and your role, and the Party's role in collaborating with Shawwaaf."

"I still don't know what you are talking about; you want me to fabricate stories? What guns...what Shawwaaf? I don't even know who he is! I had never even heard of his name until now. And where are the guns that I have smuggled?"

"Take your time and write everything down, or else! Don't forget to write your name and sign it!"

I filled up a sheet of paper with my story from the telegrams until my arrest, signed it, and handed it over to them.

That "confession" got me nowhere. The sergeant was not satisfied with what I had written. He presented me with a typewritten "Confession," which said I had been a collaborator with the dissident forces to overthrow the government, and that I was known to be "antipeople" since my young years, and that I was headed to the Iranian border to facilitate transfer of arms to help the Shawwaaf revolt. He asked me to sign the document. I refused. How could I sign such a false, incriminating document?

"I can't sign this, because it is not true, it is all fabrication," I said. "All right, you are not cooperating with the revolution, you all are alike, you traitors! I'll make you confess, I gave you all the chance, and you are not cooperating."

With that, he signaled the others to wrestle me to the floor and tie my feet together on a bar, for falaqa (flogging the soles with bamboo sticks). The real party now was on its way; two soldiers held my feet up for falaqa, as the third lashed them with full force, whereas two others kicked me indiscriminately on my face, head, and body, anywhere. Torture had started in earnest!

Falaqa, as a form of disciplinary action or punishment is common in the Arabic and Turkish cultures. It was a standard disciplinary punishment for the unruly, unrepentant, students in the nineteenth-century Anatolian, including Armenian, schools. Armenian folkloric literature is full of such stories about Der (priest) Totig and his methods of educating pupils. We used to read these funny stories, and laugh, and laugh. However, this was no laughing matter, this was no funny story; whereas Der Totig's falaqa was one or two gentle lashes, this was endless, struck with full power, thrust, and authority, intent on inflicting both physical and psychological damage.

With each lash, I felt as if my brain would jolt out of place. The kicking soldiers kept pace with the falaqa. They kept on beating me, beating me, and beating me some more. In all that, I had a glance at the bamboo hitting my feet, it had become red, and dripping; I felt the wetness of my blood on my soles. My screams were so loud that Iliya could have heard in the Christian Science Reading Room, across the street.

"Khaatter Allah bess" (for God's sake enough), I was screaming, "I can't take it anymore."

"You bastard traitor, you the enemy of the people, you son of a bitch, you conspire against our sole leader? Working against the people's revolution?" Lashes landed in synchrony with his cursing.

"I don't know what you are talking about, I swear, I have done nothing against our leader, or the revolution, or anybody. You have the wrong man, please stop. . .!

Torture never stopped. At the beginning, I was hurting a lot but, after a while I did not feel the pain, the soles had become numb, shielding the body from pain; with each stroke I felt pressure.Through it all, I was petrified but defiant. That wasn't wise. You must not defy your torturers, because your life is in their hands, but I stupidly did! The more they hit the more foul language I used to insult them, which made them hit harder. I was crying, but after a while, there were no more tears; it had dried out. My mind had jammed. I could think of nothing other than getting out of that situation. I can't say how much time Act One of this tragic comedy lasted, but it seemed like ages.

They must have decided to get to the next step. They stopped the beating, and helped me to a chair, handed me a pen and asked me sign the "Confession."

> "How can I sign a confession, which is not mine?"
> "You have to trust the revolution; you have to trust us. Sign or the party will continue!"
> "How can I sign? How can I sign? This is not my story; I have already given you a true story, the way it happened."
> "All right, we gave you a chance to end this; you refuse to sign it voluntarily; we will make you sign!"

With a signal from the sergeant, the soldiers knew what to do. They hung me from my handcuffs, like a side of beef, from an iron peg driven into a wall, high above the floor. That killed me! My wrists and shoulders felt dislocated!

As if the hanging was not enough, three sergeants stood up on benches and started hitting me as if I was a punching bag. Punches landed anywhere and everywhere above belt. As I turned to avoid a punch, one hit my face from the opposite side. The stomach punches were the worst; with each blow, I felt faint. I remember yelling, "You bastards, you cowards, if you are men, get me down and come at me one by one, you sons of bitches, you brothers of whores. Three men against one, I spit on you, you cowards!"

That was stupid of me. I agitated them even more and made them torture me with vengeance. After a while, they got tired. They must have thought that they had reached a maximum limit, short of killing me, which they obviously did not want; their goal was to unravel secrets of a conspiracy, rather than kill. They kept telling me, "C'mon, we will stop if you agree to sign." My refusal must have made them conclude that they had failed to fracture my will, so they tried another tactic while continuing to punch: They said, "Look, we know you have two sisters. If you don't sign we will get your sisters here and have the soldiers have fun with them, right before your eyes."

I wasn't tolerating the torture as it was, but this one really broke my defenses. I couldn't take it anymore. I didn't want to die in vain. I thought I had proved my resilience and manhood, "All right, I'll sign, get me down!" I said. They did! When I grabbed the pen, it fell off my hand; my fingers were numb. They thought I was deceiving them, so they beat me some more.

I read the confession again and rationalized that this would not stand in a court of law because, there wasn't a shred of evidence that I was involved with the rebellion in Mosul, there wasn't a shred of evidence that I was a Nasserite, or Aflaqi, and there wasn't a shred of evidence that I was smuggling guns. The only gun that I had bought was the Parabellum, and they might have thought that I was engaged in arming an army, hence the suspicion and the accusation. I also thought that if they wanted to kill me, they'd kill me anyway, with or without evidence or justification. So, I rationalized and signed their drafted, typed, false document.

Much later I realized that, even if there was no evidence against an accused, these sadistic "Parties" were designed to revenge from those whom they considered the enemies of the Revolution; the pillars of the old regime, the wealthy, the surrogates of the West, or just plain anti-Communists.

I had heard or read about such atrocities practiced in Soviet Armenia, Hungary, Czechoslovakia, Bulgaria, and Siberia, to name a few, and through the writings of such ex-Communists as Arthur Koestler, but now I was feeling it on my skin.

My party had ended. Two soldiers, supporting my armpits, carried me to my cell. I don't think I felt pain, but my entire body was throbbing with rapid heartbeat. Every part of my body was swollen red. Blood was oozing from my mouth, I was delirious and couldn't think. There were fleeting images flashing before my eyes, none of which registered. My feet were beaten red, there was blood under the toenails, my lips were swollen, and I could feel there was a bleeding tear inside my cheek as I was spitting blood. Sitting or lying down was almost an impossibility.

I felt hatred toward my torturers. I hated especially that son of a bitch Adnaan; yet I felt time, and this torture, had vindicated me. I had told him, a decade ago, in the Iraq Pharmacy noon gatherings, about the cruelty of Communism and the Soviet regime. I had told him about that murderer Stalin, but he had labeled what I had said as Western propaganda. What can the son of a bitch say now? How can he justify what they did to me now? Where is the humanitarian doctrine of his? Communism, my ass, they are all cruel murderers!

In the middle of all this I remembered my father. I felt indebted to him for preparing me for this kind of a beating. He used to use the stick for minor offenses that I may have committed, which was the Ottoman way of disciplining your child.

On one occasion he had left three striped black and blue marks on my left arm, and when things had cooled off, I had told him, "Dad, you have promoted me to sergeant." We both had laughed and made up.

I understood my father's psychology and modus operandi. He was orphaned at a young age, and then he hit the trail of the Armenian deportees after the 1915 Genocide, through the desert, to Aleppo, and then to Mosul to join his brother, Uncle Krikor.

With my father it was crime and punishment. I was used to that, but what I was going through now was punishment without a crime. That wasn't fair! I could forgive my father, but never that son of a bitch, Adnaan. He could have saved me by just being objective and without betraying his dedication to Communism, but he didn't! He really had a vendetta against me, and this was a perfect occasion to teach me a lesson, which I had refused to learn in our conversations and debates in the Iraq Pharmacy, a decade earlier.

Why did he have to "wash" his hands? Did he really wash his hands out of friendly gesture, or because of guilt? That brother of a whore, that Communist bastard! You mother fucker you. . .you son of a bitch you! Wash his hands my ass. . .he wants to wash his hands because it is stained with blood, that's why he wants to wash his hands! What would he have done if he didn't know me so well? Is this the behavior of a human being? What human being? Fuck humanity, man, fuck humanity! I spit on humanity, if this is what It is. I hate you world, I hate you!

They used to tell me there is no justice in this world. Aunt Victoria too used to tell me that, but I was somewhat skeptical. Well is there? Is there justice in the world?

There is no God either! Aunt Victoria was right there too! Had she not concluded, after reading Raffi and other stories of the Armenian Genocide that if there was God, then why did He permit such atrocities to befall God-loving Christian people? No, there is no God, either, and humanity sucks. But how about Akram? Wasn't his behavior that of a noble human being? Didn't he restore your faith in humanity?

I kept fuming and deliberating for sometime then I realized that this time they did not tie me from the door. I thought, no, they don't want to kill me that's for sure, otherwise they would have done it upstairs. They want me broken, but alive.

I lay down on my bed, thanking God for keeping me alive, and sparing my bones. But my body hurt, my face hurt, my lips and cheek were torn and leaking blood, my front tooth was loose, and my toenails were full of blood, ready to fall off, which they eventually did.

These are manageable, I thought. I'll live. All of a sudden, I felt hungry. I wished I hadn't returned the "Suli Kufta" that my "adopted" Mora (aunt) Dzovig, had sent for lunch that day. Because I had returned the food untouched, Dzovig Mora had concluded that I must be in a serious trouble, "Otherwise he would not have returned his most favorite dish, untouched."

But how did Dzovig Mora know I was here? How did my folks find me? God has mysterious ways of doing things. Yes, of course, there is God!

I suspected that Akram could be the one who told my father where I was. I was happy about that, hoping that he would get me out of this place, soon.

I must have fallen asleep. When I woke up, the room was still a cage; the place still smelled of urine and excrement, including mine. Gone were the scents of Kurdistan's flowers; gone were the vistas of Kurdistan. The events of the previous few days paraded in front of my eyes. In the afternoon the door opened:

Put your shoes on, we are going!
Going where?
To Baghdad! We have to take you to the train station.

I was shocked, didn't know what to think. What started in Qalah Dize rolled over to Suleymania, then Kirkuk, now we were going to Baghdad.

Is that good, or bad?
How can it be good?

If it weren't serious, why would they send me to Baghdad? Questions, which I kept asking myself, and could not find an answer to them.

I was put in a jeep escorted by Military Police, handcuffed, and stripped of the brass stars that indicated my rank.

The car got out of the archway and made a right turn on Awqaf Street. We passed the Military Hospital on the left, El-Alamaine cinema on the right, the Iraq Pharmacy to the left, and the house where I grew up, on the right. We had moved out of that house, earlier, and now only my father's dental clinic was there.

I peeked through the canvas cover to look, but couldn't. When we made a left turn, I knew we were passing Ahmed Aghas' chaikhana, and were on the Station Road. The car was speeding, so was my heart, as we passed in front of my father's newest house.

I yelled, the loudest I could, "Daaad! They are taking me! Daaaaaad, please do something, they are taking me Dad, please do something." No one could hear my voice, not even my guards who were sitting across from me, indifferently. My pleas echoed in my head, same as the echoes of the bullet I had fired for the first time, in the mountains of Kurdistan. This time however, the echoes did not give me a sense of security. Daaaad!

I had a flashback to my childhood, to that moment when I was being kidnapped in a sack, and was rescued by Saleh, the Jewish shoeshine boy. "Saaaleh, they are taking me away, Saaaleh they are taking me away." He had heard my voice and rescued me. This time no one was hearing my pleas and there was no Saleh to come to my rescue.

The train station was abuzz with soldiers and civilians. I had never seen that station that crowded. I knew the station very well, since we used to pass through it to get to our village home in Tiseen. I knew many villagers, but I couldn't spot one to send word to my father that they are taking me to Baghdad.

We passed the first-and second-class cars, and searched for seats in the third-class. Finally, we found empty seats. There were rows and rows of double benches crowded with people, cramping the small car. Smoke and sweat-odor filled the stationed train. Sweat smelled even more peculiar when mixed with the smell of acid Phenique, the toilet and hospital disinfectant, which was sprayed generously in the car as a health measure.

The MPs helped me climb into the car, which was loaded with ordinary travelers, some sitting quietly, and some arguing a point aloud. However, our entry to the car changed all that. As soon as they saw a handcuffed, unshaven, military man, they became agitated. They waged an animated demonstration chanting, "Maku Za'im illa Kareem [Qasim] guwaaweed Ba'thiya" (there is no leader but Qasim, you bastard Ba'this). In a flash, the situation became belligerent and aggressive. Some twenty people were on their feet, waving their fists, spitting at me calling for lynching this, "Shawwaaf collaborator." They could have killed me, the "Enemy of the Revolution, the traitor, the Ba'thi, the Aflaqi, the reactionary," right there and then.

Somebody stood up and recited a spirited revolutionary poem, which agitated the crowd even more; they applauded enthusiastically and made threatening gestures, shaking their fists at me. They were only four or five feet away from me when one of my guards stood between us, pulled his revolver, and threatened to shoot "Anybody who dared to harm the prisoner."

I was alarmed, but not scared, knowing full well that my guards would protect me with their lives, not because they were such good people, concerned with preservation of a human life, but because it was their responsibility to deliver a top traitor like me to the highest authorities in Baghdad, alive.

One older man stood up and said, "Let us leave him alone, let us get him alive to the highest authority; they will extract valuable information from him, which will help the Republic get rid of the last vestiges of the condemned old regime, the British agents, and the agents of traitor Nasser, and his puppets the Ba'this." The crowd applauded and then gradually simmered down. My guard nodded, in approval, and put his gun back into its holster.

Soon the noise level dropped, and the chugging of the train took over, singing a lullaby to my tired soul. I was made to climb up and stretch on the luggage rack, with my hands cuffed to the post. I used somebody's shoes and a small luggage as a pillow; there was no blanket. I slept through the entire overnight journey to Baghdad.

I woke up the next morning with the sound of the locomotive bellowing gentle steam, after having belched a big one, before coming to a full stop. We were in Bab El-Sharji station of Baghdad. It was busier than I had known it to be. Trucks, soldiers, and passengers, getting on and off the trains, formed a panorama akin to that of an opera stage. Luckily, I was an extra, an unnoticed figure!

I had arrived at that station many times before. It consisted of a brick building with some high arched gates painted half white and half forest green in some parts, and half white and deck gray in some others. It was a colonial building constructed, at the conclusion of WWI, by the British Expeditionary Forces.

There was an office for the stationmaster and a control room with telegraph equipment abutting the police security room. Just outside the building were some vendors selling "laffa" (boiled eggs, tomatoes, pickled mangos, rolled in flat bread), and tea.

The station had seen many British Army personnel's arrivals and departures; officers in khaki Bermuda shorts, carrying mahogany sticks under their arms, embarking and disembarking leisurely. I could visualize an "Old Chap" biting on his pipe, stopping to exchange a few words with another, occasionally lifting one wing of a perfectly trimmed, balanced moustache, to reveal a faint insincere smile, or lifting one eyebrow to express suspicion.

One could imagine seeing a miserable coolie hurriedly hauling officer's trunks to catch up with the master. There is the stationmaster trying to solve a last-minute hitch.

One could see village women from the nearby marshes, carrying on their heads in balance, six or seven pots of buffalo yogurt, stacked one on top of the other. There were the police carrying clubs ready for any disturbing eventuality.

Outside were the taxis manned by specially selected drivers who would report to the Secret Police. They would wait patiently in designated areas to fetch the trunks and load them in their cars for a short trip to Hotel Samiramis, or Sindbad.

One could spot dozens of Arabs, and Indians, in the service of His Majesty's government "Yes, sahib-no-sahib"-ing the officers, providing assistance to facilitate flow of the troops. After all the activities, the coolies would sweep the walkways clean, and sprinkle it with acid Phenique.

I had arrived at that station only seven years previously, on a first-class cabin, to go to the Medical School. At the time, I was full of hope, enthusiasm, and energy; the future was ahead of me! But, all that was in the past. This time I had arrived traveling third-class, with handcuffs. The entire seven years of life in Baghdad flashed before my eyes, as if a moment. Here is where I met Ann and married her. Here is where my son Vatche was born, only a year ago. Here is where I consolidated my Armenian identity, and learned more about my mother tongue, literature, history, and national aspirations.

Here is where I had the good fortune of knowing and intimately associating with the troika: Dr. Papken Papazian, the great patriot and intellectual, Levon (Carmen) Stepanian, the poet and the intellectual, Haigaz Mouradian, the Philosopher, and Aram Duzian, the founder of our pride and joy, the *Koyamard Weekly*. Here is where these people molded my public character; here is where I blossomed and opened up to the world.

"C'mon, lets go!" commanded my guard awakening me from my trance. Right by the train an army truck was waiting for us. I couldn't climb on my own;

my shoes didn't fit, I couldn't step on my soles, I could hardly stand up straight because of pain in my back and the rest of the body. By now my black and blue marks had not yet turned into yellows and greens, my face was swollen, a tooth was loose, and my cheek ripped. Despite all that, I was tranquil; numb is more like it!

Despite the pathetic physical condition I was in, I rationalized that I was OK; I had come out of this without injury to my brain and with my vision intact, I could compromise with the rest!

They loaded me in the back of the truck, like a sack of potatoes, and we were on our way to Mu'askar Al-Rasheed (Rasheed Military Base), on the outskirts of Baghdad.

19

Room # 11

I was now back where I had started. This was the camp where I got my military training: how to walk with authority, how to salute and address a senior officer, how to receive a subordinate, etc. Except, this time it was a totally different situation; we were in the barracks as detainees fenced in with barbed wires. There were soldiers everywhere armed with stenguns, pacing the grounds, guarding us. There wasn't much activity, and the noise level was down—way down as if it was a cemetery. In fact, it was a cemetery for the dead souls of the detainees.

They took me to a barrack, opened the door to Room # 11 and pushed me in. Inside, men were sitting on mattresses, on the floor, frightened, looking at me with sallow eyes.

They must have anticipated something worse, but looked relieved when they realized that the door opened for delivery, not pickup. "Here," the soldier yelled, pushing me in, "Here is another traitor, you bastards!"

When the door closed behind me, I found myself in the company of thirteen men squeezed into a 16 × 20 room. At first, there was silence, but when the guard left, the room broke into whispers. They showed me a place to sit, on the mattresses. They immediately gave me a cigarette, and tried to make me as comfortable as possible. I lit up one, and looked around. They were young and middle-aged men, most of whom spoke in a Moslawi-Arabic dialect. At the far corner, there was an old man, with a wrinkled angry face, whom I didn't recognize at first. "Is that you Henry?" he asked. I looked at him in disbelief, and realized that he was my Uncle Krikor. He looked tired, humiliated, and demoralized.

I dragged myself to his corner. We hugged and kissed. I felt secure and protected in his presence, though both of us were vulnerable and in deep trouble. He was sad and very angry. "Why giawwad oghli giawwad (oh, pimps, sons of pimps), look what they have done to you. Those Communist giawwaads! They are ecstatic that they, finally, have gotten hold of Astarjians. Their dreams have finally come true; do you think they would let us skip their hold? For years they tried to get their hands on us, they couldn't, and now we are in their paws, it is their perfect chance to finish us."

He sighed, and then continued, "We knew about them from our immediate past history, from our experiences in Armenia. The stories were not exaggerations! Now we feel it on our skin. It is like 1921 all over again, except this is not the first Republic of Armenia, but the first Republic of Iraq." "Let me tell you" he said with obvious pride, as if triumphant, "What you have on your face, and our very presence here, is a badge of honor. Everybody is going to die sometime, there is no escape from it, but our death would be different, we are going to die for our beliefs; it is going to be an honorable death."

His reflections and anger continued, "What do these Arabs know about us? Nothing! These Arabs know nothing about us, it is our bastard Armenian Judases who put us in this situation, otherwise how would these people know about our stance against Communism? Arabs are a noble people, I have written volumes about them! It is our bastards, our bastards!"

"Us, Armenians, have no claims on an inch of Arab land, to the contrary, we have been eternally grateful to them for their noble stance in taking our Genocide survivors and refugees into their midst and helping them live in peace and prosperity; they fed us, they housed us, they protected us, and they made us citizens of their countries. What else do we want? Why should we even think of betraying them? But the Communists are bastards; they are Arabs and Armenians only in name. They are Internationalists; they bulldoze anybody who stands in their way. Their ideology is hostile and intolerant, and this incarceration is a proof of that; they are falsely accusing us of participation in a revolt which we know nothing about, and that is an excuse to kill us, legitimately."

When I finally settled down, our roommates welcomed me, and doubly so for being Doctor Astarjian's nephew.

Most of them being from Mosul, knew my uncle, or something about him. He had practiced medicine in that city for decades, and had written books and articles about Armenian and Arab literature, and because of a famous and unique Japanese-style mansion (Qassir Astarjian), which he had built in the late 1930s, on the site of ancient capital of the Assyrian Empire, Nineveh, just outside Mosul.

The room we were in had a wide window overlooking the courtyard. A bare bulb hung from the ceiling, like a noose, high and beyond reach, and the walls were bare. There was no switch inside. This must have been a storage room, or something like it.

Mattresses were spread lengthwise, around three walls, the fourth wall was bare, left for entry and piling up a mound of thirteen pairs of shoes. There was no space for me on the mattresses; the only available space was the bare floor in front of the bare wall, at the entrance. The floor was my mattress, and the pile of shoes and army boots my pillow. Someone gave me a dirty bedsheet, which I folded and spread on the floor; that was my mattress! I didn't need a cover; our body heat, the cigarette smoke, and abundance of adrenalin was enough to keep me warm.

A man in his mid-thirties came and sat next to me, and said his name was Jameel Sabri Al-Bayaati, Baghdad's Chief of Security Police, before his arrest. He must have been a participant in the July 14 Revolution, or at least a strong supporter, otherwise they would not have entrusted him with that kind of sensitive job. Now he was accused of being a Shawwaaf supporter, or at least an opponent of Qasim, which is why they had detained him. But then he was not tortured yet, so he was not fractured. In fact, aside from me, nobody else in that room was tortured, but many were already fractured.

Jameel gave me all the sympathy, and tried to console me. "Don't regret what we have done, what we have done is right for the country, the country was deteriorating under Qasim!" he said. I don't know why he said "we" including me with the rest? It, probably, was to establish camaraderie, but I didn't feel as a part of "we." I had nothing to do with what had happened. I was a victim of circumstances.

He talked about Shawwaaf's bravery, and the heroism of Mosul. He told me about the three pilots who had unsuccessfully bombarded Qasim's den, the Ministry of Defense. "They were here, in this room," he said. "They were taken out of here, yesterday, and summarily shot to death without trial." I thought these pilots were not heroes because, they couldn't drop their bombs accurately, and they were ineffective. For God's sake, they couldn't even bomb the undefended radio station!

Jameel, having established the preliminaries, introduced our roommates before hearing my story:

General Abdul-Azeez Al Uqayli, a famous, highly respected soldier, commander of the Third Army Division.
Colonel Azeez Ahmed Shihaab, one of the original Free Officers and one of Shawwaaf's right-hand men, a co-conspirator.
Colonel Abdul Ghani Al-Raawi, one of the original Free Officers and a staunch nationalist.
The rest were a bunch of fighter pilots who had bombed Qasim's Defense Ministry, conspirators with Shawwaaf in his failed coup.

These were the Army's luminaries. These are the revolutionaries, who had overthrown the Hashimite Kingdom, and changed the political landscape of the Middle East. Once in command, now they were my prison mates, how funny I thought! What had I done to deserve such an honor? I hated what they stood for. I hated Nasser for his stance against the West. I also hated Ike for his stance in the War of Suez in 1956, which stopped Britain, France, and Israel from toppling Nasser. I hated to see the end of the Hashimite Kingdom. I was laughing at this tragic comedy, which victimized me. My being here had absolutely nothing to do with the events; I was caught in the eye of a hurricane, accidentally.

My roommates eagerly listened to my story with amazement, but not surprise. They were not surprised at all because, "The Communists have taken over the country and this is their opportunity to finish all their enemies, the nonprogressive elements, and you are one of us," they said. That put me in an unwanted position of camaraderie and parity with the people who had plotted and revolted against Qasim, and were facing the firing squad. I was not one of them, and didn't want to be one of them, but I had no say in the matter.

Soon, I learned that the day before my arrival, they had shot eleven Shawwaaf-pilots, three of them from our room. I also learned that Abdul Salaam Arif, the Vice President of the country and the actual organizer of the Revolution, was held in our compound. I discovered that Abdul Rahman Al-Bazzaaz, the professor of Law (later, one of the founders of OPEC [Organization of Petroleum Exporting Countries], and Prime Minister of Iraq) was in Room # 10, next to us. In the same room was Abdul-Razzaq Arif, one of the Free Officers who had fought in Palestine, as a pilot (later held very important ministerial posts, and then became Prime Minister).

I felt really, overwhelmed. To be in the company of such people was awesome! I thought, no, I didn't deserve, or want this honor. Here I am, an ordinary military doctor, totally innocent, accused of smuggling arms for a revolution that I never knew about, or believed in, which was led by a man whom I had never known, never even heard his name before, and whose god Nasser I despised. I was an Armenian Nationalist, brought up in the traditional British colonial style, whose hero was Winston Churchill. What was I doing here? I thought this whole thing was a joke!

I was horrified: first, for being imprisoned in such a dangerous place, and second, for being lumped together with important and famous people who were being executed by the dozen, every day.

All these events generated anger, resentment, defiance, and sarcasm in me. I had become a cynic! I considered this as a tragic comedy, like life itself, displayed on a stage so big that it was beyond my imagination, comprehension, or control.

I thought Communism is evil and the Communists are a bunch of bastards, I refused to succumb to them, and yes, my Uncle was right I should be prepared to die for my principles! Some degree of "la-belle-indifference" fell upon me, which shielded me from the serious realities of the day.

Each of us, the detainees, had come from a different background, had a different outlook on life, had different spheres of imagination, and roamed in different galaxies. We had but one element in common: fear of torture and fear of being killed brutally—in one word "fear."

This feeling was multiplied every time the iron door opened at night or past midnight. We knew that "parties" were held at night. So, when the door opened during the day we knew it was to deliver food, or to let us out for a ten-minute exercise, or to go to the unbelievably overflowing and crowded toilets; there were two in our section, for a hundred-plus people. There were no showers.

They opened the door yelling profanities at us, hurling insults, and beating us indiscriminately. They beat us at random with a cane, and since I was right there in front of the door, I got the brunt of the beating.

It was two in the morning, one day, when the door opened. We all sat up terrified, knowing that one of us would be the honored guest at the party. Each of us, I am sure, hoped that it was somebody else's turn, not his. They called the name of one of the pilots and took him away. The rest of us felt sorry for him, but were relieved that it wasn't us. When he came back at 5 AM, four soldiers were carrying him on a blanket. They tossed him onto the floor, as if a he was dead dog; we thought he was dead. He couldn't as much as make a single sound. His body and soles were swollen; his eyes had turned into slits. Ours, however, were wide open; we had stayed awake all this time holding vigil and fearing for our safety; nobody could sleep. In a sense, ours was a torture too, without a party!

I sympathized and empathized with the victim, I felt his pain, felt sorry for him, and subconsciously also felt sorry for myself, because I had experienced the same kind of a party, myself.

When the victim could finally talk, he described the torture, scaring the hell out of those of us who had not gone through it yet; I had; I knew, and I understood. I was hoping that I had already paid my dues, and I wouldn't have to pay it again. Luckily I never did, not in this camp, perhaps because I was not important enough to deserve priority consideration.

But, those who attended the "party" in their honor, told us that they were hung upside down from a hook used for the ceiling fan, high enough to have the head touch the floor. After flogging him to bleeding, they would pull on the rope until his feet touched the ceiling, then let go to make him land on his head.

We could hear the torture across the courtyard. With every strike and screaming, we turned paler and paler, as if blood, indeed life, was being drained from us. We all wondered about our turn, and trembled like a Parkinsonian.

I kept begging: Oh, Lord spare me, I've had my share, I am barely beginning to heal. Please God don't let me go through it again!

We heard stories about Chinese torture being employed on a "traitor"; it involved dripping water on a victim's head, nonstop, for twenty-four hours, then fracturing his arms and legs, all four of them. Reportedly, a London-educated surgeon (Fellow of the Royal College of Surgeons), visited this man, for show, and walked away without treating him.

This doctor was a known Communist. Whether he was a Fellow of a prestigious college like the Royal College, an ordinary doctor, or a peasant, it made no difference; a Communist is a Communist, cruel and inhuman!

All these events had negative effects on all of us; especially my roommates were totally demoralized. They would often cry when beaten at random not because of pain, but in anticipation of what was yet to come. They knew that their future was: most probably, the firing squad. For them that could have been honorable, but to be humiliated like this was degrading? They couldn't take it!

I was astounded! How would Generals and high-ranking leaders of a nation allow themselves to cry? What kind of revolutionaries were these, what kind of men? It would be alright for an ordinary man to cry, but leaders of armies to shed tears? They are supposed to be above such emotional reactions!

There were hours during the day that would pass without an event. We knew that "Parties" started after midnight, so we used the quiet times to catch up with sleep, or reminisce; both provided escape.

One high-ranking roommate would say:

"Oh, if I get out of here I wouldn't stay in this God-damned country for one minute. These God-damned people don't deserve to live like human beings, they don't deserve our sacrifice. Look at the shit that's going on. Nouri Sa'id was right when he said, 'Iraq is a cesspool, and I am its cover, if you remove me the stink will overwhelm the world.' He was damn right, look what is happening now. But again, we killed him; we executed the Revolution."

"Do you remember when we were at Sandhurst?"

"If I could only be in Soho, do you remember the blonds? My God were they beautiful babes!"

"I'll definitely settle there and have my pension sent over; that will provide me with a decent living in London; but London is expensive, may be just outside London; at least the kids will get decent education."

"Oh, how I miss my wife," one of them said, with tears running down his cheeks.

They all wished to have been in a cafe in Soho, sipping espresso, chatting with friends, while watching the passers by, especially fashionable girls.

"Who the hell gives a damn about this rotten country, let alone risking his life for it?"

This statement, uttered by some, and shared by many, compelled me to lose respect for these men, the possible future leaders of Iraq, if they got out of this trap, alive.

As I evaluated the fabric of these leaders, an Arabic proverb kept on replaying in my mind, it says:

"If your leader was the crow, it will inevitably lead you to the garbage dump."

This, already, was the dumps and if these people came to power, they would continue managing the same dump, therefore, I concluded that I didn't want to live in a dump, I wanted out. Besides these so-called "Leaders" talked so much about leaving the country that it started making a dent in my head too: I thought, if by any chance, I got out of this place, I too would pack up and go to the safe shores of the West. After all, I thought, Kirkuk is my birthplace all right, but Iraq, in reality, is not my fatherland.

Yes, I am a loyal citizen of this country, but Iraq is not my true homeland, my true homeland is Western Armenia. That is where my parents came from, that is where my roots were until the Genocide, and that is where I belong, not in some

Arab land! However, living in my fatherland was impossible, at that time; Turks had deported the majority of the Armenian population, including my parents, and forced some to convert to Islam, and I could not live there!

In this, my situation was similar to that of Jews who had lived in their Diaspora for centuries, had been loyal citizens, but never lost the sight of Jerusalem or the hope of return.

Such inner conflicts, and feelings of double loyalty, created instability in my psyche, and I did not like it. However, it was ridiculous to have such thoughts when your very existence, for the next minute, is very much, in doubt.

I could not believe what I was hearing in that room, I was astounded. These assumed "Nationalist" and patriotic leaders, were denouncing their country. They were dreaming about Britain, the very Britain that they so vehemently condemned, yet so dearly loved. They wanted to live in a kingdom and enjoy a democratic life, the very system, which they just rejected.

In all this, my uncle showed remarkable resilience. His torture was psychological. He could not contain his anger over the fact that the Communists finally got him, and now he was their prisoner. His ego was extremely hurt.

I had arrived in the barracks just in time for a meal. I was hungry. There was nothing to eat, but soon the door opened, and a hot meal of "Bamia ou Tmmen" (okra and rice) was dished out. It came from Tajraan, a favorite and popular restaurant in Bab El-Sharji. I hadn't had anything to eat for a long time. This was heaven.

The Holy Qur'an was the only reading material allowed in the prison. I had a chance to read it, even though, by tradition, it is forbidden to those who are not circumcised, to touch the book ("La yemissuhu illal muttahaaroun"); they made an exception, and allowed me to read the Book. I thought this was good education, and a continuation of what I had learned in high school. The teacher would allow me to stay, hoping that I would convert and he could secure entrance to paradise for his efforts. I thought it made no difference; it is God's word, whether delivered through Islam or Christianity.

The prison authorities allowed the detainees, mostly Muslims, to conduct a collective prayer that day. They did not permit it again! I don't know whether it was to join the crowd in camaraderie, or to bribe God, or to have solace, I took quick recourse in praying the Muslim way, and joined the crowd. I found myself praying behind the leader, who in this case was none other than Abdul Rahman Al-Bazzaz, a highly respected professor of law, and one of the founders of OPEC. He was held in Room # 10, therefore I had no chance to know him the way I knew my roommates.

Within a few days, I became acclimatized. There were no more "Parties" given in my honor. My wounds were healing; the black and blue marks were now turning greenish yellow, but my toenails were loose enough to be pulled out, or fall off by themselves.

At dusk, one evening, we heard the rumbling and squeak of wheels. Two tanks had taken position in the yard, with guns pointed at our rooms. The guards rushed to close the doors of our rooms. We all panicked, worried that the tanks may run us over, or else open fire pulverizing us. "My God, they are going to kill us, en masse!" someone yelled.

Everybody was mumbling some sort of a last prayer; I recited the only one I knew, the Lords Prayer. I couldn't think of anything, my mind was jammed. My uncle was also frozen and had that worried look on his face, but I doubt that he said any prayers, at least not aloud; he was an agnostic, and this situation was not about to make him surrender to God.

Minutes passed like hours, each weighing a ton. I thought this is it, a brutal death! But, no. Five minutes passed, leading to a half-hour, then an hour, and still we were alive. All of a sudden, the tanks rumbled again, this time to pull back. We breathed a sigh of relief. A deadly silence fell upon us. We looked at each other in relief, but none of us uttered a word; we were numb.

The following morning our suspicions were confirmed; soldiers told us that the Communists had brought the tanks in without the government's knowledge or approval; their intent had been to fire upon the barracks and finish everyone, but at the last minute the "Sole Leader" had gotten the whiff of the plot, and ordered immediate cessation of that "Illegal operation."

At first, I had an alternative explanation to the event: I thought the "Tank Plot" was a part of a psychological war against us. However, later I accepted the original explanation, which made sense: There had been a rupture in Qasim-Communist Party relationship. The Communists staged the "Tank Plot" to:

(a) Get rid of their imprisoned enemies, en mass, and
(b) Challenge Qasim's authority, and demand decision-making partnership.

Six weeks had lapsed since my incarceration, yet I, like the others, had no visitors. I was sure that my family didn't know where I was. One day the door opened and a soldier called my name and ordered me to accompany him to the front building. "You have visitors," he said. It was Ann with our infant son, Vatche, in her lap. I was surprised and happy to see them; also the visit restored my identity.

Ann tried to look brave and encouraging, but I could tell she was terribly worried, and looked scared. She didn't say much, she couldn't. She could only say that they had turned the world upside down to locate me, but she didn't say how. Akram, my loyal orderly, may have given her a lead about my locations. "You have lost weight!" said Ann.

"It's all right, it will be light on the ropes!"
"Don't say stupid things like that. This will be over soon, I know it will; you'll come home, and I'll cook for you again, and you will be all right."
"So, how are you?"
"I am fine, how are you?"
"I am fine."
"How is Vatche?"

"He is fine; he eats like a horse, and sleeps through the night. He misses his daddy, ha, Vatche?"
"Do you want to hold him? Here!"

I felt so strange holding my son. I kissed him and gave him back to Ann. Maybe I didn't want to feel the sweetness of fatherhood, only to lose it to the cruelty of reality, in minutes. I had already been demoralized, and resigned from life; that kind of rekindled love would have exacerbated the agony of losing it again, also it would have pulled me out of reality, and make me cling, unrealistically, to life. I couldn't take additional torture.

"So, how are you?" asked Ann again searching for a topic for conversation.
"I am fine, how are you?"
"Oh, this is my friend, Miss Tikriti!"
"How do you do!"

She was the sister of Hardaan Abdul-Ghafour Al-Tikriti, Commander of the Air Force, a participant in the July 14 Revolution, and a Shawwaaf co-conspirator. [Years later Saddam agents liquidated him in Kuwait]. Hardaan joined us briefly.

He was a man with an imposing figure, dark complexion, and thick lips. His voice and demeanor were gentle, concealing deep-seated anger. I thought, despite having been in high places, he was a transparent person who had not lost his tribal simplicity and mannerisms.

The visit felt like a moment, but long enough to have ones entire life pass in front of his eyes. I tried not to be emotional, but such meetings, under the circumstances tend to destabilize ones psyche.

"Death is easier if one doesn't look back," a roommate told me philosophically.

Hardaan and I headed back. On our way, we saw an imposing figure, standing in front of an open window overlooking the yard. He was returning the military salutes of the detained officers who were out on their ten-minute walk.

As we came close, I recognized the man, General Nadhim Al Tabaqchali, under whose overall command I had served in the Second Army Division, in Kirkuk. He was not allowed to leave his room for fresh air and exercise, like the rest of us. Hardaan told me that in order to insult him, humiliate him, and demoralize him, he was made to sweep the floor, wash the dishes, and handle trash.

I too gave him a military salute, with feelings of solidarity and prison camaraderie. He returned my salute with gesture and words. He had recognized me, even though we had met only once before.

Some nine months back, I had arranged for a Mass in our church in Kirkuk to celebrate "The dawn of a new era," as it was called, the July 14 Revolution. I had invited Tabaqchali, one of the architects of the revolution and one of the Presidential Troika, to attend. When he entered the hall, the place burst into applause. His entrance, surrounded by his entourage, was graceful. He was a handsome man in his late forties, I would guess. He had an imposing figure, sporting a neatly trimmed mustache, which delineated his upper lip. His wide forehead led to a shiny crown. He had thoughtful eyes, which reflected his inner feelings. His demeanor was that of an Arab aristocrat, exuding gentleness and kindness. One immediately felt that he was in the presence of a great person, which he was. One wondered: how could such a man get angry, let alone become a revolutionary leader, and spill blood? But he was!

In that gathering, after my welcoming remarks, he had delivered a speech, delineating the aims of the newly formed Republic. His speech was received with polite applause, most of it disingenuous. Armenians, being the post-Genocidal generation, did not like more radical changes, which this was, in their lives. We collectively were content with the Royal regime, which had hosted the survivors of the Genocide, and provided them with opportunities for a decent life. Now this revolution had disturbed the status quo, leading to an uncertain future; we did not like it! But what difference does that make; we had to show our support to the Republic.

Tabaqchali was articulate, soft spoken, and radiant, he was genuinely happy to be with us, and told us, "You are the children of this Revolution," but nobody really felt that; our hearts and minds were with the British, and the Royal regime.

Later I talked to him in private. I had many thoughts to convey to him, but I chose to talk to him about hijacked revolutions. That subject was of paramount importance to me since I could see what the Communists were up to. I knew how the Communists operated; my experiences at the Iraq Pharmacy had schooled me well!

I told him about Armenia's experience with the Communists in 1920–1921, when they axed some 1,500 nationalist prisoners to death. I cautioned him from the evils of Communism; I told him about this sinister doctrine, and the brutality with which they had dealt with the people of Armenia. I reminded him of 1956 events of Hungary. I told him about how untrustworthy these people are, and how hard they were at work to divert and hijack his Revolution.

He listened attentively then said, "Dktore, everybody tells me that they are scared of the Communists; who are the Communists? What powers do they have in this country? How many of them are there? What is their significance? If we come up with agrarian reform laws, if we dismantle the tribal system, if we apportion land to the peasant, if we provide him with a tractor and seeds, who would want to become a Communist? These are poor, Muslim, religious people, nobody is going to trade the gains he has made because of this Revolution, to become a Communist! They have nothing to offer!"

He accepted my polite, but firm, disagreement gracefully then, expressed gratitude to the community for supporting the Revolution. I told him, "Seyyidi (Sir), I cautioned you, I have done my duty."

All that had happened only about nine months previously. Now he was standing at the window, composed, as if still in power, but he had no spark in his eyes.

He returned my salute, and almost immediately turned to my companions and said:

> "Ya Jamaa'a (folks), I know the dktore, I met him in his church. He gave me some important advice; he cautioned me about the Communists, but I didn't listen to him. I am terribly sorry for that! Look where we are now! Had I listened to him, none of us would have been here today. From now on, if we live, I want you to listen to him and to the Armenians who have been there before us. They have history behind them, they know the Communists well."
>
> "It is never too late, seyyidi, there is still hope!" I said.
>
> "I don't think so, ya dktore, may be for the next generation, but for us there is no hope, they'll never let us go!"

We couldn't talk any longer; we had to move on. I was amazed and ecstatic that he not only remembered me, but also remembered what I had told him, at the celebration of the "Dawn of a new era," in my church hall. We saluted again and continued our walk.

That was the last time I saw him. On September 20, 1959, he was shot to death in Umm Al-Tbool together with Rif'at al-Haj Sirri, the original founder of the Free Officers in Palestine, and Azeez Ahmed Shihaab, another Free Officer, my roommate. Umm Al Tbool became a shrine, and inspiration, and a rallying symbol for anti-Qasim and anti-Communists forces. Saddam, a decade later, built a mosque on that site.

By their elimination, another chapter in the battle over Baba Gurgur folded in favor of those who opposed joining the United Arab Republic: Qasim, the Kurds, the West, and the Communists.

The walk ended very fast. When I got to the room, my Uncle called me to his corner; he had just awakened from a nap.

> "You wouldn't believe this, Henry," he said, "I had a scary dream just now! I was walking in a dark, dark, underground sewage canal. The sewage was up to my knees. I kept going, and all of a sudden I saw light and headed toward it, and I got out to a bright sunshine."
>
> "Well, do you believe in dreams? Sometimes they come true!"
>
> "Don't give me that dream bit, I hardly believe in God, let alone dreams. It's easier to believe in Jesus because, at least, he was a historic figure, and people could touch him and talk to him! But dreams?"
>
> "Well, no! Scientifically dreams are reflections of ones suppressed feelings, but man has always interpreted dreams to predict the future. It gives one a sense of controlling his destiny, or maybe just satisfies ones curiosity."
>
> "That's a lot of garbage, interpretation of dreams is for the superstitious, and I am not one of them!"
>
> "Well, let me tell you, I am not superstitious either, but there are things in this universe which could not be explained. I say your dream tells me that you are getting out of here soon!"

"I wish, but don't daydream. They have gotten us by the balls, and you think they are going to let us loose? They are not that stupid!

"Your dream tells me just that! Not all these believers can be wrong; there must be some truth in it, look! The Bible is full of such examples, as you know."

"Don't talk to me about that chronicle of pornography!"

That night the door opened, they called our names. I thought here we go again, how wrong I was in thinking that there wouldn't be another "Party" for me! Here it is I am invited again, this time to hang from a fan hook upside down. Oh God, what have I done to deserve all this? I was scared to death.

They wanted my uncle too. We were to go for interrogation. Very much to our surprise, they handcuffed us, and loaded us onto a truck and drove away. By the time we reached our destination, it was almost two o'clock, past midnight; we were at the Ministry of Defense.

Ministry of Defense? I thought this is it, it is our turn, the waiting is over; they will consider our case and give us a mock trial, like the others, then make us face the firing squad; in my uncle's case, the gallows.

We sat in an anteroom to this salon and waited. There was a party going on inside! A man was shouting, and crying and making all kinds of noises. We heard angry shouts and commands, but couldn't understand, through the thick mahogany doors, what was being said; for sure it was not a conversation, it was beating and torture, and we were right there to hear it!

We must have waited for at least two hours when the noises subsided. The floor-to-ceiling doors opened and four soldiers, each holding a corner of a blanket, carried the victim out. He was semiconscious. It was our turn. They called my uncle in, first. He gave me a look of resignation, and inched his way into the interrogation salon. I thought this old man would not survive any kind of physical torture; he is barely surviving the psychological one. I remembered; he was hit in the prison once with a stick, on his shoulder. His ego was hurt but the shoulder pain, from which he had suffered for years, had gone. He was happy about that; a sort of gallows humor, I thought.

I gave him an encouraging look, and wished him luck, before he went in.

I was left alone and unattended. They had freed my wrists. The second floor appeared empty, except for the interrogation room, which also was amazingly quiet.

Immediately, escape played in my mind. Escape! But, escape to where? How could I get out of this complex building? What would I tell the guards if they saw me? That I was an officer on duty, or some such nonsense? My disheveled appearance would have been enough to deceive me. Yes, escape was appealing, but not practical. It was a fleeting crazy idea, which reflected man's eternal wish for freedom. Anyway, it is better to stay and face the consequences, rather than be recaptured, and retortured endlessly. I dismissed the idea!

Uncle Krikor entered the room. The door closed behind him. I could hear some incomprehensible conversational sounds, but nothing to indicate that there was physical torture; there were no whoosh-thud sounds like in the previous case.

His one-hour interrogation felt longer than Lent. There was every indication that the interrogation was low-key. When the doors opened and he walked out, unscathed, looking even victorious. I knew that he was not physically tortured.

He sat next to me and said, "They had a copy of my book *History of the Armenian Nation* [In Arabic] on the table, and that son of a bitch Colonel Jalaal Balata! I couldn't believe my eyes! That Kurd was sitting behind the table interrogating me! I had treated his entire family, his parents, his relatives, for years, and seldom charged them for my services. I knew him when he was a little kid growing up in Zakho (a town in Mosul). They are good Kurds, but I didn't know he was a Communist. He sat there questioning me about the contents of my book. He said "Dktore Astarjian, you belong to the old condemned Royal era; here it is, you can't deny it; you have praised the Hashimite dynasty in your book; here it is, black on white." He then turned around and said, "You are the chief of the Tashnag Party, what is this party?"

I gave them a lecture about the ideals of this party, told them it is a nationalist party, which was born out of necessity, to fight the Ottoman Turkish tyranny, and Sultan Abdul Hameed, The Red Sultan, just like you fought the injustices of the Royal regime. The Tashnag Party, indeed all Armenians are loyal citizens of this country, and have no territorial claims against this country or the entire Arab world. And no, I am not the head of the Tashnag Party, and to the best of my knowledge, there is no such organization in Iraq, but the ideology lives in the hearts of all Armenians."

Then he said, "Colonel Balata told the others that I have really been good to the people of Mosul; that I have treated them and taken care of the poor; that kind of talk! I must say they didn't hit me once. The interrogation was more like an educational session for them, which is why I am happy. These people should know who we are, and what we stand for."

I could see his relief and contentment. He looked like he had skillfully argued the Armenian Cause in The Hague, and won. Probably he had received a favorable ear because his audiences were among those leftists who hated Turkey for its membership in CENTO, and its anti-Soviet stance.

I barely said a word before they called me in. I was hoping for the same kind of a session for myself. He wished me luck and uttered some encouraging words, as the guards took me in.

The salon was cavernous. A twenty-foot conference table was facing the entrance door. Sitting behind it were two high-ranking military and a civilian. They looked determined and angry. My uncle had told me about Colonel Jalaal Balata, I spotted him because he looked like his brother who was a medical student in my school, but the other two were total strangers. Later I knew who they were! One was Hashim Abdul Jabbaar, a notorious Stalin-style Communist who had vowed to cleanse Iraq from all "Reactionary forces," and the other, another notorious Communist lawyer, Dawood Khammaas. The tribunal had been, and was, everybody's nightmare.

I sat on a chair facing Dawood Khammaas. The second I sat down, there landed a lash on my shoulder, passing my ear: whoosh! That set the tone for the rest of the interrogation.

The party began in earnest when music started. They were playing one of Elvis' rock-n-roll records. I hated rock-n-roll, at the time, because, to me it was the music of the hedonists; the hoopla-hoo, merry-go-round Westernized Iraqi youth known as "Americano," who imitated Hollywood lifestyle; wore above-ankle tight pants, short-sleeve shirts, white socks, loafers, and greased hair. I used to hate that culture and style. However, in their minds playing rock-n-roll and calling me Americano would weaken my resolve and force me into submission.

They ordered me to get up. I did! The sergeant took me to a huge ornate fireplace, in front of which was stacked a pile of bamboo canes, some thick, and some slender.

"Do you know what these are?"
I didn't answer.
"These are my rockets, from V1 to V8; I'll break all these on your back if you don't tell us the truth. You understand?"
I didn't answer again.
He brought me back to my chair. Now that they drew the parameters, questioning started.
"All right," asked Khammaas, "who were you smuggling arms for?"
"Sir, I wasn't smuggling arms at all?"
"You were going to Iran to smuggle arms for Shawwaaf, weren't you? Do you deny it?"
"I don't know what you are talking about, seyyidi! I am not involved in gun-smuggling, I don't know who Shawwaaf is; besides, why would Shawwaaf send a high-profile man like me to smuggle guns? It is insane!"

Bang, whoosh, whoosh—the canes passed my ears hitting my shoulders. My neck hurt. Bang, bang, bang! For the rest of the half-hour interrogation, the beating continued regardless of my answers.

The soldiers kept calling me "Americano" and played rock and roll music, while beating me, seated.

"So, then what were you doing on the Iranian border?"
"Sayyidi, I had gone for medical inspection of villages for outbreak of disease, as ordered by the Ministry of Defense and Ministry of Health; my commander knew about it, he provided me with police escort, you have the copy of the telegrams which I had received, right there, in my bag!"

Luckily, my doctor's bag was there, it was "Exhibit One." Khammas opened the bag and took out the two official telegrams. He read them and passed it along to the others. The more time they spent on the telegrams, the more I felt hopeful of resolving this comedy. I thought any reasonable man would conclude that there was no case, no conspiracy, and no plot.

> "Are you a member of the Tashnag Party?" one of them asked.
> "There is no party in Iraq for me to join, but yes, ideologically I am a Tashnag; every Armenian who believes in the Armenian Cause, struggles to recover our fatherland from Turkey, and holds Turkey responsible for the crime of the Armenian Genocide, is a Tashnag."

I am not sure if they bought my arguments. They really didn't have much more to ask. I thought this session didn't make or break the case. I thought, if not the military, at least the civilian, who is a lawyer, will see that there is no case. However, I had no hopes of being released, my uncle's words were ringing in my ears: "After all these years the Communists have finally trapped us, do you think they will let us go?"

While the beating never stopped, I was not flogged, or brutally beaten, like before.

The interview ended with those silly questions and I was handed over to my custodians to return to my detention camp.

I thought, despite the beatings, I got out easy. My shoulders were swollen and hurt a lot, but I was hopeful that soon, I'd be out of detention. I was satisfied that, finally, finally, someone looked at those telegrams, and hopefully made some sense out of it. It was proof positive that I was innocent, and justification enough not to refer me to the kangaroo court of Colonel Mahdaawi, the People's Court.

On our way back, my uncle and I were satisfied that at least we had a chance to plea our case. Dawn had broken when I hit the floor to sleep.

A few days after our interrogation, they released my uncle, and transferred me to another room. I was happy to see him go; I considered it a good omen. I thought that these people have finally decided that we are small fish, and that there were no legal bases for our detention or prosecution. I felt that my uncle's dream had vindicated "dream believers," and I postulated that there are some invisible powers and energies in the universe, which we, humans, have not been able to comprehend, or harness, yet.

Compared to where I had been, my new habitation was luxurious; I had a mattress and a pillow, albeit dirty. My immediate neighbor, on the floor, was General Abdul 'Azeez Al-Uqayli, who was also transferred from my room, earlier. Until his detention, he had been the Commander of the First Army Division. He had been one of the original Free Officers, which was formed after the defeat of the Arab Armies in Palestine, in 1948.

He had been an active participant in the July 14 Revolution. Prior to the Shawwaaf Revolt he had been transferred to the Foreign Ministry, in the rank of ambassador, and was awaiting assignment when he was detained as a Shawwaaf coconspirator.

This man was an avowed Muslim, following the teachings and the philosophy of Khalif Omar "El-'Adil" (The Just), the third Khalif of Islam who succeeded Prophet Mohammed. He was educated in Britain, and was considered one of the foremost and the ablest military minds in the country. Needless to say, he was a fervent Nationalist, but I didn't get the impression that he was a Ba'thi or a Nasserite. Regardless, he was an anti-Communist.

Our conversations were about general topics; we both were cautious not to say anything that might incriminate us later, under the circumstances, neither of us trusted the other. Being anti-Communists, and cellmates, were enough to create a sort of camaraderie between us, otherwise lengthy conversations revolved around religion. Omar El-'Adil brand of Islam was his conviction and passion; he kept educating me about his Khalif who was "Just and fair minded."

He said, "Omar, upon his arrival to Jerusalem was taken to a Christian church, to pray. He had refused, arguing that if he prayed there the Muslims would build a mosque on the site, and "That is not right; it will inflict injustice upon the Christians, this church belongs to the Christians!" he had said. "He then chose a site away from the church, and prayed there, and that's where they built a mosque, which later became known as the Dome of the Rock."

On the other side of me was Colonel Abdul Ghani Al-Raawi who was another revolutionary, and a fierce nationalist. I never knew if he was a Ba'thi or a Nasserite. He was a nice, good-hearted person, albeit very emotional, volatile, and flammable.

A day or two had passed since my transfer to this luxury room. We were comfortable, and there were no parties, and no terrorizing. To continue a noncontrovertial conversation, I asked the General whether he believed in dreams.

"Of course I do," he said, "The Qur'an provides for interpretation of dreams, even the Bible . . . remember Jacob's dream?"

"Well, in that case, I'll tell you, I just had a revealing dream! We were three. We were ushered out of a mud hut on a bright sunny day. There were three horses waiting for us. One was white and the others chestnut. I jumped on the white horse and galloped away. The second man mounted, the horse galloped, then he fell on his back with his feet still in the stirrups, and the horse dragged him for a distance. Then he managed to erect himself back on the saddle, and caught up with me. The third fell off the horse, and couldn't get back on. Well! What do you think of that?"

"You are going to be released soon! Mark my words!" he said.

I told him about my uncle's dream, and how it was realized in a few days.

"You see? I am right." That injected a healthy dose of hope in me.

The following day the door opened, the soldier called my name and the name of another roommate. They told us to get ready to go to the Ministry of Defense for further interrogation. Soon, we were in the back of a truck, handcuffed. There was a third "conspirator" with us from another room. A short while later we were on the second floor of the Ministry, sitting in the same waiting room adjacent to the boardroom where, a few days earlier I had had a party. They took me in first.

I found myself facing Dawood Khammaas who was alone in that room, sitting behind the huge table. I was in military uniform, all buttoned up, but without a hat, or any sign to indicate my rank. I clicked my heels in military salute. There was no acknowledgment.

> "Are you Hiniry Astarjian?"
> "Yes, seyyidi, I am."
> "What is your rank?"
> "Second lieutenant, seyyidi!"
> "Where are your stars?"
> "I don't know sir, they were stripped off my shoulders."
> "Sergeant, give him two stars!" he ordered. "Now you can go, you are free. Contact the Administrative Offices at the Ministry of Defense for further instructions and orders."
> "Yes, seyyidi!"

I saluted the civilian sitting behind the huge table with another clicking of the heels, but this time with the stars on my shoulders. My heart was jumping with joy!

I walked to the waiting room and waited for the others to finish their ordeal with Khammaas, before heading back to the barracks. Their appearances were short, too; one was released on a 10,000 dinars bail, and the other referred to the People's Court for trial before that famous monster Colonel Mahdawi and the television cameras, for the whole world to see.

"My dream has come true, to the scene!" I told my friend the General, who was happy for me. He kept telling me that there is merit to dreams. "Sometimes that's how God communicates with his creation," he said, "here is one proof."

I had neither the time, nor the desire to argue. Why should I? After all, my dream and my uncle's were realized, and I was going home. Why argue?

I got a ride to Baghdad to join my wife and my child.

At the time, our release remained a mystery to me. I didn't know who had conspired to put us in, and I didn't know why we were released. I couldn't believe the ease with which the case was closed, just like that. "Where are your stars? Here, take it and go!" Three and a half months of torture and agony disappeared, like Act Three of a tragic comedy!

Regardless, I was happy to go home. My physical wounds had healed, and my toenails were starting to grow again, but the psychological effects, mainly fear, were still dominating my senses.

Within a month or so, they discharged me from the military. Now I was a civilian doctor in need of a job.

20

Courts, Kurds, and the Communists

It was late July 1959 when I was released. The entire political atmosphere in the country was unsettling to say the least, especially because of the famous "People's Court," a supreme court headed by Qasim's Cousin Colonel Fadhil Abbas El-Mahdaawi. The court was created especially to try the "Old regime and the Traitors of the Republic," but after the Shawwaaf revolt, the trials of the Old Regime were set aside, and the trials of the "New Traitors" started. It was like watching a new soap opera. The chief prosecutor of that court was Colonel Maajd Ameen who, together with Mahdaawi, ran a circus, the like of which was never seen before anywhere in the world.

The court was anything but a legal forum; these two clowns used it primarily as a theater to degrade, ridicule, and attack Nasser and all those who had subscribed to his ideals of uniting the Arab land under one flag. They degraded Syria, which was being ruled by the rival Ba'th party.

Among those who were tried were General Ghazi Al-Daghistani, Sa'eed Qazzaaz, Bahjat Attiya, Tabaqchali, Rif'at Al-Haaj Sirri, and the rest, all big names in the Iraqi government and the military. They were insulted and humiliated in front of the television cameras. The ad hominem attacks extended to their families and relatives.

They condemned the Baghdad Pact, insulted Britain, and Anthony Nutting, the British ex-cabinet minister-turned-journalist, who was visiting Cairo. They called him Anthony Nothing. They despised him not so much, because he was an Englishman, but because he was Nasser's friend. Nutting spoke fluent Arabic. He had played an important role in the 1956 Suez campaign, something that they interpreted as a skill to spy on the Arabs.

The court sessions opened with an hour or two of uttering obscenities and insults directed toward the enemies of the Republic. The concept of Arab unity was ridiculed and denounced, over and over again. Friendship with the Soviet Union, "the fighter against Imperialism and the liberator of all oppressed people," was stressed and praised. Lengthy lectures on patriotism would follow. Then there would be a counterattack on Ahmed Sa'eed, the eloquent stinging Egyptian broadcaster, whose venomous prose degraded Qasim, his regime, and Mahdaawi's court.

The court audience, as if in a theater, would applaud, demonstrate, and read poetry to praise its sole leader, Za'eem Abdul Kareem Qasim, and insult Nasser, Shawwaaf, and "all the reactionary forces."

"This court belongs to the people!" would shout Mahdaawi from the bench. The audience would respond: "Hang them! Hang them! Hang them! Maaku Za'eem illa Kareem (there is no leader but Kareem)."

Then Maajd Ameen, the chief prosecutor, would interject with a threat: "The people of Iraq have learned a new technique it is called 'sahhl' (dragging), which is the Iraqi way!" The audience would go wild, "Kill them, kill them, they deserve to be dragged, give them to us, we have the ropes! Mahku mu'amara tseer wal-hibaal mawjooda" (there can be no conspiracies when ropes are available).

Then Mahdaawi would continue: "Our Za'eem al Awhad (sole leader), despite plots against him and the country, has liberated the country from the colonialists, the reactionaries, the feudalists, the American Imperialists, the enemies of Iraq, Nasser's agents, and these traitors who are here, assembled before me. Whose interests do these people serve? They are after our oil and other riches, we will not allow that to happen, we will defend our country and the revolution, we will cut their hands!"

Now Maajd would pick up: "Nasser cannot poke his long, ugly nose in the affairs of our free and valiant country. He created the United Arab Republic and converted our beloved Syria into his subjugated Northern Territory. We will not allow him to subjugate us and create a North Eastern Territory out of Iraq. He wants to extend his dictatorship to Iraq and eliminate our hard-earned liberties, the way he has done it in Egypt and Syria; he is also fighting the Communist patriots there!" He would then, belittle and ridicule Nasser, yet again, for being the son of a mailman, and the audience would sarcastically break into a popular song, "El-Postaggiya ishtekoo min kithri maraaseeli" ("the mailmen complained of heavy mail"). He would ridicule the idea of Arab Unity and entice the Syrians to rescind the union with Egypt. He would wash dirty linen in public, and fling obscenities and insults at the enemies of the Republic.

This was night court live with all its theatrics presenting drama, comedy, musicals, vulgarity, and literary trash, all at the same time.

People would be glued to their TVs, every evening, to watch this soap opera.

"Did you see what Mahdaawi did last night?"
"I couldn't believe my eyes and ears; this General turned into a mouse in front of him, he couldn't even say a word, he just froze."

"Yeah, but did you see Sa'eed Qazzaaz? He is a real man; he wouldn't let Mahdaawi humiliate him!"

"He is a Kurd! A very brave and proud man, he wouldn't take shit from anybody, let alone Mahdaawi. He hurled back all the insults and he defended his record as Minister of the Interior. Did you see what he told Mahdaawi? The guy really has balls!"

When Mahdaawi sentenced him to death by hanging, Sa'eed Qazzaaz responded, "When I ascend the gallows and look down, I'll see under my feet people like you who are unworthy of living."

Qasim's speeches and Mahdawi's pronouncements had clearly defined Iraq's identity and stance vis-à-vis union with the United Arab Republic. The West could not have been happier; the man was opposing Union with Nasser, thereby denying Nasser control over Baba Gurgur. The oil was flowing without interruption, and its prices had not gone up. They could not have wished for more.

This situation fortified the hypothesis of the conspiratorial theorists that it was the British who, preemptivly changed the regime in Iraq, and that Qasim, who for all these years was known to be pro-British, was indeed Britain's man on-the-spot.

The same people also explained Qasim's internal policies in the same manner; British-led conspiracy! Whether these people were smart enough to make such assumptions or not, the political situation on the ground vindicated them, Qasim successfully played a major role in a serious matter, which the previous governments had failed to do. He acknowledged peoples' rights to sovereignty, and allowed them to exercise unprecedented liberties, freedom of speech, and freedom of assembly, of course for as long as they did not clash with his political stance.

This policy gave the Communists a false sense of security and encouraged them to come out of their hideouts in droves. Now the entire Communist party and its leadership were exposed to the public, ready to be destroyed at a suitable time. But not yet! Of course, the British and the Americans were happy: Qasim had done what the previous governments had not been able to do!

The Communists exploited their newly found freedom to the fullest. Their strength forged a symbiotic relationship with Qasim. At this point, the Kurds and the Communists worked in unison and formed Qasim's political base. So, the country was divided in more than one way: Qasim, the Communists, and the Kurds on one side, and the Arab nationalist, Ba'thists, and Nasserites on the other. The most aggressive, therefore the most influential, were the communists who were set to protect their gains by attempting to control the events through not only denying the opposition every opportunity to succeed, but also persecuting them in the name of their sole leader. They gained control of the country in the name of the sole leader; so much so that people believed that Qasim was a Communist! "If he wasn't he would not have condoned their excesses," people believed.

The Communist militia, the Muqaawama al-Sha'biya (People's Resistance Militia) was terrorizing the country from the north to the south, intimidating, arresting, and torturing people arbitrarily, and then killing them at will. Another Communist organization that surfaced was Anssaar al-Salaam, which was instrumental in organizing and mobilizing the masses to support Qasim, but in reality, their aim was destruction of their opposition and securing dominance of their party. The country, undoubtedly, had become Red!

For the Kurds it was time for not only revenge, but also renewed hope for a better life under Qasim's new regime. So the Kurds had every justification to help Qasim by working with Anssaar Al-Salaam and the Muqaawama in defeating their enemy by any means possible. Its interests dictated that kind of conviction, and they did not shy away. They supported Qasim and hoped that he would remove all the injustices that they had suffered at the hands of the Royal regime and before that at the hands of Ottoman Turks.

To understand Kurdish support for Qasim, it is important to understand the Kurdish Cause: They had lost in Lausanne what they had gained in Sevres. Syria, Iraq, and Iran were treating them as second-class citizens; they were neglected, oppressed, and often persecuted for no good reason. It is no surprise then that Kurdish intellectuals and political-military leaders, felt shortchanged and were angry with those who formulated the post WWI policies and reshaped the geographical map of Asia Minor. Kurds had no choice but to resort to armed struggle, whenever possible.

There were numerous armed uprisings against the central governments of Turkey and Iraq. In the 1920s, the Turkish government crushed Sheikh Obeydullah's, then, Sheikh Sa'id's uprisings. In Iraq, Mala Mustafa Barzani, the Chief of the Barzani tribe, an already experienced warrior and strategist, never ceased to struggle through armed uprisings, for a better future for the Kurds of Iraq. He became the symbol of Kurdish nationalism, and the nightmare of Iraq's rulers. Northern Iraq, which is Southern Kurdistan, never ceased becoming the ulcer that eroded the body of the Iraqi entity, bleeding at times, and quiescent at other times, but never healing.

These uprisings rendered the Iraqi government financially anemic, and militarily impotent to the start of hostilities against Israel. Arab Nationalist observers blamed the West, who controlled the levers of power in the Middle East, for this strategy. Indeed the Iraqi army, regardless of its intent to fight Israel, was distracted by these side wars.

Not only was the West involved in this game, but the Soviets, the Iranians, the Israelis, the Syrians, and also the Turks were in it too; they manipulated the Kurds in general and the Barzanis in particular throughout the twentieth century to pursue their own national interests. For example, at different times, Iraqi Kurds sided with Iraq to create insurgents in Iran, and Iran manipulated them to pressurize Iraq. In 1975, Henry Kissinger negotiated a peace agreement in Algeria, between the Shah of Iran and Saddam Hussein, striking a fatal blow to the Kurds who found themselves caught in the crossfire.

Barzanis were very patriotic, very brave, and very experienced fighters but unlike the present, they lacked political maturation and foresightedness. Perhaps, because of their isolation in landlocked mountains, they had developed certain characteristics unique to mountain dwellers: Respect, naiveté, chivalry, noblesse oblige, trust, and an unyielding pride.

It was mainly for this psychological makeup that they paid dearly. They defied death, but feared humiliation. They carried the spirit of the mountain breeze in their souls, and the freedom with which it moved from valley to valley.

In Iran, in the immediate aftermath of WWII, Kurds declared the formation of the Kurdish Republic of Mahabad. Mala Mustafa Barzani was their defense minister. The Republic lasted for over a year before its demise in 1946. Barzani managed to escape to his mountains in Barzan, northern Iraq.

Upon his return, there were more clashes with the Iraqi army, which was having the upper hand in these hostilities. Additionally Iran, Turkey, and the West, cornered him politically and militarily. The rugged mountains of Barzan were no longer a fortress for him and his people; they had no choice but to seek a safe haven in some friendly territory. They found it in the Soviet Union where they went, via Turkey, and Armenia. In Yerevan, Armenia, the Soviets gave them asylum then dispersed them all over the Soviet Republics. This was in 1948–1949.

Armenia had her share of these escapees, and accepted them with open arms. They incorporated the refugees with the indigenous Kurdish community of Armenia. This distinct community already had its own theatre, Kurdish language newspapers, and Academy of Kurdish Studies. It is no wonder, then, that the Kurds were very much pro-Soviet, an attitude that was erroneously interpreted as being Communist.

July 14, 1958, brought new hope for the Kurds. The Revolution stressed the "Brotherhood of Kurds and Arabs" under one flag, led by its champion Qasim. The Kurds supported him wholeheartedly. They, in conjunction with the Communists, were determined to protect the gains brought about by this Revolution. Part of this protection was to annihilate the opposition; and that's what happened on the ground.

On September 11, 1958 Arif was excused of his duties as Deputy Commander in chief. Nineteen days later he was excused of all his duties, and arrested.

Power, now, was solely in the hands of Qasim, but he had lost the support of a huge number of people, collectively and loosely known as the Ba'thists, or Aflaqis. That left him with the Communists to include the Kurds who became his conduits and power base without which he could not survive. This evolving situation couldn't suit the Communists better. They mobilized and solidified their forces. They organized farmers, teachers, students, women, and others into labor unions and organizations. "Anssaar Al-Salaam" ("Allies of Peace") and Al-Muqaawama Al-Sha'biya (Peoples Resistance Forces) were the latest.

To protect the Revolution from evil, they set up checkpoints to control or arrest the dissenters, the remnants of the old regime, the traitors of the revolution, and above all the Aflaqis; in essence, all non-Communist elements. They said, "You are either with us, or against us."

Taking advantage of the emerging neodemocratic situation, they held huge demonstrations, almost every day, carrying banners of support to the Za'eem and shouting, "Maku Za'im illa Kareem, guwaaweed Ba'thiyya" (there is no leader but Karim [Qasim], bastard Ba'this). They would denounce the Aflaqis; shout slogans promoting Iraqi-Soviet friendship, and glorifying various unions, and the proletariat.

These demonstrations electrified the atmosphere, destabilized the street, and unsettled the already stressful lives of the ordinary Iraqi.

The newly acquired Communist hegemony pleased the Soviet Union for many reasons, not the least of which being the replacement of the Western experts with their own, a development that would give them an opportunity to shape the policies of Iraq to their liking.

Nasser was livid, and the West was terribly concerned. Oddly enough, these two found themselves on the same side of the fence. They were united in fighting the Communists, albeit for their own different reasons: Britain, for losing influence and possibly future control over Baba Gurgur, and Nasser for losing an opportunity to have control over Baba Gurgur.

Anssaar Al-Salaam (Allies of Peace) consisted of Qasim supporters, opportunists, the disenchanted, and the hooligans who had come under the banner of the Communist Party. The Party, which was growing in influence by the day, utilized them to fight their enemy, the nonprogressive elements.

Since Mosul was the bastion of Arab Nationalism, the communists decided to flex their muscles in that city and shrink the Aflaqis to size. They organized the "Festival of Peace" in that city. In fact, the festival was a cover to their real goal of controlling the city and destroying the infrastructure of Arab Nationalism, once and for all.

In late February 1959, preparations were made for such a parade to take place on March 8. The Moslawis objected and demonstrated in advance opposing such a parade, but to no avail. On that day, trains provided gratis by Qasim, loaded with armed civilians, left Baghdad for Mosul. Immediately, demonstrations and counterdemonstrations filled the streets. Verbal exchanges and arguments led to skirmishes, then clashes, which evolved into armed fighting. Soon, as planned, Mosul was turned into a battleground between the Communists (to include the Kurds, who had descended onto the city from their villages on one side), and the Nationalists (to include Ba'this, Aflaqi's) on the other.

The army had to intervene. Troupes entered the battles on the side of the nationalists/Ba'this. The commander of the Fifth Battalion in Mosul was Abdul-Wahaab Al-Shawwaaf, a unionist, and a member of the "Free Officers" who had played a major role in the Revolution. He had gone to Baghdad to plea with Qasim to disallow these demonstrations. He had begged him, threatened him, and done his utmost to prevent Anssaar Al-Salaam from going to Mosul. But, Qasim had declined, "People have the right to express their views," he had said, "after all this is a republic."

Shawwaaf, a volatile man, had promised "A coup to adjust the direction of this revolution to its original path, if Qasim did not stop the Ansaar from coming to Mosul." Well! Qasim did not!

Within hours of their arrival, Shawwaaf kept his sworn promise and revolted against Qasim. A few of his lackeys took off from Mosul and bombarded the radio transmitters in Baghdad, and the buildings of the Ministry of Defense. The young pilots missed their targets, all of them; a few bombs fell on some buildings, causing minor damages.

Apparently, Shawwaaf had conspired with Nasser's people in Syria for his plans, but on the day of the precipitous revolt, Nasser's people were nowhere to be found, and the promised help did not materialize, except for a portable radio transmitter, which broadcast on a wrong wave-length with feeble reception. Later, it became evident that Shawwaaf's move that day was a knee jerk reaction, rather than a planned revolt, which is why the Syrians were not ready to help. At least that was Nasser's and Syria's excuse.

In any case, from the beginning, it had become evident that this revolt was destined to fail because of bad timing, poor planning, and inadequate logistical support.

Shawwaaf's coconspirators, like Rifa'at Al-Haj Sirri (the founder of the "Free Officers" movement), the Chief of Millitary Intelligence in Baghdad, and Nadhim Al Tabaqchali, Commander of the Second Army Division, in Kirkuk had advised Shawwaat not to revolt because they "...were not ready yet." But the obsessive-compulsive Shawwaaf had ignored their advice.

Qasim's pilots, in a counterattack, bombed the rebel's barracks and killed Shawwaaf. The whole thing was over in hours, and the country entered into a new phase of violence and turmoil.

While things were over for Shawwaaf and his revolt, big problems were starting for those participants, and nonparticipants who survived the events.

Of the officers who survived the military assaults, Qasim loyalists, primarily Communists and Kurds, captured a large majority of them and sent them to Baghdad to face The People's Court of Colonel Mahdaawi (Qasim's cousin). I met some of these people in Room # 11 at the Al-Rasheed Military camp. One day before my arrival there, thirteen of them had already faced the firing squad in Um al-Tbool, and there was more to come.

Qasim and the Communists were, in a sense, jubilant with this turn of events. It meant their survival, and a renewed opportunity to destroy their opponents. In Baghdad, Qasim purged the military of the undesirables. He arrested the conspirators, the reluctant coconspirators like Rif'at al-Haj Sirri, and Nadhim al-Tabaqchali, and the sympathizers; they were all jailed at the Rasheed base.

In Mosul, the Muqaawama Al-Sha'biya (Peoples Resistance forces, Communist militias) embarked upon mopping-up activities; they attacked shops, homes, and institutions, killed civilians indiscriminately, and the known Aflaqis selectively, and hung them from telephone poles. Amongst these were women of

Mosul's prominent Sunni Arab families, like the Omaris. Kurds were participants in these atrocities. They descended from the surrounding mountains; for instance, "Aqra," and helped finish the job. In two days 5,000 citizens of Mosul were brutally murdered, still hundreds faced "People's Tribunals" for a few seconds, and then were summarily executed. When the news of the massacre spread, a blanket of fear descended over Iraq. The country had never seen such mass murders since Holako.

The ethnic, as well as political divide, grew to outright animosity. Revenge became the driving force in people's conduct. Qasim was blamed for all of this whose support eroded amongst ordinary people, even amongst the Communists, who being encouraged by their deeds began to demand power sharing with Qasim.

> For the next four months, the mopping operations continued day and night. Communist "Commissars" had pretty much taken over the day-to-day operations of the government. Authority was slipping off Qasim's hands; he was being isolated more and more. More and more people were detained just on the suspicion that one day they could pose a danger to them.

Kurds who wore two hats, one of their ethnicity and one Communist, had planned on July 14, 1959, a pogrom against the Turkomans of Kirkuk. They wanted control of the city because "Kirkuk is Kurdistan." They had massacred a score of Turkomans, and buried dozens in a ditch, alive. Two of my friends were amongst the victims, Mohammed Awtchi and Jaheed Fakhri. At the same time they had killed two prominent Turkoman brothers, Dr. Ihsaan Khayralla and Colonel 'Atta Khayralla, two prominent Toranis.

Qasim's government had interfered after the fact, and those who had committed the crimes were tried, and sentenced to death. Qasim did not carry out the executions, possibly because of Communist party pressures. It is quite possible that Qasim was unaware of this heinous act; however, it was certain that he became aware of the fact that his authority was shrinking, and the Communists were destroying the country at his expense.

For the ordinary person, this pogrom and the deferment of their execution added to their suspicion that he was indeed a Communist, otherwise why wouldn't he carry out the executions? The Turkoman community continued to live in extreme fear, and was angry, demanding justice, but justice never came! Needless to say, as a result of this pogrom, animosity between the Kurds and the Turkomans grew a thousandfold.

21

Triumphs and Defeats

The Shawwaaf revolt jelled the political situation in the country and the region. There was no confusion about who stood where, and where was the country headed! One thing was crystal clear: the project of joining Nasser's United Arab Republic was dead. The Wihhdawis (advocates of wihhda = union), newly budding Ba'thists (whose spiritual father was Michel Aflaq of Syria, therefore called 'Aflaqis), and the Arab Nationalists who backed Arif were the losers. The Communists, the Kurds, and the Christians who backed Qasim, were the winners. It is interesting to note that Christians opposed the union for fear of fanatic Islamic domination in case it became a reality. Today the same thinking dominates the geopolitical calculations of the United States and Europe.

Qasim also had strong but covert support from Britain and the United States because of the same fears, and because his oil policy remained unchanged: free flow of oil and cheap prices. Qasim had kept his promise, which he had made to the British and American ambassadors

On the day of the revolution, by eleven o'clock, Qasim had arrived at the Ministry of Defense and assumed power. By noon, he received a request from the British Ambassador Michael Wright to meet with "The Leader of the Revolution." Qasim agreed. The Ambassador then asked Qasim's people, "How should I address him, 'Your Majesty'?" He was told "Brigadier General" would do just fine.

By 3 PM the two met for all of ten minutes, after which they appeared on the steps of the Ministry of Defense with broad smiles on their faces. Colonel Khaleel Ibrahim Hussein, who was present at the meeting and was taking minutes, writes:

> The Ambassador's first question was about union with Nasser. The Ambassador said, "Britain objects to Iraq's union with the United Arab Republic, and if Nasser's hands

reach the oil wells, Britain will have a different posture, the British forces are in Jordan, and the American forces are in Lebanon. Oil must flow." He then returned to his hotel where he had moved temporarily, because of a fire in the Embassy, which had started accidentally while burning sensitive documents.

Qasim, standing on the steps of the Ministry of Defense with the Ambassador by his side, announced, "Oil will be produced and exported as before, and the prices will remain unchanged." OPEC did not exist then. The West won yet another battle over Baba Gurgur!

Britain immediately recognized the new Iraqi regime.

On the second day of the revolution, this time the American Ambassador met with Qasim at the Ministry of Defense. He too appeared on the steps of the Ministry with Qasim. He too had a broad smile on his face when he left. The same day, an official government spokesman announced,

> Iraq affirms its adherence to all the International Treaties, obligations, and decisions that were passed by the United Nations. That included Iraq's membership in Baghdad Pact.

This declaration was a slap in the face for Nasser, the Unionists, and the Soviet Union, who were vehemently opposed to the pact. This Pact was a military coalition between Iraq, Turkey, Iran, and Pakistan, in conjunction with Britain and United States as observers. The aim was to contain the Soviet Union from the south.

Immediately after this announcement, the United States recognized Iraq's new regime. Other countries followed.

These pro-Western decisions reaffirmed people's belief that Qasim was indeed Britain's man. British and American recognition of the new regime, with Qasim at its helm, gave Qasim a tremendous boost; now he was the preeminent leader of the pack. The power struggle between himself and his deputy, Arif, was in his favor. Utilizing this, and to further consolidate power in his hands, he stalled, and then rejected forming the Revolutionary Council, as was agreed upon by the planners of the coup, the Free Officers.

All these realities deepened the chasm between the two broad political currents in the country: Those on Arif's block and those on Qasim's. This is exactly what the West wanted!

Qasim's positions on these vital issues, which were the same as that of Britain and the United States prompted many to postulate; indeed they believed that the coup was cooked in the kitchens of Whitehall, in the first place. That may or may not be true; the fact was that Britain and the United States liked the direction that the Revolution had taken.

In a classical "divide and conquer" policy, Britain helped widen the gap between the two factions. For instance: in a daring operation the British Embassy intercepted and decoded a telegram that was sent to Nasser by his Ambassador in Iraq, who had met with Arif on July 17, three days after the revolution. In that telegram Egypt's Ambassador had reported Arif's profound enthusiasm about joining the United Arab Republic immediately, in effect handing over the revolution to Nasser without any conditions.

What the British embassy did was to insert a false statement in the Ambassador's report, supposedly made by Arif, which read, "Arif may be forced, at any time, to get rid of Qasim." The British Embassy conveniently handed this telegram over to Qasim who, according to many sources, was already suffering from paranoia, and this made it worse. He now had a document, which would vindicate his actions. He apparently finalized his decision, right there and then, to get rid of Arif. Later, the Egyptian Ambassador swore that he had never written such a telegram, and that Arif had never said such a thing!

22

Baghdad

With all these disturbances, Baghdadis struggled to retain their city's old structure and flavor. For them what had happened was a coup, not a revolution. Baghdad was the same, minus the royal regime and the statue of King Faisal I.

Like New York City, Baghdad was a mosaic of different "villages" spread along the banks of the Tigris, which delineates the Eastern flank of ancient Mesopotamia. Civilizations have come and gone, each inscribing its mark on both sides of the river, but it is the Eastern side, El-Rassafa, which was more developed. That might have been because the most illustrious of these civilizations, the Abbasid Dynasty, had settled on this side of the river and built their mosques and institutions here rather than El-Karkh. The ruins of El-Mustansirriyah and many other buildings that still stand bear witness to the glory of this University before Hulako and the Seljuks destroyed it in the twelfth century.

History books tell us, "these savages destroyed the University and its gigantic library, and threw hundreds of thousands of manuscripts into the Tigris; the river ran black for three days." Baghdad, indeed Iraq, was seriously wounded, from which it has never recovered even today; Iraq has never been the same!

The villages constituting Baghdad fall into place like a colorful jigsaw puzzle: A'adhamiya, Kadhimiya, Waziriya, Gog Nazar, 'Agd El-Nasara, and many more, each with its distinct flavor and local cultural traditions, form the mosaic of Baghdad, which is intricate, artistic, and unique like the cerulean-blue inscribed tiles of its many mosques!

The milieu of life in these villages was centuries old, and continues to date; it had its own sensitivities and idiosyncrasies unique to a culture that emphasized family ties, kinship, "noblesse oblige," and camaraderie.

The elders of a village, and its "shabaab," the youth, saw to it that their neighborhoods stayed the way they wanted them to be: quiet, tranquil, and protected from intruders who might have roamed around for sinister reasons, such as having an eye on a neighborhood girl whose honor was the honor of all who lived there. They were to take care of their poor and the sick, and no one was to remain isolated, everybody shared in the joy and the tragedy of a neighbor; people walked hand in hand through life. People attended weddings in the neighborhood without invitation; they all went, participated in the joy, dined, and danced. In death, they all mourned and highlighted the virtues of the deceased, even if it was scanty. Tradition did not allow saying a bad thing about the one who went to face his creator, no matter how undesirable he was in life, or if he was a Christian, a Sunni, or a Shiite. They would always say, "May God forgive his sins."

When the Ba'thi militia accidentally killed my brother at age twenty-three, the entire neighborhood, mostly Muslims, came to console us, recited from the Qur'an, and told us stories and words of wisdom to console us and share in our pain and sorrow. Many participated in the military funeral given him. "Al-Baqaa'u Lillaah (eternity is for God only), he concluded God's will," they told us. They never denied us sympathy and support because we were Christians.

Tradition aside, Baghdad was a modern city impregnated with Western culture, mostly British, but that too was changing before the revolution.

The centuries-old Shar'i El-Rashid, the main street of Baghdad, ran parallel to the Tigris and, like the river itself, gave the villages a window to display their varied, but colorful lifestyles, to the passing world. I don't know the exact length of the street, it must have been about five to seven miles long, but that didn't matter, it was long enough to hold centuries of history and loads of modern life.

At the west end there was The Royal College of Medicine, the crown jewel of the Iraqi educational system. The bus would drop off one at a very busy square, Bab El-Mu'adham, before continuing its route to the other colleges: Law, Teachers', and Commerce.

The newest and the most exciting school was the Institute of Fine Arts where they taught performing arts as well as creative art, painting, sculpting, music, and theatre. Some of the artists like Jawaad Seleem who graduated and later taught there, became so famous and his work became so valuable that the government prevented exporting his work. They were considered to be national treasures. Jawaad's gigantic work, in the form of relief on a flat surface, is a landmark in Bab el-Sharji, even today.

The Institute also gave courses, some in the evenings, in classical Arabic music, also classical European music. Arab musicologists taught the oud (lute), qanoon (kanon), dmbug (percussion), kamaan (violin), and other instruments, while the vocalists learned the Iraqi Maqaam in the hands of the masters, such as Gubbanji, Ghazaali, and the others.

Professors Sando Albo and Julian Herts, teachers of violin and piano, brought up a generation of Iraqi music lovers and performers in classical European music.

Guitar and other instruments were also in the curriculum. King Faisal II music hall had seen Bach, Brahms, and Beethoven concerts, as well as dramas and variety shows.

One of these students who attended evening classes was my good friend Garo Kishmishian, a civil engineer who studied violin under this Italian professor. Well, neither Garo nor Sando Albo could predict what the future held for them. The original objective was for Garo, to learn music and violin, as a hobby. However, things changed as he advanced in his avocation: upon the insistence and guidance of Dr. Papken Papazian, a renaissance man himself, Garo formed an Armenian choir group and named it after Gomidas, the greatest Armenian composer and musicologist ever. Sando Albo eased him into this task.

The Armenian community, the diplomatic community, and the Arab elite used to crowd the auditorium of the Armenian Youth Club to listen to the performance of Gomidas Choir, the cultural event of the year, indeed. That choir group is now nearly a half a century old and still performs under the baton of Garo Kishmishian, enriching the cultural life of the Armenian community and Iraq.

Another Institute graduate-teacher was Miss Gladys Boghosian, a piano virtuoso whose work led her to the highest civilian Medal of Honor a few years ago.

There was Loris Chobanian of the same Institute, an Andre Sagovia to us, who mastered the guitar, and now is a professor of music in Ohio. There was Vartan Manoogian, a Violin Virtuoso, a brother to Archbishop Torkom Manoogian, now Patriarch of Jerusalem.

There was Haig Balian, another accomplished violinist who came to the United States. I believe he played with the Los Angeles Symphony Orchestra until his passing away a few years ago.

On the folkloric side, there was "Qrnatachi Arteen" (Arteen, the clarinet player), the Benny Goodman of Baghdad, whose performances on Baghdad radio, music lovers awaited eagerly, every week.

Before the Jewish migration, there was a band composed of all Jews, which played live on Radio Baghdad; "Chalghi Baghdadi" delighted generations of Iraqis with their special brand of music. People, sorely missed their music, when they migrated to Israel. Now, I believe, they perform on radio, from Tel Aviv.

Other Arab performers captured the hearts and souls of music lovers. Amongst the most prominent were Mohammed El-Gubbanchi, Nadhim El-Ghazaali, Siddiqt-El-Mullaya, 'Afifa Iskender, Seleema (Pasha) Murad, Munir Beshir, and many other luminaries of Iraqi music. Such was life in Baghdad, colorful, tranquil, exciting, and enchanting.

El Rashid Street connected Bab El-Mu'adham (the Great Gate) with Bab El-Sharji (the East Gate), where all the municipal buses and taxis loaded and unloaded passengers. Streets from all directions met at this square, which never slept. It was also a cultural crossroads of sorts. One could spot the old, the new, the fashionable, the Bedouin Arab, and modernized girls, all intermingled. Like Baghdad itself, this place displayed a colorful demographic mosaic.

The centerpiece of the square was the classical, ornate, movie theatre, the King Ghazi Cinema. It looked more like an Opera House than a movie theatre; Velvet seats, velvet double-hung curtains raised with thick golden ropes and tassels to reveal the screen just before playing the National Anthem. The audience would stand up and salute the image of His Majesty, or pretend to anyway, then settle down to watch the movie. I remember seeing Charlie Chaplin's *Limelight* there and admiring his genius. I still whistle its theme-tune the way I did on my way down the regal set of stairs, after seeing the movie.

Not far from the King Ghazi were the twin movie theaters, Rex and Roxey. I remember seeing the *Spellbound* there.

El-Hamra was a few streets down. Doris Day, June Allison, Jane Russell, Ginger Rogers, Fred Astaire, Esther Williams, and the entire Hollywood contract actors and actresses were on parade there.

The American Cultural Invasion had begun. Bookstores and magazine shops on the square were flooded with periodicals and magazines for men and women. Aside from *Time*, *Newsweek*, *Look*, *Life*, *Collier*, *Readers Digest*, and *Argosy* that were on the shelves, there also were *Vogue*, German *Burda*, and other bridal magazines. Import of pornographic periodicals was banned, though there were undoubtedly some smuggled into the country.

Stereo, mono, and hi-fi records were very popular, and Elvis Presley was the favorite of "Americanos": the youth who dressed in narrow blue jeans short enough to reveal white socks and loafers, and wore their hair with a heavy dose of Brylcream to give it a greasy look, like Elvis. These people also carried a comb in their back pockets and a pack of Chesterfield or Camels in their shirt pocket, otherwise rolled into their short sleeves. To them, looking American was a sign of sophistication and modernity, a rejection of the classical Arab and English way of life.

I despised both the look and the mentality of these people. It clashed with the colonial-English cultural upbringing that I had adopted. To me these people were a "cult" of sorts, though they were not. It was I, who rejected the new; the feeling was mutual, they too discriminated against the rest of us.

Though there was free flow of information in the country, occasionally, one could feel that it was not total; a page would be missing from *Time* or *Newsweek*, something that could be considered anti-Arab or pro-Israel, for instance. You knew the censor had been there.

There was another feature of American "invasion" of the Arab culture: fashionable fast food. Cafeterias ala Horn and Hardart of New York, opened their doors for business. McDonalds or Burger Kings were not around at the time, but American-style hamburger was. There was also a corporate-style cafeteria called "A la Americaine" and next to it was "Mexicana," a more upper class conventional restaurant. The elite would go there to impress their dates.

Physically and culturally juxtaposing these restaurants were the curbside food stands, which sold anything from liver or meat kebabs, boiled calf's tongue, roast beef or chicken sandwiches, to boiled eggs with tomatoes, scallions, and parsley with a touch of amba (Indian pickled mango) stuffed in "sommoun" (a variant of the French baguette). That was a sure recipe for heartburn, and yes, we did have Alka-Seltzer. There was no shortage of up-to-date medicine, American Pfizer, Eli Lilly, and many other drug manufacturers were there doing good business.

There were no cabarets in this square; they were all lined-up, together with bars, casinos, secret love nests of madams, a few blocks away on Shari'e Abu Nawwaas, the cornice on Tigris. Rows and rows of mansions and luxury high-rise apartments overlooking Tigris were located further down on this palm tree-lined street.

The immediate riverbank was studded with bonfires burning a few meters away from each other, roasting shabboott, a variant of carp, unique to Tigris. This fish was the favorite of Baghdadis and foreigners alike; there would be no diplomatic banquet without shabboott cooked into masgoof gracing the table.

Before going to a bar, one would select live shabboott, which is then cooked on wooden posts stuck in the ground facing a bonfire. While fish faced the bonfire and roasted, people faced Tigris and enjoyed the scenery of rowboats silhouet-ting against the reflected lights from the Karkh side. A gentle breeze, like Um Kalthoum's songs in the background, blew, cooling the otherwise hot and humid evening.

When ready, masgoof was delivered to one's table at the designated bar. It is eaten with fingers and sips of Arak, with music, belly dancing, and merriment going on until the wee hours of the morning. People used to have fun! Some had so much fun that they had to be carried away on shoulders and put to bed.

In Abu Nawwaas, indeed in all of Baghdad, every night was an Um Kalthoum night, but one Thursday night a month was very special. That night Um Kalthoum sang a new song, live, from Cairo, broadcasting to the Arab world. Radios in chaikhanas and homes tuned in to Cairo to listen to her, and lived up, with each poetic verse, their personal experiences of love, and the heartaches, the disappointments, and the hopes associated with it. Poetic Baghdad lived in "One thousand and One Nights," and Um Kalthoum was its interlocutor: the undisputed Queen of the Arab heart! Her "Anta Umri" (You're My Life), "Al-Hubbi Kida" (Such Is Love), and "Ya Dhaalimni" (Oh, the one who has tyrannized me) made people reach to the depths of their emotions and respond "Allaah, Allaah..." in admiration and ecstasy. It was said that her audience numbered one hundred million. When she died in the 1970s, the entire Arab world, bar none, went into mourning. Decades after her passing away she still remains the number one Arab Chanteuse, ever.

Abu Nawwaas was also a cornice for innocent pleasures. Couples walked hand in hand at dusk for fresh air, and also to watch the sunset while having ice cream. Abu Nawwaas, like its namesake, the poet, was an avenue for lovers, a street for romance!

Running in the opposite direction from Abu Nawwaas was Rasheed Street, the vitrine of Baghdad! It connected Bab Al-Sharji Square with Bab Al-Mu'adham. At the entrance of the street, there was Hasso Ikhwaan (the Hasso Brothers), the showcase of English clothes for men. Diagonally across from them, there was Les Arcade, a very expensive boutique for women owned by Armenians. Further up the street was Vogue, another fashion boutique also owned by Armenians, the Fesjians. Further up was Photo Antran, a brother of Archbishop Torkom Manoogian, now the Patriarch of Jerusalem, who specialized in photographing antiquity and museums. In that vicinity, Nshaan Kumrigian's shop displayed American-made auto parts. The bakery of Cakeji Samuel (Samuel the cake maker), another Armenian, provided the passersby with a variety of cup cakes and pastries. Across the street from him was the shop of coffee roaster Garabed Kaptanian. He roasted mostly Brazilian, Colombian, and Yemeni coffee. His son Ohannes was my friend. Behind this shop and a few streets down was Dr. Stout's School for Boys, an American school, which I had so badly wanted to attend but could not, because of my mother's veto.

On the left, there was a showroom for Opel cars, which whetted my appetite every time I passed by, but couldn't afford it.

On King Faisal Square there was studio HAAS, a well-known gathering place for some Armenians, a club of sorts at the photography studios of my friend Tsolag Hovsepian. Here ideas, politics, literature, and current events were discussed with our only published poet, Levon (Carmen) Stepanian, and our friend Haigaz "Imastoon" (Wise) Mouradian; both were the intellectual leaders of the community. The rest of us participated, expressed opinions, made mistakes and ridiculous arguments, but always learned from these two men. It was there that I first heard of the Indian philosopher and poet, Sir Rabindranath Tagore. Haigaz was an expert on his philosophy.

It was here where *Bonjour Tristesse*, Françoise Sagan's revealing masterpiece, was first mentioned. It was here that I first heard of Robin Wright, Andre Gide, and Arthur Koestler. It was here that ideas for the next issue of the community weekly, *Koyamard*, were fermented.

Koyamard (struggle for survival) was licensed to Aram Duzian, who was also its editor. The "intellectual twins," Levon Carmen and Dr. Papken Papazian, formulated the contents. While the former was a writer and a poet, the latter was a critic, essayist, a community activist, and a skilled orator. Together they carried the community's cultural life on their shoulders.

In the late 1950s I was given the duty to oversee the production of the paper. Once a week I went to the printing presses of the *Iraq Times*, the only English language newspaper in Iraq, to print the paper, all 700 copies of it. The first copy that rolled off the press and smelled of ink gave me such a high, may be because of the ink, that I used to sing an aria from an opera, to celebrate the newborn. Luckily, the noise of the printing presses drowned my voice and saved me embarrassment.

Decades later, during my Ob-Gyn rotation in Englewood, New Jersey, whenever I delivered a baby I sang the same arias, taking my lead from the pitch of the baby's cry. To me the birth of a baby was like the birth of a new issue of *Koyamard*: exciting, invigorating, and inspiring. Both gave to me and to the world a fresh start, full of messages, destined to put an unpredictable mark on humanity.

The nurses couldn't understand my behavior, though they liked my duet with the baby better than my silence. There was only one such occasion when singing was replaced with whispers befitting a stillbirth, a different kind of an opera indeed!

Other shining vignettes of El-Rasheed street were two adjacent cafes; Cafe Brazil and Cafe Swiss, both were designed and furnished in the style of European cafes where you could sit for hours to have Capucino or Espresso, smoke a pipe, read the newspapers, chat with a friend, discuss an elegant topic, or just plain feel European, in silence.

In that vicinity there were two classical hotels: Sindbad (named after the legendary sailor), and Samiramis (named after the famous Assyrian Queen). These were distinctly colonial-English hotels; cavernous salons furnished with deep leather armchairs, large Persian rugs, ceiling fans, chandeliers, and superb service given by the Assyrian and Chaldian men who had learned butlering in the Levy Forces of Britain. They were experts in serving His Majesty's officers like royalty, and now they served whoever could afford to be a customer, especially those who tipped well.

Some Armenian elite used to gather there for their midday beer, peanuts, and gossip. Most of them had graduated from Baghdad College, a Jesuit-run exclusive high school. They were snobbish and considered themselves a cut above the rest of us, maybe because they rubbed shoulders with the sons of the most powerful Iraqi families, or because they now belonged to a superior culture, American. I was on the English side of the cultural divide.

Samiramis had a glorious past; it was the hotel where the British Army officers stayed and where Iraqi politicians, and dignitaries held their meetings and cocktail parties. Now only their ghosts roamed the corridors, and inhabited the rooms. If the walls could talk, they would reveal stories about deceptions and plots that the British wove to keep Iraq under control.

Like the Tigris, which flowed in its backyard, and like its namesake, the hotel was mysterious, absolutely enchanting, especially in midmorning and midafternoon when traffic was at its lowest and the corridors were quiet. In that silence, one could feel the walls vibrating with the joyful sounds of the British Officers laced with the giggles of the girls who had reached the summit with them, as if imitating Queen Samiramis, herself. One could feel the Assyrian Queen applauding their triumph, remembering hers, when she captured in battle the man she loved, the Armenian Prince Ara Keghetsig, who had rejected her love.

Now the British officers were gone, so were the giggles and the vibrations from the rooms. The hallways were silent except for the few people scattered here and there, who would whisper their orders to the "Boy" while keeping their eyes on the *Guardian* or the *Daily Telegraph*. A voice would snap a medical student out of a trance, "Would you like more coffee, Sir?"

One famous plot that the Hotel witnessed had the Kurds as its victims. The Ba'th Government of Ahmed Hassan El-Bakir played this one, soon after the Coup d'etat, which overthrew the regime of General Qasim on February 8, 1963: The

Kurdish representatives were staying at the Samiramis Hotel, awaiting transportation to the El-Rashid Military Base for their flight to Kurdistan. They had just concluded negotiations with the government about their rights, and they were to present the terms of a newly hammered-out Kurdish-Iraqi agreement to General Barzani, their boss, for approval.

Everybody was ecstatic for this unprecedented achievement. A large number of Kurds had come out of hiding in Baghdad to celebrate the agreement. A military bus pulled up in front of the hotel and the Kurdish leaders were ushered in with utmost respect, to be taken to the military airport for their flight to Barzan. When they got to the military base, the government arrested them instead. The negotiating team, and many Kurds who had surfaced, had fallen into a trap!

This trick was not new to Iraq or Asia Minor; the Khalifs of Baghdad and Damascus, and the Ottoman Sultans, had all practiced it to destroy their enemies.

In fact, U.S. Narcotic Agents had a similar plot in Florida a few years ago; they lured the drug kingpins to a party and then arrested them all.

Once more Kurds were deceived! Regardless, negotiations between Barzani and successive Iraqi Governments continued, in one form or another.

In the 1950s Baghdad was changing! American cultural invasion of the country was winning the battle against the British. Suddenly there were Lions and Rotary Clubs. Only the well-to-do or the well-connected knew about, and joined these clubs. Owning a tuxedo became a necessity and it symbolized social status. To wear a tuxedo and attend a party meant elevation to a new social echelon, an achievement indeed. Those who could fit the mold were accepted in these two clubs. It was an accomplishment to belong to one of them, but not the Free Masons, not any more; a clear shift of sentiments and orientation toward American way of life.

Ordinary Iraqis, indeed the entire Arab world considered Free Masons as Infidels, a spying network for Her Majesty's Government, the enemy of Islam, and Arab Nationalism, and as such surrogates of Israel. Iraqis called them "Farmassone."

When the American clubs appeared, they were perceived differently, perhaps because of America's demographic makeup, which included Arabs and Muslims, and because the United States did not have a colonialist past, in the classical sense of the word.

They were right! America was a different country then; we knew about it through USIS (United States Information Service) and from Hollywood movies: Christianity was dominant, people were churchgoers, and religious norms governed societal behavior. God was everywhere, in schools, Congress, and other institutions. Christmas was a religious event celebrated by all. We became aware of the constitution, and more importantly, the Bill of Rights. Hollywood showed us beautiful schools, neatly dressed students, and teachers who were respected, and revered. It showed movies about the FBI, and how the good guys always won.

The world loved America for its ideals: freedom, justice, fairness, charity, and lawfulness. She was the antithesis of colonial Europe who had sucked the blood of its colonies; the world knew the difference, and that's why they loved America. America was good, America was great, and Americans were proud to flaunt their passports wherever they went. The world dreamt of America, and wanted to live there.

American Presidents were considered larger than life. For the Armenians and the Kurds, one president stood above all, the twenty-seventh president, Woodrow Wilson. It was his philosophical stance and the academic background that made the League of Nations, which had coined the Treaty of Sevres, to delegate him with the task of apportioning land to Armenians and Kurds after the demise of the Ottoman Empire.

After meticulous, laborious work, which had lasted for three months, he had produced the Wilsonian Map delineating the boundaries of Western Armenia and Turkish Kurdistan, thus giving what belonged to Armenians to Armenians, and what belonged to the Kurds to the Kurds.

Unlike Syckes-Picot designs for dividing the defeated Ottoman Empire, Wilson's design did not materialize, but to date that Map remains to be the modus vivendi of all Armenians, globally! Yes, that is how America looked to the Iraqi youth, at the time!

University students, who frequented the USIS, liked the casual friendly atmosphere. They compared it with the British Institute, where culture was aplenty, leather armchairs spelled authority, and four o'clock tea was served in the proper manner, it felt too formal and restrictive. I liked it!

A decade later, at the British Medical Association (BMA) in Edinburgh, I felt at home as if I was at the British Institute of Baghdad. Throughout the building, people spoke in whispers; discussions were just that, not shouting matches; there were no distractions except for the gently falling snow, seen through floor-to-sealing windows. Tea was served in style. How civilized, I thought!

Why can't Iraq be like that? Is it really worth going back to Iraq? Can I go back to Iraq? Do I have anything in common with Iraqi culture? Questions, which for years to come tortured my mind and the minds of other Iraqi compatriots, engaged in postgraduate studies in Scotland.

In this Anglo-American cultural battle, it was clear that America was winning, and Iraq was on its way to modifying its orientation.

In the aftermath of the 1958 coup d'etat, the successive governments closed these clubs, and prosecuted only the Free Masons as traitors. Years later the members' list of a Mason lodge was found in an unclaimed safety box of a bank. Those on the list were arrested and sentenced to long-term imprisonments, accused of being British agents. A prominent, eighty-year-old Armenian Professor Dr. Hagop Tchobanian was amongst them. He too was tried, and sentenced to a ten-year imprisonment. After serving some time, he was released, possibly because of his age. A few years later, when Saddam Hussein assumed power, he decorated him with the highest civilian medal, the "Rafideyn Medal," for being one of the founding fathers of the Royal College of Medicine.

The Medical School was one of the accomplishments of the Royal regime. Its founders, Professors Saa'ib Shawkat, and Haashim Al-Whitri, medical doctors in King Faisal I entourage entering Iraq, joined Dr. Sinderson and Professor Tchobanian in starting the school. This was one of the positive things that colonial Britain did for Iraq. Within a decade, the school rivaled that of the American University of Beirut (AUB). However unlike AUB, Baghdad University had not expanded, there were the Law School, Teachers' College, School of Engineering, School of Pharmacy, and the School of Commerce.

In the 1950s Baghdad University was expanded to include many other colleges and institutes, and each college expanded to accommodate more co-ed students, who were pouring in from all over the country and from all classes of society, seeking education. That was progress! Women from all social strata attended the university without restrictions. Contrary to popular American belief, Iraqi women were free, in fact I personally know of a woman who in the 1920s was licensed to drive a car in Baghdad!

The university setting, however, was a fertile ground for fermentation and crystallization of political ideologies, which, in turn, propelled into a more effective dissent and action, in the street. Communists, Ba'this, and other nationalist organizations were at work, fiercely competing to win the hearts and minds of students. At times, the opposition united in demonstrations against their common enemy, the Royal regime.

Leaders emerged, who later became instrumental in changing and directing the course of political events that determined the future of Iraq itself. Some of what Adnaan Azzawi, and people like him were doing in the Iraq Pharmacy, in the late 1940s, had come to fruition in the 1950s; in the political battleground, there was a cadre of hardened Communists who were competing with Nationalists, Ba'this, and other dissident currents for position and influence.

Azeez Al Haaj, for instance, one of the more ardent and prominent Communist leaders, emerged from the student ranks of Teachers' College. Those of us who were not participants were considered outcasts, and outcasts we really were! At least I was, because I hated both Nasser, and Communism, therefore had no reason to protest. Besides the system had been good to me, it had accepted me in medical school regardless of my race or religion; I was an Iraqi, period!

The University was established based on British system and curricula. However, American competition in Iraq was not far behind. Boston's Jesuit Fathers, who had established Baghdad College decades earlier to cater to Arab elite, and propagate Jesuit ideals, expanded to become the Al-Hikma University. This university, like Baghdad College, educated and indoctrinated pro-American cadre that believed in the American way of life. Their alumni still meet in Boston, and other American cities, once every two years, for nostalgia and camaraderie; the majority of them have prospered. Britain had no such institution.

Thus, a golden age of education dawned in Iraq; Now Iraq had, for the first time since the twelfth century Abbasid era Mustansirriyah University, two universities that educated and produced scientists, teachers, and intellectuals who were the envy of the Arab world. They were very much needed to educate the country, which had 90 percent illiteracy.

Progress was also in areas other than education. In the early 1950s work had already begun on gigantic water projects. The Dokan and Derbendi Khan Dams, both in Iraqi Kurdistan, were built over the Greater and Lesser Zabs. The Haweeja irrigation project in Kirkuk was in progress, nearing completion. These projects were to irrigate millions of acres of fertile, rain-dependant land, and settle otherwise nomadic tribes.

There was talk about expanding Habbaniya Lake and Habbaniya air force base, which was an active British Royal Air Force (RAF) base. From there the British had exerted air control over Baghdad, especially during Germanophile Rasheed Ali's coup, which briefly brought Nazis to power in 1943. The base also served as a symbol of Britain's presence in Iraq.

This base had great strategic importance, which is why, during lengthy negotiations with the British aimed at ending their mandate on Iraq, both sides fought bitterly over it; Britain was adamant about its continued control, and the Iraqis wanted to remove the last vestiges of overt British presence in their land. Also in 1948, when the Portsmouth Treaty was negotiated, Habbaniya was the nidus of their discord, the plum to fight over. Habbaniya was Britain's strategic base to control not only the skies of Iraq, but also that of the region, especially the oil fields of Abadan, the Baba Gurgur of Iran.

Habbaniya was a real British colony within independent Iraq. There were some Armenians, who worked there in civilian support capacity, and lived in camps set for families, but the majority of the inhabitants were Assyrians of Tiari and Jeelo tribes. These were mercenaries, the Levy Army; a military force, which the British recruited to project might, influence policy, and impose its will on Iraq. In fact, in the 1920s the Levy forces were used to quash the Euphrates Uprising of the Arab tribes against the British. In 1924 the Tiari-Levys were brought to Kirkuk with the intent of sending them to Suleymania to quash the Kurdish independence movement led by Sheikh Mahmoud Al-Berzinji. While in Kirkuk, they raised havoc in the city and committed a number of murders of the local Turkomans. A trivial dispute with a butcher in Qoriya bazaar had triggered the event. They had done the same in Mosul on August 15, 1923, around the time of the League of Nation's Plebiscite. In 1914, Tiari Assyrians had declared war against the Ottomans and fought on the side of Britain. This had created a negative view of the Assyrians:

Arabs hated them for fighting Arab uprisings, and considered them a Fifth Column in their midst, despite the fact that they were Iraqis. Turkomans hated them for their fighting against the Ottomans and for committing atrocities in Kirkuk, and Kurds hated them for helping to destroy their independence movement by fighting with the British against them. All these events had created a very big ethnic divide in Iraq, which continued for decades.

Britain never let the Assyrians down. When the Levy mercenaries retired or got discharged from the Army, they were employed by the IPC. When I was in the IPC, I was lucky to have an Assyrian, Lazar, in my employ. He had had an excellent training in the British officer's mess in Habbaniya, his certificate said so, and it bore the signature of a Colonel Johnson who was recommending him for employment, without reservation. Lazar held on to that piece of paper the way a traveler would hold onto his passport, with pride and care: it was his lifeline. Colonel Johnson was honest in his recommendation; Lazar discharged his duties as if still serving a British officer who was enjoying the spoils of colonialism.

Not all these projects and progress made an immediate impact on the lives of the ordinary Iraqi. Trickle-down economy was leaving masses of people behind. Although a core of middle class had formed, statistically it was negligible; the poor remained poor, and the wealthy got wealthier. That distinction did not clash with the social understanding of Islam: since Allah was the giver and the distributor of wealth, he had given to some more than the others; some were meant to be poor and some wealthy, that was Allah's will. What one owned was his kismet and naseeb (luck and fate), decided by Allah! Everything belonged to Allah, and the wealthy were only custodians of this wealth; Allah has mandated that it is their duty to take care of the poor and the needy, on his behalf. Sometimes they did! This was the conviction of a Muslim, which set a social milieu.

This centuries-old conviction was of course rejected by the atheist Communists who were blaming poverty on the corrupt wealthy, who had monopolized every avenue of wealth leaving the masses behind, wanting and needy. "These people have raided Allah's treasury, these people have no conscience, no morality, they have robbed the people in the name of Allah," they argued. They presented Communism as an alternative social order where justice prevailed, where all shared wealth equally, and where there was only one class. They did their utmost to disrupt the status quo by setting the poor against the wealthy.

The Winds of Change

It was the mid-1950s. The country was bubbling with political problems: The "shame" of the losses against Israel was still lingering, and the Palestinian Issue was a big negative infesting the Arab thought. Opposition against Britain and the West was getting more intense; people still considered them as colonialists and blamed them for transplanting a "cancer in the Arab body," in the form of the European Jew.

Exploiting the situation and spearheading the opposition was the Communist Party, which, despite the hanging of Fahad and the Communist hierarchy a decade earlier, was still strong, and the Al-Qai'da was still in circulation.

Events in Iran gave the ICP a big boost in morale: Mohammed Musadegh, the Prime Minister of Iran had just nationalized the Anglo-Iranian Oil Company in Abbadan (1952–1953), and led a coup against the Shah who fled the country with his wife, Empress Soraya. They landed in Baghdad unannounced, on their way to Italy. My friend Tsolag Hovsepian of famed Photo Haas, was summoned to the airport to document the event.

The Musadegh coup was a big gain for the Soviets, and a big, big loss for Britain and the United States. They were concerned that Musadegh would nationalize the Anglo-Iranian oil company of Abbadan, which could spill over Baba Gurgur. Musadegh did nationalize the company, and yes, it did spill over Baba Gurgur, though not directly and not immediately.

The Musadegh coup shook the world, not only because of Abbadan, but also because the new anti-West government's willingness to facilitate Russia's access to the warm waters of the Persian Gulf and the Indian Ocean; a fulfillment of centuries-old Russian dreams.

Musadegh was an aristocrat, and definitely not a Communist or Communist sympathizer, regardless Tudeh Party (Iran's Communist Party) falsely claimed credit for deposing the Shah. Musadegh nationalized the Anglo-Iranian Company and returned it to its "legitimate owners, the people of Iran."

The new situation was not acceptable to the West, especially the United States. Tudeh was so strong that even Musadegh government was not stable. Iran, de facto, was in the hands of the Communists, which threatened its oil rich neighbors, especially Baba Gurgur.

For the United States in particular, the coup was a defeat in the Cold War Theater, and more importantly a loss of strategic territory. Ike had to react swiftly, and that is exactly what he did! The CIA in collaboration with General Zaahidi, a Shah loyalist, launched a countercoup engineered by General Schwarzkopf (General Norman Schwarzkopf's father), and restored the Peacock Throne. The countercoup also restored, though in a modified way, Western authority on the oil industry in Abbadan, the Baba Gurgur of Iran.

The Iranian events could not have passed without adversely affecting and alarming the Iraqi Royal family. The Middle Eastern political climate was unstable, so was the Hashemite throne in Iraq. They were on a state of high alert, taking all necessary precautions. So was Britain, which had learned a bitter lesson in Iran and was not about to allow the same to happen in Baba Gurgur.

Two additional events contributed to the instability of Iraq in the mid-1950s and strengthened the hands of the opposition:

(a) The 1956 Suez Campaign in which Britain, France, and Israel attacked Egypt, and
(b) The decision the United States had taken to deny financing the Aswan Dam project.

Both these issues proved to the Arab street once more that the West was pursuing their sinister intentions against the Arab world. Their stance fueled the fires of dissent against Iraq, which was siding with the West anyway.

On the other hand the pro-British, or let us say the anti-Nasserites blamed the United States for its amateurish foreign policies; they could not understand why America:

(a) Issued an ultimatum to Britain, France, and Israel and aborted the Suez campaign immediately. They wanted Nasser out, "Ike should have let Anthony Eden beat the shit out of Nasser, that Commie," they would say; and
(b) Did not finance the Aswan Dam, and missed a golden opportunity to win the hearts and minds of Egyptians and Arabs at large. They thought that allowing the Soviet Union to build Aswan, would give them high marks in the Middle East. People would say, "Americans are naive, they

don't know foreign policy; the Middle East is going Red." In other words, American action on one subject, and inaction on the other weakened the hand of pro-West Arabs, and this aggravated the Middle East instability.

Paradoxically, the Nationalists who blamed the United States for not financing the dam, praised her for stopping the trilateral aggression.

A day after Ike's ultimatum, the Soviets issued a similar ultimatum of their own to stop the Suez campaign. This gave the Communists tremendous propaganda ammunition, which they used to its fullest: their propaganda machine highlighted the West's Imperialist stance, praised the Soviet Union's role in stopping the aggression against an innocent Arab nation, and portrayed them as champions of peace. They successfully obscured the fact that it was Ike who stopped the aggression in the first place, not the Soviet Union.

In this kind of a regional turmoil, a new era of economic progress and prosperity was dawning on Iraq. The progress excluded political reform.

Though there was a parliament with upper and lower houses, its members had earned their seats through fraud and deception, rigging the elections. The Parliament consisted of "yes" men. There was no effective opposition, and whatever there was did not deviate from the government line. In one word, there was nothing resembling democracy in Iraq.

But Iraq has never had democracy in its glorious past. Yes, millennia ago, Babylonian Hammurabi's Codes governed society, but that never provided for plurality. Even the glorious Abbasid Dynasty, with its Khalifs, mathematicians, astronomers, chemists, physicians, poets, and military leaders, did not have democracy, or plurality rule.

Ruler-subject style of government has always been the norm for Iraq, indeed the entire Arab and Islamic world. The rulers have always hoped for obedient subjects, and the subjects have always hoped for a just ruler. They both have failed.

Iraq of the 1950s was not different; there were no plans for political reforms. Iraq was busy with major construction projects and creating a modern infrastructure for the country rather than pursuing the so-called Arab Cause; Uniting the Arab countries, getting rid of Israel, and getting rid of the neocolonialists.

Iraq's solidarity with the Arab world was not solid; it never really exceeded lip service to this or that Arab problem. The League of Arab Nations of which Iraq was a founding member, was a joke, a club of sorts where the foreign ministers or their deputies got together to discuss pending issues facing the Arab world, then release a routine communiqué full of rhetoric fed to them by their Western handlers. It is fair to state that at no time, since her founding in 1945, has The League seriously addressed issues vital to the Arab nation, to the satisfaction of the Arab public opinion, nor have their decisions and efforts resulted in tangible results.

As the Arab individual became more and more educated, acquired political skills, and accumulated experience, he lost faith in his rulers and their system of governance. People demanded political freedom, prosperity, and respect for human rights; they had none. They demanded healthy and just replacement to the antiquated and corrupt Ottoman system, which was still infesting the Arab constitution.

This kind of a situation angered not only increasingly educated Iraqis, but also the ordinary citizen. Despite the political stagnation, the economic development was progressing in oil rich Iraq. The government had formed the "Construction Board" consisting of highly qualified technocrats, and empowered it to manage Iraq's transformation into a modern State. They had two tremendous assets at their disposal to achieve that goal: oil and water.

Aside from the fully developed Baba Gurgur fields, there was virgin land awaiting exploration. Drilling for oil had already begun by petroleum companies, all Western concessions, in E'in Zala near Mosul (now Iraqi Kurdistan) and Basra in the south.

Global demand for oil had increased, and Baba Gurgur was destined to stand up to the challenge. Increased production required a larger pipeline to bring oil to the Mediterranean shores. In 1948, after the creation of Israel, or thereabouts, Iraq had shut down the "H" line, which originated in Baba Gurgur, and passed through Jordan to Haifa. The only operational pipeline was the "K" line, which also originated in Baba Gurgur and joined the "T" line, at the Iraqi-Syrian border, after passing through K-1, K-2, and K-3 pumping stations. The faucets were in Tripoli on the Mediterranean.

Turrif-Burden, an Anglo-American company was at work laying a new thirty-two-inch pipeline under the sand to replace the twelve-inch line. This line also originated in Baba Gurgur, and headed west to end in Tripoli and Banias. I saw these American experts laying the pipeline and admired their capacity for hard work and consumption of beer and thick, juicy, steaks; I was an IPC medical officer stationed in K-2 then K-1.

Water was prominently and permanently on the agenda: The construction Board created projects to harness the waters of Zab El-Kabir and Zab El-Sagheer (The Greater and the Lesser Zabs), the two main tributaries of the Tigris. These originated in the mountains of Kurdistan, including Qalah Dize where we had met workers measuring the depth of the snow, to predict the water flow in the spring into these tributaries. I believe one of the reasons for trying to harness waters pouring into the Tigris was Baghdad's vulnerability to flooding, which almost paralyzed the city every spring.

Plans were drawn, and soon implemented, to build the Dokan and Derbendi Khan Dams on these two rivers, in northeastern Iraq. The projects displaced dozens of Kurdish villages, adding to the frustrations of the people who had no say in the matter.

Tigris originated in Turkish Kurdistan and flowed down to Mosul and Baghdad without major restrictions. Turkey had not yet built dams on it, and could not ration what can flow to Iraq. There were constant consultations between Iraq and Turkey for control of the waters of the Tigris. So the present dispute between the two countries over water, stemming from the newly built Ataturk Dam projects, had originated over half a century ago. Regardless, water, like oil, was aplenty in Iraq, Mesopotamia: the eastern pole of the "Fertile Crescent."

These huge projects did not deter the Communists, the Nasserites, the Nationalists, and the Kurds from pursuing their political agenda and their goal of getting rid of the monarchy. This internal instability rendered Iraq vulnerable to outside forces that were desperately trying to get control over Baba Gurgur.

Despite vigorously fighting the dissidents and the subversives, and gaining some ground, the Royal regime continued to remain unstable and vulnerable. Britain had to do something different, something preventive, to take the initiative away from the others: a coup perhaps? Perhaps!

If this is a rational approach to the problem it is then not illogical to conclude that a general, Abdul Karim Qasim, who was known to be pro-Britain, and enjoyed the trust of the Prime Minister was entrusted to lead the coup of 1958 on behalf of the British Government. Logical deliberations conclude that, to prevent repetition of the Iranian disaster, Britain did plan and execute this preemptive strike.

To further this hypothesis the observers of the time cited the British Ambassador's meeting with Qasim some hours after the coup and his declaration that, "Oil will flow, as before, and the prices will remain the same," as proof positive to their belief.

Approximately one year into the Revolution, the political dynamics of the country had changed significantly: the Nationalists, the Ba'this, and the Nasserites were nullified as effective forces and the Communists were on the go—they gained strength by the day! Their demands for power grew, and grew, and grew—so much so that it overwhelmed Qasim and posed a challenge to his authority.

On May 1, 1959, the International Labor day, about half a million people, organized by Communists, demonstrated in the streets of Baghdad demanding power-sharing with Qasim, and appointment of at least two Communists to the Cabinet. They were raising banners depicting the usual Communist slogans of peace, friendship, and socialism. Their standard slogan for the day was "Asha Za'imi, Abdul Karimi, Hizb Al Shiyou'i bil hukum matlab Adheemi" (Long live the Chief Abdul Karim [Qasim], Communist party's participation in government is a grand demand). The "sole leader" perceived this as an ad hominem attack and a threat to his authority.

By July 1959, the aftereffects of the Mosul massacres, the massacres of the Turkomans in Kirkuk, and the Communist power sharing demands were still disrupting people's minds. The People's Court added tremendous anxiety and created profound instability to the situation.

It was obvious that the Communists had controlled the country, and their militia, the Muqaawama al-Sha'biya (People's Resisting Militia) was raising hell from the north to the south, arbitrarily arresting, torturing, killing, and intimidating people. Whether Qasim himself was a Communist was irrelevant, the country was red.

The situation in the country was tense also because the Communists had committed on July 14, 1959, a mass murder in Kirkuk. They had massacred a score of Turkomans, and buried tens in a ditch, alive. Two of my friends were amongst them, Mohammed Awtchi and Jaheed Fakhri. At the same time they had killed two prominent Turkoman brothers, Dr. Ihsaan and Colonel 'Atta Khayralla.

Qasim's government, cognizant of the massacre, had interfered and those who had committed the crimes were tried and sentenced to death; but Qasim did not carry out the executions, possibly because of Communist party pressures. This act added to peoples' suspicion that he was indeed a Communist. The Turkoman community was angry and felt shortchanged and demanded justice, to no avail.

Iraq's problems did not end by removing the Royal regime. Yes, a republic was established, but hours after its birth the political landscape was already jaundiced indicating a sick infancy and a sicklier adolescence. The prerevolution agreements and understandings struck between its leaders were now null and void. The struggle that had ensued between Qasim and Arif was now magnified. Each leader had an ideological motivation to implement. Arif's: to unite with Nasser, and Qasim's: to block it. They could find no common ground, and the argument evolved into personal hatred. Yesterday's comrades in arms were now avowed enemies.

The dispute came to a potentially criminal end when Arif pulled a gun on Qasim and pointed at him, but couldn't fire, then broke into tears. When those present disarmed him, Qasim asked him why he wanted to kill him? Arif said, "I didn't want to kill you, I wanted to commit suicide," to which Qasim replied, "Why don't you go home and kill yourself there?"

The ideologues that backed Qasim and Arif brought the dispute to the fore through newspapers, demonstrations, liquidations, and violence. The discord, leading to opposition and enmity, was soon established amongst the Iraqis at large.

A "U-Turn"

All these events took their toll on Qasim. He felt ostracized and increasingly vulnerable. He had successfully fended off demands to form the Revolutionary Council, he had successfully isolated Arif and the idea of joining Nasser's train, and now he was facing a Communist takeover—the threat was real! The fact that the Communists had committed the atrocities and were demanding cabinet posts was a real threat to his authority. In appearance and de-facto he was not the strongman he once was! They had taken over the country doing as they pleased in his name. People blamed Qasim for all the ills, and the anarchy that befell the country; Qasim had no choice but to launch a campaign to remove this threat by destroying them. He did!

In a speech delivered on July 19, 1959, to Christian worshipers in Mar Yousif Church (Saint Joseph Church), he clearly and forcefully, denounced Communism. He called them "fawdhawiyoun" (anarchists) and condemned their atrocities: the pogroms of Mosul, which was committed on his behalf to quash the Shawwaaf uprising, and the pogrom of Kirkuk.

Now he portrayed the Communists as criminals, something, which the ordinary citizen knew, anyway! But the questions people asked were simple! Why now? If Qasim were honest he would have condemned all these atrocities when they happened, better yet he could have prevented them from happening in the first place. The answer was obvious: he had to use the Communists to destroy his enemies, and then destroy them because they rose above their shoes and posed as a real threat to his authority.

The parishioners received the speech with honest, thunderous applause; it was a pleasant surprise for them and the world. The ordinary Iraqis, who were listening on the radio and TV, were jubilant: they had had enough of roadblocks, checkpoints, extortions, assassinations, and plain oppressions, imposed on them by the Communists, for a whole year. To the outside world his action indicated change of policy in favor of the West, and that it was! People looked at Qasim as a man of high moral standards, a man of justice. Qasim came out smelling like a rose!

The freedoms that Qasim had brought to the country had exposed the Communist party structure. Qasim and, most importantly, the West knew them. Some say that his original tactic of unleashing the Communists was a ploy to expose the entire organization. It could very well have been! It bore fruits for him, and the West: it weakened the Aflaqi opposition, thus preventing union between Iraq and the United Arab Republic, and it exposed the entire Communist organization, something that the Royal regime and the British Intelligence had failed to do in the past.

Now, he and the West were in a good position to make their long-anticipated move. They knew who the Communists were and who was their Central Committee; all they had to do was pick them up, one by one, like ripe berries. And pick they did! Qasim launched a campaign of mass arrests against the Communists. He arrested and incarcerated all of them. The prisons were now full, this time with Communists who had changed places with us.

In his book *Testimonial for History* (April 2002) Azeez Al-Haaj of the Communist Party Central Committee, states that the decision to challenge Qasim and insisting on sharing power was the biggest mistake that the party made at the time. He is right! Qasim shredded the Party into pieces; however by doing that he also debased himself and now his support, feeble as it was, came from ordinary people who had no political affiliations, savvy, or even inclination.

The shift in direction opened the doors to a new era, but also created a new political vacuum, new political realities, new challenges, and new problems, which Qasim had to face.

The Mar Yousif speech was a turning point in the political climate of Iraq: It was radical, it was effective, and it was a shrewd political move on Qasim's part. Thousands like me, who were incarcerated—except for the conspirators who had actually participated militarily in the Shawwaaf uprising—were released immediately, but almost everybody was bitter and not supportive of Qasim; by releasing us, he did not win our hearts.

The Aflaqis who, started to intensify their political activity and gain notoriety, prominence, and power to control the street, immediately filled the political vacuum created by the paralyzed Communist Party.

In September, Ba'th party propaganda and publications, such as Michel Aflaq's doctrinal *Fi Sabeel Al-Ba'th* (On the Path to Revival), flooded the stores. However, that was only a prelude to mobilizing the people for the pursuit of their agenda of union and socialism ala 'Aflaq. Demonstrations and Ba'th political influence was now clearly a force to reckon with!

Despite Qasim's tolerance of Ba'th's newly acquired notoriety and political gains, their enmity toward him did not cease; first for the harm that he had done to them, and second for the genuine ideological and political irreconcilable differences, which had separated them.

Anti-Qasim, and pro-Nasser forces, now collectively seen as Aflaqis, accused him, and rightly so, with breach of initial contract, agreements, and understandings: He had deviated the course of the July 14 Revolution from its intended goal, away from joining the Arab caravan. Qasim had to go!

Opposition was not confined to just demonstrations and shaping public opinion, it included covert plans to eliminate Qasim, partly for revenge, and partly for what he had done to them and their cause. Revenge they attempted on October 7, 1959!

On that day I was working in the office of one of my colleagues who had gone to Lebanon on vacation. The office was in Raas Al-Greyya, an area of narrow passageways, so narrow that the windows on either side of the alley were in kissing proximity. To the left of my desk was a high window overlooking Shari' Al-Rasheed (street), which was only about forty feet away. It was late afternoon. I had just given a Bedouin patient the bad news that she was suffering from cancer of the throat. Both she and her daughter were devastated and I consoled them by saying, "Everything is in God's hands. He alone knows who will live and who will die." I had barely finished the sentence, when I heard the rata-tat-a-tat of a submachine gun followed by a bomb explosion. I looked out of the window and saw a damaged car, scattered shoes and sandals, and people running in all directions in panic. We didn't know what was happening! My doorman immediately shut the main door, and we ducked in front of the window, in fear and curiosity.

Within a minute or so, I saw two soldiers carrying Qasim from his armpits and desperately asking anyone for help. They appeared to be in shell shock heading toward my office. I heard them beg, "Ya ahli khair, ya ahli sawaab, ilhhagu, az-Za'im indherab! (Oh good doers! help! the Chief is hit).

No one responded, neither did we! For a moment I surrendered to my humanitarian instincts and wanted to help; after all, I was a doctor pledged to help the sick, but within an instant, I decided otherwise; I wasn't prepared to take a risk to save someone who had caused my incarceration and torture. Yes I was also a Christian, supposed to forgive, but not to that degree!

Having received no response from our alley, the guards returned Qasim to the street where the car stood, ruined and smoldering. Soon an ambulance arrived and whisked him away. The street remained paralyzed and in darkness. To date, it is not clear who turned the lights off!

We were shocked too, and didn't know what to anticipate except more danger, more turbulence, and more uncertainty. Was this the start of something big? Whose work was it? How badly did they wound Qasim? If he makes it, how is he going to take revenge? All these were questions that cascaded into my thoughts within seconds. Events of the passed few months rushed before my eyes with thundering speed.

A half hour or more had passed when things had finally settled down. We let the patients out, and closed the office. I thought the best thing for me to do is to go to a safe place until the situation becomes clearer. Dr. Tchobanian's house, which was close to my office, was the practical refuge. Mrs. Tchobanian received me with her usual optimism and compassion, and tried to alleviate my fears.

After an hour or so, I was calm enough to go home, on foot, passing through the narrow alleys of Raas Al-Greyya. Later I learned that I had walked the same escape route as the assailants, one of whom being a young man named Saddam Hussein. He and his colleagues must have been real amateurs in planning and carrying out the attack; they had fired from both sides of the car, unintentionally hitting each other: One of them had died, and Saddam was wounded in the leg. By all measures, the operation had been clumsy, leaving behind a wounded Za'eem, his dead chauffeur, a dead comrade, and a few wounded coconspirators.

Rumors started circulating, but the Ba'th Party put an end to it by claiming responsibility. They had decided to eliminate Qasim soon after Shawwaaf and Mosul, to avenge the atrocities supported, possibly engineered, by him, and also to remove the main obstacle blocking union with Nasser, and to end the Communist domination. His liquidation would have redirected the Revolution to its originally intended path. Remove from power a man who had deceived his comrades in arms, monopolized power, and refused to form the Revolutionary Council.

> He was the one who had given Communists a free hand to raise havoc in the country; he was responsible for the incarceration and death of thousands of people. For all these reasons and more, his elimination was "haqq"(just) the opposition argued.

The government captured seventy-eight Ba'thi suspects to face Mahdaawi's court. Saddam was free; he had managed to flee to Syria, and eventually to Egypt to become Nasser's guest. Now, these assailants had the priority before the court; the old regime and Shawwaaf conspirators had to wait for their turn to appear on stage again.

Within a few hours of the shooting, Qasim appeared on television with his left arm in a cast. He assured his "beloved citizens" that he was alright and that he would lose no time in working for their prosperity and well being, even from the hospital. He accused these traitors of being "agents of the enemies of Iraq" and promised swift action against them. After a brief hospitalization he was released, looking triumphant and in the saddle again.

Qasim's assassination attempt did not augur well for the country, for it was a precursor to rigorous events, an indication of Ba'th's resolve and popularity.

The following day of the assassination attempt, the authorities told us to stay open that night, with all the lights on. Colonel Mahdaawi and Colonel Maajid Ameen, the chief prosecutors, were to visit our alley for inspections. I was scared to death, not because I had done anything wrong, but because I had just come out of detention, and I was on their black list, still a suspect. If they were thorough in their questioning, they may spot me, and detain me for questioning, which meant more beating and more torture.

The investigators were late. We waited for them. Finally they came! An entourage of submachine-gun-wielding soldiers protected them with their gun barrels pointed upward toward the windows. They looked left, they looked right (as if inspecting), did not question anyone, and left after a minute or two. I breathed a sigh of relief; obviously, fear had led me to give them more credit than they deserved. It was all a part of poorly staged and executed comedy by both sides.

The assault on his life must have had an impact on his thinking; in January 1960 Qasim announced legalization of all political parties except the Communist party, which remained barred from official functioning. Once more, the Communists went underground to start rebuilding anew, but they were so weak that they couldn't play an effective role in influencing policy. The country, at least on the surface, quietened down for a while.

With all these convulsions, IPC kept on pumping oil, albeit on borrowed time. Qasim, having lost his base, exerted pressure on the oil companies for change, so that he could regain some lost credibility. IPC obliged and made some concessions: establishing and implementing the "Iraqization Program," a program that mandated replacing the British experts with qualified Iraqis. The agreement was not without economic benefits for IPC, since the Iraqi employee, with the same qualifications as his British counterpart, cost less. Qasim looked good!

This program went well; a number of American- and British-trained Iraqi engineers were already in place operating oil production units. There were others, like my friend Nafi' Abdullah, Iraq's ex-Air Attaché in Washington, who held high administrative positions; he was one of five Assistant General Managers.

I dare say that none of these Iraqis were dissidents or held anti-British sentiments. Having studied abroad and modified their culture to Western norms, they were misfits in both cultures: to the British they were Iraqis, not to be fully trusted, and to the Iraqis they were Westerners with suspicious loyalties, especially those that had returned with British or American wives. Regardless, in the eyes of the law, they were Iraqis and that fit the Iraqization bill.

Though this bill changed the demographic makeup of IPC, it did not change the political orientation of the company; the key posts remained in the hands of the British. Some Iraqis, who replaced the British, had stronger pro-British sentiments than the Britons who were repatriated. For all practical purposes, Baba Gurgur was still in British hands!

I was one such Iraqi. One day, my friend Levon Carmen (Stepanian) who was an employee of Khanqin Oil Company, headquartered in Baghdad, told me there was a job waiting for me in IPC Kirkuk. Unbeknownst to me, he had arranged it through his boss Mr. Clerk. I was appointed on the spot after filling some forms. I was very happy! Almost overnight, I had moved from the dungeons of the death row cell, to the luxury of life in IPC, where I had a chance to live up my childhood dreams of an English lifestyle, akin to that of Allen Chapman.

My first assignment was in K-2, a pumping station near Baiji, located south of Tikrit, Saddam's birthplace. The station itself was a fenced-in gigantic compound, which housed a huge pumping station, homes for the workers, homes and gardens for the top brass, a soccer field, a club for the workers, and a posh one for the hierarchy. There was a dispensary for the workforce and their immediate family, and another health station just outside the fence for the neighboring tribes. I was in charge of both.

The top brass of K-2, like the labor force, was diverse: The station administrator was Colonel Dawood Salman Al-Badr, a Kuwaiti who had just retired from the Iraqi Army. The chief mechanical engineers running the gigantic pumping station were Isma'eel Ibraaheem Al-Raawi, an Arab nationalist and a staunch supporter of Nasser, from Raawa near Ramadi (Now al-Anbaar province), and Yuwaash Ibraaheem, an Assyrian, whose father-in-law, Soski, had been an officer in the Levy, and whose loyalty to the British Crown was unquestionable.

Bahaa'addin Wali, Chief of Transportation, was a Turkoman transferee from Kirkuk whose job was to oversee transporting material for the thirty-two-inch pipelines being constructed by Turrif-Burden, to take oil to Banias, on the Mediterranean. I was the fifth man, an Armenian.

Though this arrangement of diverse ethnic makeup represented a microcosm of Kirkuk, it was not entirely without deliberate intent and design. The management had arranged it thus in order to guarantee security, safety, and smooth oil pumping operations: having five people, one Kuwaiti conservative Arab, one dissident Arab, one Assyrian, one Turkoman, and one Armenian made conspiracy and collusion to sabotage Baba Gurgur, impossible. Smart planning, I thought! Given the political climate of the day, this kind of a scenario was prudent, not paranoiac.

Work at the outside dispensary was hectic. I used to see dozens of Bedouins a day and send them away with medicine provided by IPC. That was nothing new; for years IPC had substituted negligent Baghdad in providing health care to these people, who claimed to be the cousins of the cousins of some third-rate laborer. But now the political climate had changed the dynamics of the IPC-Government relationship. IPC was no longer feeling obligated to be generous beyond its official commitments; to spend money and provide health care for people that did not belong to the IPC family. So they decided to terminate the services at the out-of-fence dispensary and stop extending this help to the tribes. That did not sit well with the laborers.

The labor union considered this as an unfair policy; their families and the tribes were left without health care, and without free medicines; they were adamant to restore the status quo.

IPC maintained that they are not the government, and that it was not their legal or moral obligation to provide health care to ineligible people.

The obstacle was the language of the agreements, reached previously, between the two sides, which had dictated that, "IPC was to provide health care for the worker and his family and dependents." The misunderstanding was in the interpretation of the word "dependents"; for the worker it meant his extended family numbering dozens, and for the IPC it meant the wife and the children, and those who actually lived with the worker, under one roof, within the confines of the K-2 Station.

There was a deadlock! Both sides held a confrontational posture, a tense situation indeed! The workers were threatening to strike, which would have shut down the pipeline, creating turmoil in the global oil markets.

Being the medical officer who was running both health facilities, I could not avoid the issue. My initial casual conversations with the Union evolved into unofficial negotiations, which then became formal.

The union leaders, who had been my patients at one time or another, considered me as their representative. They accepted my offer of providing everyone with medical examination, but not medicine; it was a compromise that the union accepted reluctantly. Strike was averted, and oil kept on flowing to the Mediterranean.

I notified the management of this agreement. The next day, my superior Dr. William (Bill) Bain summoned me to Kirkuk. When I entered his office at K-1 Hospital, he greeted me warmly and wasted no time in getting to the subject:

"Henry!" he said, "Who gave you the right to negotiate on behalf of IPC? Who authorized you? Who do you think you are, some kind of a lawyer? How can you do such a thing without my knowledge?" He went on, and on, and on, to put me in my proper place. When he felt he had said enough, he continued: "Now tell me the terms of the agreement!"

When I told him what I had achieved and the reasoning behind it, he said, in a much gentler and appreciative voice, "Henry, you have done a marvelous job which our negotiators couldn't do, but don't do things like this again without our authorization. Promise me that you will never again engage in such matters without my permission!" With the next breath, his anger gone, he expressed thanks for settling the dispute, and averting a potential disaster.

I am not sure if it was my reward, but almost immediately he arranged for a medical scholarship for me in Edinburgh, an event that changed the course of my life.

More Turmoil

It was the spring of 1963. I had just returned from Edinburgh. Now I was transferred to K-1 Hospital, which was the central hospital for the entire company, including Syria and Lebanon.

In a Ba'thi coup Qasim had gone. He and his cronies, including Mahdaawi, were shot in the presence of his old comrades, on television, live. His last wish had been to keep his eyes unmasked, because, "I want to see the bullet coming," while his cousin Mahdaawi had soiled his pants, begging for his life, and blaming Qasim for all his misdeeds.

With Qasim and the Communists gone, Kirkuk had a semblance of tranquility, but not quite! Now Ba'th was in power, and the fighting between Barzanis and the Ba'thi government was at its peak. There were many dead and wounded on the army side, also amongst the Kurdish tribes, collectively known as Jahshas, who had allied themselves with the government against the Barzanis.

A seriously wounded allied Kurdish agha was admitted, as a favor to the Army, to K-1 hospital in Kirkuk. This was an exception. Two of the most competent English nurses were assigned to take care of him, Miss Hollbrook and Miss Johnson. One afternoon, the commander of the 2nd Army Division, accompanied by five armed soldiers, came to the hospital unannounced and headed to this agha's room at a time when the nurses were tending to his wounds. The commander had entered the room, without permission, and without knocking at the door. The disciplined nurses were very angry and did not allow him to visit. They angrily ordered him out. The commander told them who he was. They told him they didn't care who he was, he was not allowed to visit, because first of all it wasn't visiting hours, and secondly the patient was half naked and they were tending to his wounds.

The commander was terribly offended and humiliated by "these women." He walked out of the hospital in fury and returned to his headquarters. As soon as he sat at his desk, he issued a written order extraditing these two nurses out of the country immediately, to never return again. They had twenty-four hours to pack up and get out.

My boss, Dr. Bain, was very worried because their departure would have meant an acute shortage of nurses, also a blow to IPC's pride and prestige. The company's General Manager and his assistants attempted to interfere, but to no avail; the commander refused to see them. Even Nafi' Abdulla, an ex-military comrade, was rebuffed; the commander didn't allow him to even enter his room, let alone negotiate or mediate.

I asked Dr. Bain's permission to try my luck with the commander, only because I had done him a favor or two, taking care of his wife and daughter, who were not eligible to have treatment at the company hospital. Dr. Bain checked with the administration, got their OK, and wished me luck. Now I was an accredited mediator.

It was around noon when I reached the headquarters of the second Army Division and requested to see the commander. In less than a minute, the commander himself was at the door welcoming me to his office. He had a few other visitors in his spacious office. He introduced me as the doctor who takes care of his family. I thought that was a good sign. Tea and cigarettes were offered, as is the custom amongst Arabs.

After he finished talking with the others, he turned to me and said he knew why I was there. He said he respected me but no, he couldn't help me. I didn't say a word! He continued his litany, this time with profanity, "Who the hell do these English whores think they are to stand up to me and expel me from the hospital? I'll show them who I am! I can't accept any delays; they have less than twenty-four hours to leave the country." He kept pouring his anger, and I let him ventilate. I didn't utter a word and kept on drinking my tea, which in Arab societal symbolism means friendship.

After about ten minutes of profane monologue, he ordered another tea for me. I knew I was making headways! When he finished with a sigh, I said:

"I am in full agreement with all that you have said, Excellency, I too demand that these girls pay for their misbehavior, who the hell are they to insult a commander of the Iraqi Army? If they think they still are our masters, they are mistaken! Our revolution freed us from that kind of subjugation. What I am concerned about is the harm to Iraq that might come out of their deportation; they would land at Heathrow and immediately hold a news conference trying to trash you and the Iraqi government. Bad publicity is one thing we cannot afford to have at this point, and if this matter is not handled properly, it will give us just that. What will happen to the girls? Nothing! They will find employment in their country in no time! We will be the losers! So, here is what I am saying: what they have done to you does not take away from your honor and dignity. People know you and respect you, regardless. For the good of the country, you have to sacrifice your pride a little bit. I am suggesting to you to let the girls get out of Iraq for two weeks, as if on vacation, and then return to their stations to help the poor Iraqi oil workers. You will save face! People will know that you were firm and your orders were carried out, and the company will save face claiming that the girls were going on two weeks vacation abroad."

He listened carefully. I could see his face relax with a sigh. I knew it was a yes and it was! Case closed! It was a good solution!

The year 1960 was crucial for Iraq and the world. Under Qasim's auspices and through the work of Abdul Rahman Al-Bazzaz (my next-door neighbor in Room # 10 at Al-Rasheed Military Base, and our Imaam in prayers), Perez Alfonso of Venezuela, and Abdulla Al-Tareeqi of Saudi Arabia, a meeting was held in Baghdad, which lasted from September 10 to 14. The meeting gave birth to OPEC (Organization of the Petroleum Exporting Countries). Its founding members were Iraq, Iran, Saudi Arabia, Kuwait, and Venezuela. The idea of forming the organization probably had originated in Saudi Arabia; regardless, its maiden meeting in Baghdad was a trophy for Qasim; he had won another battle over Baba Gurgur!

Creation of OPEC appeared to have loosened Britain's grip on the Iraqi oil industry, and portrayed Qasim as a patriot concerned with Iraq's well being, rather than chasing the dream of Pan Arabism and handing over Baba Gurgur to Nasser.

His opposition had mixed feelings about this new organization, because it tied Iraq's petrol with six other nations, slipping it from Nasser's grip; also, because Qasim would capitalize on this achievement and score big in the public opinion arena. Their position was that OPEC was a good idea, but only after the actual union of all Arab petrol-producing countries under Nasser.

Pan-Arabists, in addition, accused him with inconsistency: While attempting to rid Iraq of the British influence, he was introducing his new ally, the Soviet Union, into the equation of controlling the Iraqi oil industry. For them the Soviets were just as bad as the Imperialist West, if not worse.

The writing was on the wall. Since its infancy, OPEC became a force to contend with, but at the time neither Iraq nor the other members could predict the impact of their creation on the world events. The intent of forming OPEC was to protect the interests of oil-producing nations, nothing else. They didn't know or couldn't imagine the role their organization was destined to play in war and peace.

Soon after the creation of OPEC, another major event shook the oil industry: in 1961, in a bold move, Qasim formulated and passed "Law # 80 0f 1961," which restricted IPC (Iraq Petroleum Co.), MPC (Mosul Petroleum Company), and BPC (Basra Petroleum Company) from drilling outside their existing leased areas. The old contract, which had allowed these British outfits unlimited access to drill anywhere in Iraq, was rescinded.

This law, of course, was unfavorable to the British, but at least the new arrangement guaranteed uninterrupted production from the existing wells. Qasim became the undisputed winner in this battle over Baba Gurgur.

The Soviets were jubilant not because they gained something from Qasim's actions, but because his actions hurt the West by denying them valuable assets and prestige. Nasser received the news with mixed emotions; he was happy that Britain's wings were clipped, but disappointed that he too, gained nothing; his ambitions of controlling Baba Gurgur in the name of the Arab Union had evaporated. It was a lose-lose situation for both of them.

Despite Law # 80, matters did not change much for IPC. Production was the same, and oil flowed as before; however, the company feared that sterner measures were yet to come. They did, a decade later. With the stroke of a pen, the company was nationalized ending a longtime speculation. Thus, almost half a century after first tapping oil in Touz Khurmatu and waging crucial battles over it, Iraq finally became the sole proprietor of its Baba Gurgur, but not necessarily its destiny. Did Iraq really win the war over Baba Gurgur? Did the West lose? Act Three of this saga was not over; the struggle to win the war over Baba Gurgur was to take another form at another time, and it did!

In 1963, three other major events shook the world.

For the United States, it was disastrous: President Kennedy was assassinated, and the country plunged more and more into the Vietnamese quagmire, which claimed many American lives. I felt sorry for both events.

In Iraq, there were three major events, one of them personal. On February 8, in a Ba'thi coup Qasim's regime was toppled, and he was shot in front of the television cameras for the whole world to see. So was his cousin Mahdaawi and the prosecutor Maajd Ameen, the two clowns of the "People's Court."

Reportedly Qasim had asked Arif to spare his life the way he, Qasim, had spared his, but Arif had denied the request stating that the verdict was unanimously reached by the revolutionary council, and that he personally pardons him, and washed his hands off his blood. He must have had terrible inner conflicts: a duel between emotion and logic. He being a sentimental, emotional man, couldn't have voted to exterminate a comrade-in-arms, a "brother," a man who spared his life. On the other hand he could not have voted against the unanimous will of the coup leaders who were about to eliminate Qasim, the comrade who deceived the original ideals of the Iraqi Revolution, the traitor of the Free Officers, the obstacle to Arab unity, the ally of the Communists who destroyed their beloved Iraq.

Despite all that Arif had no choice but to vote; he asked to be the last to vote, and he was! He followed suit with the majority, but minimized his guilt: being the last, his vote carried no weight; the man had to be executed for the common good, for Iraq. He could have taken the noble high road and voted to spare his "brother's" life; but he didn't! He had no noblesse oblige.

When I heard this, I remembered Adnaan Azzawi, my "pal," the Communist who "washed his hands" off my case using the same excuse during my torture in 1959. I thought it didn't matter if one's torturer is a Communist or a Ba'thist; it takes a certain humanoid type to become a cruel extremist, a criminal bastard.

Just before the execution, Qasim's last wish was granted: he was not blindfolded. He must have seen the bullet, which lodged in his forehead, like a badge of honor. I thought it took a certain intestinal fortitude to face bullets; it spoke of the man's character. Thus, by his execution a chapter in the Iraqi saga folded, only to have another, equally rotten, unfold.

The country was, now, in the hands of the Ba'this, with Abdul Salaam Arif as president. Like the Communists who had created the notorious Muqaawama Al-Sha'biya troops, Ba'this created their own notorious Hharas Al-Qawmi (Nationalist Guards). They too, armed them with submachine guns and semiautomatic weapons to terrorize and control the public, and subjugate them to their will. They too, like the Communists, were engaged in a one-party dictatorship. They too, were charged with the "Protection of the Republic against all enemies, foreign or domestic," which meant the Communists and whoever opposed the Ba'th.

For an ordinary Iraqi nothing had changed—the Hharass was the other side of a dirty coin; Ba'this committed, in revenge, the same kind of crimes, murders, incarcerations, and terror, as the Communists in Kirkuk. Their new government wasted no time in executing those death row Communists, mostly Kurds, who had committed the Turkomani pogroms in Kirkuk and whose sentences Qasim had not carried out.

One of the hanged was my sixth-grade classmate Hussein. He was a Kurd. When I saw his pendulous short body swaying in mid air, I was petrified. I couldn't believe that my classmate, a shy, gentle, playful kid with shabby clothes, was hanging from the gallows with his hands and feet tied, head tilting to the right and tongue protruding, just the way he was in class trying to concentrate on the lesson.

I hated death, and still do, but I hated violent death even more. I thought some people are born under unlucky stars; Hussein was one of them. He was born with odds doubly stacked against him: his parents were very poor, and he belonged to an oppressed ethnic group, the Kurds. He must have felt trapped; he had no chance in life. Even if he had, the society in which he was to function would have given him a real uphill battle, outstretching his capabilities, and denying him opportunities. No wonder he became a Communist! A "religion" that promised him social justice, equality, and prosperity, and gave him the justification for hating the wealthy; those "capitalist bastards who have exploited human beings and sucked their blood," as he said

Unlike other religions and ideologies, Communism was about here and now, on earth, not in ethereal heaven. This was a gratifying "religion" indeed, worthy of sacrifice! The Communists had undoubtedly lured Hussein, like the others, into believing that once the old regime was toppled, he would have a prosperous life, and, to topple the old order he had to kill. Kill he did, and now he was swaying from the gallows.

The twenty-seven bodies hanged in public in three different locations to make examples of them, and also to win the hearts of the Turkomans who were seeking justice. They were to stay on display long enough for people to see, before handing their bodies over to their relatives. Through these bodies, the new government also intended to project power and the will to crush their opposition.

I witnessed this scene with feelings of sorrow, disgust, fear, uncertainty, and worries. All of a sudden, it was night in the middle of a hot, sunny, morning: foggy, cold, and unbearable. I remembered myself in the death row cell with my friends, the cockroaches and the mice, running around happily. I smelled the pungent odor of urine and excrement.

Hussein must have been held in my death row cell. I bet he was in my cell! Yes, he was! My gut feeling told me he was; we had shared a classroom before, why not a cell? But he would not have known that I had been there before him. Was Hussein really detained in my death row cell? Did he write his last will and testament with shit, on the wall?

That was ridiculous; what difference did it make if it was the same cell or the one next to it? He was now dead, swaying from a rope, and I was alive trying to negotiate the ropes of life. I had seen and experienced enough. I asked my happy Turkoman driver to take me back to K-1 Hospital where I worked.

On my way back, Saalih, the driver, kept on talking and talking about justice, revenge, the Kurds, and the Communists, but nothing was sinking in. I was absorbed with what I had just seen and experienced; it was juxtaposing, in flashes, with scenes of life in Britain, which I had recently enjoyed.

I made that trip to London a thousand times in an instant. The overriding question in my mind was my future in this country. I knew that the prosperous life that IPC had provided me would be short-lived. The question was whether I was prepared to face the uncertainties of the future, in Britain!

By the time I reached the hospital, I had arrived. I concluded that I was not in any danger because my prison mates were in power; they were holding important cabinet and subcabinet posts. In incarceration they had offered me, should they come to power, any position that I desired, short of a cabinet minister. At the time, it was laughable and rightly so: for one I never believed that they stood any chance of coming to power again; and second, talk of that nature is nothing more than prison talk, made under morbid circumstances as a psychological defensive mechanism. Now they were in power, but I was not going to join their march to the abyss, which was sure to happen! I had seen their weaknesses and unpatriotic statements in prison, and questioned their competence to govern. These same people while in prison had displayed soft character: had cried, denounced their country, and yearned for the cafés of Piccadilly and Soho, and now they were at the helm of the State ship heading to disaster. Regardless, I was not in immediate danger. But, how about the future? What guarantees my safety? What guarantees the stability of this country? How do the uncertainties of Iraq compare with that of the West? These questions and more kept my mind busy.

All these deliberations came to a decisive end with a family tragedy: my brother Noreeg, twenty-three, was accidentally shot at a Hharass al-Qawmi checkpoint, and rendered quadriplegic. The army officer on duty who caused the accident happened to be his friend. He died in my arms at the El-Rashid military Hospital, in the same base where I was incarcerated.

I was devastated! So was my family. Our friends and the community wept as he was buried with military honors. Muslims of our neighborhood, like the Armenians, came to console us, and they recited the Al-Faatiha for the soul of the dead. Through it all, I had to display composure and strength for my old parents. I didn't cry; I wish I had; it would have brought closure, which I have not achieved yet. I am still crying!

I never memorized the name of the man who shot Noreeg, and in compliance with my brother's wishes we did not bring charges against him. We received no apologies from him or his family, nor did he express remorse. A decade or so later he too, I hear, was shot and killed in the Iraq-Iran war. Such was life in Iraq for us, and thousands like us, under Qasim and the Ba'this, after the demise of the Royal regime in 1958!

26

"Your Destiny Is Charted for You the Minute You Are Born"

(An Arab belief)

Noreeg's death changed our outlook on life. Sadness descended over our household and grief never left us for a long time. We became more acutely aware of the fragility of human life. We philosophized a lot, and for us death became a yardstick of life.

One day at his graveside, I reached a decision: I am leaving! Living in Iraq was not for me, or my children any more. True, I'll be leaving Noreeg behind, but now Noreeg was not a person whom I could hug and kiss and talk to, he was only a precious spirit, whom I could take with me anywhere I went! All of a sudden, I felt Noreeg's spirit become a part of my soul. Now he was with me, I could go away without looking back, I concluded.

The next day, I started working on the arduous task of obtaining a passport. I had to obtain approval from the Ministry of Health to leave the country, post a thousand dinar (equivalent of $4,000) bond to guarantee my return, and then apply for a passport. I paid, and I got permission to leave. It took me several more weeks to get the required clearance from the Police Security, and get the passport. I was ready to say goodbye to Iraq and hello to the West; I was on my way to a new life filled with hopes, illusions, successes, disappointments, and a new reality. I was looking forward to my transformation from an oppressed subject to a free citizen of a democratic country; the Bill of Rights was too enticing!

My leaving broke my family's back. My father couldn't believe his ears when I told him. With tears in his eyes he said, "I lost a son, now I am losing a second son, it is not fair." I looked at his face: the wrinkles appeared deeper, the greenish-blue eyes duller, as if the tears had washed away the tint. He had aged some more since the night before. He lit up a cigarette. "Dad," I said, "You have lost a son, you don't want to bury another son; I better be far and safe, than another grave for you to visit; you will come to see me!" He understood but couldn't accept it; to him this was another tragedy that was "written," allocated to him by God the minute he was born. That was, and is, an Eastern myth, "Your destiny is charted for you the minute you are born."

My mother and sisters continued crying, and were lost for words. My wife was sad, but hopeful, because she and the children were to join me in a few months, and they did!

That was the last time I saw of my father. He died nine years later, yearning for his sons. The rest of the family eventually got out of Iraq, leaving my grandmother's, father's, and Noreeg's graves behind.

Despite all this, I was happy to leave Iraq when I did. My predictions for the future of Iraq materialized. I know that had we stayed in Iraq, the first or the second Gulf wars would have claimed the life of at least one of my sons, and I know that I would have been, for some trivial reason, like my friend Hussein swaying from the gallows; it would have been all a part of the battle over Baba Gurgur.

27

A Chitchat

I left Kirkuk for London in 1964, but not psychologically. Like Noreeg, Kirkuk became a spirit, which I carried with me to America, and as time passed, it, like the flames of Baba Gurgur, grew eternal.

I chose to come to America because I wanted to be a citizen, not a subject. To me the one absolutely tempting attraction of America was not its modernity, or the opportunities it offered, but the Bill of Rights that had set Americans free, and made them what they were: respectable and guardians of morality.

Since her birth, America had earned not only the respect of the world, but also its love; a huge capital of good will existed with the peoples of the world. That capital has now eroded partly because of our shortsightedness, adventurism, mismanagement, ineptitude, and plain amateurish conduct of the foreign policy, and partly because of the dirty battles for Baba Gurgurs of the Middle East, which we have waged for the last two decades. We are especially not respected because of our duplicity in conducting Foreign Policy, and because of violating our own moral standards.

When Saddam invaded Kuwait, we waged war under the false pretence of liberating Kuwait and reestablishing democracy in that sheikhdom, a democracy that Kuwait never had. The war, however, was just! The world knew that we waged war for oil, not democracy. The world knew that our excuse was a lie, yet we insisted on that falsehood hoping that the world would change its mind. Why couldn't the administration tell the American people the truth that we were going to war to protect the American interests in the region, provide gas for your car, heat for your home, and energy for your factories, which would protect your jobs? That would have been the truth, and would not have insulted people's intelligence.

Whatever Saddam's justification, the fact remains that his goal was control of the oilfields of the Gulf. Previous Iraqi governments, starting from King Faisal I in the early 1920s, to General Karim Qasim in 1961, had also claimed Kuwait as part of Iraq, which historically it was, but they had failed; Karim Qasim even mobilized his army for invasion. But for Britain's threat, he would have invaded! When King Faisal made his claim, oil was not an issue; Kuwait was a desert sheikhdom producing pearls, not oil.

After Desert Storm President Bush (41) asked the Shi'as of the south to rise against Saddam, and they did, but he failed to support them; we did not even attempt to help them and the result was several hundred thousands dead, buried in common graves, which we now call Saddam's atrocity.

The Kurds had the same fate in the north; it was a repetition of the Bay of Pigs fiasco! Additionally, in negotiating the articles of surrender, we disallowed the fixed wing aircraft from flying but allowed helicopter gunships. Saddam used this with impunity; they pounded the Kurdish territories mercilessly, and they lost lives; we lost face, their trust, and respect; it took us a decade or so to regain what we had lost.

In putting a United Nations resolution together to liberate Kuwait, the administration, whose will dominates the Security Council, formulated a shortsighted resolution that did not include the overthrow of Saddam, the excuse being, "...we would have been an occupying power charged with running Iraq, and may be not even finding Saddam" (Bush 41). A decade later, his son proved him right; we went there totally unprepared, totally oblivious to the demographic idiosyncrasies and the political realities of the country, and mismanaged the aftermath of our invasion. Five major mistakes got us into the present chaos:

(1) We did not secure the borders.
(2) We did not secure the Iraqi ammunition dumps.
(3) Instead of purging just the top brass, we dissolved the army unnecessarily, which created a half a million jobless soldiers and two million of their dependants without income. They hated us and became our enemies!
(4) We allowed the mobs to loot stores, institutions, homes, and museums; destroy property, burn cars, destroy all but the Ministry of Oil, which we were protecting.

   All this happened right before the eyes of our military, and they did not raise a finger to prevent the disaster, arguing that they are not the police; it was not their job.

   All this and we stood there dumbfounded, asking ourselves, "Why didn't Iraqis welcome us with bouquets of flowers the way the French did when we liberated them in WWII?" It is a fact that most Iraqis were prepared to do just that if we knew how to manage the situation.

   Iraqis also discredited us for being inept, incapable of restoring the very essential utilities: electricity and water. For months, and now for three years, people's water and electricity, are rationed. Iraqi's couldn't believe that this technological giant, America, is so inept that after three years they haven't been able to repair what they have destroyed. To them, omnipotent America has failed to improve the quality of their lives, some believe intentionally. Today many ordinary Iraqis yearn for the Saddam years, when the basic services were functional despite the international economic sanctions. Still, we are asking ourselves rather naively, why don't they like us?

(5) Not hunting Abu Mousab al-Zarqawi, who was nestled in the northeastern corner of Iraq away from Saddam's sphere of influence. Colin Powell, in his presentation at the United Nations, showed a map with the camp's exact location; why then didn't they fire missiles to get him and the other members of the Al-Qa'ida?

The Administration's propaganda machinery keeps on misleading the American public. When the horrendous crime of 9/11 shook the nation and the world, they explained the event as being a struggle between the haves and the have-nots, concealing Bin Laden's and the militant Islamist's true motivations for hitting the United States. Once again, they misled the American public opinion! They said, "The enemy wants to change *our* way of life. . ." when the reality is that the enemy does not want us to change *their* way of life; they despise the Western culture, they despise their leaders whom we support, they despise the corrupt Arab regimes that we tolerate, and they resent our support of Israel.

Furthermore, they long for the lost glory of the Arab domination of the Middle East, Africa, and parts of Europe, and blame their 1,000-year stagnation on the West. In their arguments they disregard what the Ottoman Empire, the seat of the Islamic Caliphate, did to them for four and a half centuries: they destroyed them, their Muslim brothers! They disregard the fact that it was Britain, and Lawrence of Arabia, who liberated them from the jaws of the Ottoman Turkey.

In the final analysis, not even all these are the absolute true motivations of their actions; in reality, what is going on now is only a part of a battle over the Baba Gurgurs of the Arab World. If through ignorance they do not understand us, it is incumbent upon us to understand them! But, do we?

In 2003, in order to justify our invasion-occupation of Iraq, we first used weapons of mass destruction as an excuse, then changed it to Saddam's collaboration with the Al-Qa'ida terrorists, then justified it by the necessity for regime change in Iraq, because Saddam posed a threat to Iraq's neighbors and the world. All these false excuses contributed to further deterioration in our reputation as a credible superpower, and the world; even Europe reacted to that with the simplest of all negative feelings: hate!

Aside from all this, we went to Iraq totally oblivious of the idiosyncrasies of the people. The best example of that is what I saw on television the other day: The new Iraqi army recruits were to have their hair clipped; the recruits resisted, but finally agreed. However when the barbers attempted to clip their mustache, they became angry, combative, and agitated, trying to jump off the chair; one of them said, "What am I going to tell my wife? This is my honor. I am an honorable man and you are humiliating me!" To an Iraqi, indeed for an ordinary Arab, his mustache is his honor and cutting that mustache means dishonoring him and his family. Under ordinary circumstances, a barber would never touch a man's mustache to shape it, except as instructed.

In a related story, I saw on television an amusing incident, which happened immediately before Saddam's fall, at the Arab Foreign Ministers meeting. The meeting was attended by almost all Arab countries, including Iraq, which was represented by Izzat Ibrahim al-Duri (K of clubs), the # 2 man of Iraq. The Kuwaiti head of the delegation, now the new Emir, said something that provoked al-Duri's anger, to which he reacted angrily by saying, "Curse be on your mustache," which of course is funny and meaningless to a Westerner, but to an Arab that is one of the worst curses one can utter.

Our military should have handled this and a thousand other situations like this in a tactful manner: they could have prepared the soldier ahead of time instead of catching him off guard to shave his mustache. In his neighborhood that soldier will be known as the man who surrendered his honor to the Americans in order to be employed for a few bucks. It is a stain on his honor and patriotism. It is virtually certain that we did not win that man's love or loyalty.

When I left Iraq, Saddam was not in power, but the Ba'th party was. They had employed the same tactics as the Communists, to keep control over Iraq. Arrests, murders, tortures, and cutting of the ears as punishment, became commonplace. The Ba'th party, which two Syrian Sorbonists Akram al-Horani and Michel Aflaq had established, separated. I do not know the reasons for this separation, but it was clear that Michel Aflaq was siding with Iraq, and Horani with Syria.

Saddam, who had just risen to the highest position in the Party, chaired a meeting of the Ba'th Party in Baghdad, and produced a list of names, which he read to the audience. Those on the list were taken out of the hall, one by one, and summarily executed. Saddam, with a Cuban cigar in hand, shed crocodile tears to the thunderous applause of those present. Now he had purged the party, and become its chief, the rest of the delegates pledged allegiance to him. Thus began a very short journey to dictatorship, which eventually ended in a rat hole in 2003.

Saddam manipulated this power shrewdly, and eventually disregarded the Party altogether. Members of the Ba'th became his pawns, to move according to his whims.

Thus began the Saddam Dynasty consisting of his two sons, Qusai and Udai, and his Tikriti relatives and friends. Remembering the brutal Tikritis of Kirkuk, and my classmate Mohammed Saber, the only decent boy of the bunch, I felt sorry for the Iraqi people! After all I was not wrong about the Tikritis of my teen years; time had vindicated me!

For the next twenty-five years or so, Iraqis lived under the most brutal regime, rather dictatorship, which the country had ever seen since Hajjaj Bin Yousif al-Thaqafi, who governed Iraq after beheading all the notables of Iraq, some thousand years ago.

The two major ethnic/religious groups suffered the most: The Kurds because of their aspiration for some kind of a self-rule, which had nothing to do with religion, and everything to do with the splitting of their land in accordance with the provisions of the Treaty of Sèvres and the League of Nations plebiscite of Mosul; and the Shiite hierarchy, who were persecuted because they were considered a fifth column undermining the State, in favor of Iran. They were guilty by association because their roots extended to Qum, the Iranian Shiite religious bastion, forming the Qum-Najaf axis, Saddam's "Axis of Evil."

Saddam brutalized and murdered Shiite imams of Najaf and Karbala with vengeance. Sayid Baqir al-Hakeem, and thirty members of his family were brutally murdered; dozens more shared the same fate.

But for this political reason, Iraq did not have Sunni-Shi'i problems since their seventh-century skirmishes, which separated Ali's followers from the main body of Islam, the Sunnis. From that date, Ali's followers became known as Shi'as. They have their own mosques, which they call Hussainiya and where they conduct their religious rituals, some of which are different from that of the Sunnis. One ritual, which the Sunnis do not have, is the Ashourah, which is a ten-day-long wake and penance in the month of Muharram. Throughout that month they hold religious ceremonies in the Hussainiyas and repent and mourn Hussein's murder with chest beating, self-flagellation, and hitting their forehead with a sword to gently bleed so that they may feel Hussein's suffering and repent for their ancestors' crime, a mea culpa of the Shi'a world.

With such minor differences, however, Mohammed and Islam unite the Sunnis and the Shi'a the way different Christian churches are united through Jesus Christ.

There will never be a fatwa (Islamic encyclical) by a Sunni mulla, or a Shi'a Imaam to start a jihaad between the two sects; jihaad is a call to fight the enemies of Islam. The brutal killings and blowing up of mosques and Hussainiyas is not because of religion but because of political and military positioning. The hierarchies of both sides have vehemently condemned it, and have blamed the outside forces for the crimes. People believe this; even some conspiratorial theorists believe that special interest outside—forces that vie for a civil war to destroy Iraq's social structure—are the culprits. What is happening in Iraq now is not a civil war; it will not qualify to be that until and unless the Sunni and Shi'a hierarchy declare war against each other, and that is not the case and is highly unlikely to occur.

In modern Iraq, as secularism took hold, these differences faded even further; intermarriages between Sunni and Shi'a became commonplace. Religion was a nonissue; no one was denied employment because of his religion. Not infrequently, the Prime Minister was a Shi'a, and frequently so were the Cabinet Ministers. There was no discrimination in university admissions.

There were three major political parties in the Kingdom: The Istiqlaal Party (The Independence Party, headed by Fa'iq al-Sammarraie and Mohammed Mahdi Kubba), the Hizb al Watani al-Demoqrati (The Nationalist Democratic Party, headed by Kamil al-Chadrchi), and the underground Communist Party. None of these had ethnic, religious, or sectarian orientation; all three had members from all the layers and colors of the Iraqi society.

In the 1920s, during the Euphrates Uprising, it was the Shi'a tribes, who fought the British first. In Iran-Iraq war of the 1980s, Shi'as of Iraq fought on the side of the Sunni Iraqi government against their coreligionist Shi'a Iran. Iraqi Shi'a are Arabs first, Iraqis second, and then Shi'a.

During the Iraq-Iran war, the Iranians did not spare their Iraqi Shi'a kin death and destruction, they turned the mostly Shi'a Basrah and the southern provinces, into graveyards.

During the Saddam era, Sunnis suffered as much as the Shi'a, if not more; his brutality did not discriminate, and had no boundaries.

With all these facts in place, one wonders if we did not artificially create this ethnicity issue, for reasons one can only speculate.

The Kurd-Arab division also was not, and is not, a real ethnic division. The majority of the Kurds are also Sunnis; they have no religious dispute even with the Shi'as. Their struggle has been with Baghdad to gain or regain their rights on a land that has been their home for 4,000 years.

In 1973, the two sides came to an agreement for establishing Kurdish self-rule in the old vilayet of Mosul, the very same vilayet, which Turkey had lost to the newly formed Iraqi Kingdom in a League of Nations plebiscite. That vilayet is now what the Kurds call Southern Kurdistan. Northern Kurdistan is the Kurdistan of Turkey, the Western in Syria, and the Eastern in Iran. Baba Gurgur was a sticky point in that agreement, which soon caused Saddam to renege on the deal.

Fights led to many more battles: in the Halabja Genocide, Saddam forces gassed some 5,000 people; some say Iran did it. However, the Anfaal campaign was exclusively Saddam's doing, his forces slaughtered the Kurds mercilessly. Kurds, by the hundreds of thousands, took refuge in Turkey. Eventually, the United Nations and the United States took them under their protection and brought about some degree safety, peace, and prosperity.

Throughout the past five centuries there had existed in Iraq, a large degree of ethnic balance. This equilibrium was disturbed in the WWI and II, though with minor skirmishes. The Turkoman-Kurd discord over the vilayet of Mosul, especially Kirkuk, has always been their bleeding ulcer. However there has never been Sunni-Shi'a clashes over anything. Sunnis, Shi'as, Yezidis, Assyrians, Chaldians, Kurds, Turkomans, Mandaeans, and Armenians lived together in harmony. May be the Ottomans, and then the British colonialists, wanted it to be that way.

In March 2003 we disturbed that harmony when we invaded/liberated Iraq. Now the United States' policy is capitalizing on the ethnic diversity of the country, a dangerous gamble, which might result in the division of Iraq into ethnically oriented cantons: the oil rich North to the Kurds, upgrading it from federated autonomy to statehood; the oil rich South to the Shiites; and the poor middle section, to the Sunnis. That is only a scenario! However, regardless of what happens, Kirkuk has become the Jerusalem of Iraq, a disputed territory, which needs a Saladin to its rescue, and I don't see one on the horizon! There is no doubt that the battle is over Baba Gurgur!

Index

About the Author

HENRY D. ASTARJIAN is a neurologist who grew up in Iraq. He has lived in the United States since 1966.